S0-FER-782

HUMAN RESOURCES MANAGEMENT

QUALITY AND RELIABILITY

A Series Edited by

Edward G. Schilling

Center for Quality and Applied Statistics
Rochester Institute of Technology
Rochester, New York

1. Designing for Minimal Maintenance Expense: The Practical Application of Reliability and Maintainability, *Marvin A. Moss*

2. Quality Control for Profit, Second Edition, Revised and Expanded, *Ronald H. Lester, Norbert L. Enrick, and Harry E. Mottley, Jr.*

3. QCPAC: Statistical Quality Control on the IBM PC, *Steven M. Zimmerman and Leo M. Conrad*

4. Quality by Experimental Design, *Thomas B. Barker*

5. Applications of Quality Control in the Service Industry, *A. C. Rosander*

6. Integrated Product Testing and Evaluating: A Systems Approach to Improve Reliability and Quality, Revised Edition, *Harold L. Gilmore and Herbert C. Schwartz*

7. Quality Management Handbook, *edited by Loren Walsh, Ralph Wurster, and Raymond J. Kimber*

8. Statistical Process Control: A Guide for Implementation, *Roger W. Berger and Thomas Hart*

9. Quality Circles: Selected Readings, *edited by Roger W. Berger and David L. Shores*

10. Quality and Productivity for Bankers and Financial Managers, *William J. Latzko*

11. Poor-Quality Cost, *H. James Harrington*

12. Human Resources Management, *edited by Jill P. Kern, John J. Riley, and Louis N. Jones*

Additional volumes in preparation

HUMAN RESOURCES MANAGEMENT

Edited by

Jill P. Kern
Digital Equipment Corporation
Stow, Massachusetts

John J. Riley
Jack Riley and Associates
Ardmore, Pennsylvania

Louis N. Jones
Quality Technics
Olean, New York

Sponsored by the American Society of Quality Control Human Resources Division

Marcel Dekker, Inc.   New York and Basel
ASQC Quality Press   Milwaukee

Library of Congress Cataloging-in-Publication Data

Human resources management.

Includes index.
1. Personnel management. 2. Organizational change.
3. Human capital. I. Kern, Jill P. II. Riley, John J.
(John Joseph), [date]. III. Jones, Louis N.
IV. American Society for Quality Control. Human Resources
Division.
HF5549.H8727 1987   658.3   86-29321
ISBN 0-8247-7716-6

COPYRIGHT © 1987 by ASQC QUALITY PRESS
ALL RIGHTS RESERVED

Neither this book nor any part may be reproduced or transmitted in any form or by any means, electronic or mechanical, including photocopying, microfilming, and recording, or by any information storage and retrieval system, without permission in writing from ASQC.

MARCEL DEKKER, INC.
270 Madison Avenue, New York, New York 10016

American Society for Quality Control
310 West Wisconsin Avenue, Milwaukee, Wisconsin 53203

Current printing (last digit):
10 9 8 7 6 5 4 3 2

PRINTED IN THE UNITED STATES OF AMERICA

About the Series

The genesis of modern methods of quality and reliability will be found in a simple memo dated May 16, 1924, in which Walter A. Shewhart proposed the control chart for the analysis of inspection data. This led to a broadening of the concept of inspection from emphasis on detection and correction of defective material to control of quality through analysis and prevention of quality problems. Subsequent concern for product performance in the hands of the user stimulated development of the systems and techniques of reliability. Emphasis on the consumer as the ultimate judge of quality serves as the catalyst to bring about the integration of the methodology of quality with that of reliability. Thus, the innovations that came out of the control chart spawned a philosophy of control of quality and reliability that has come to include not only the methodology of the statistical sciences and engineering, but also the use of appropriate management methods together with various motivational procedures in a concerted effort dedicated to quality improvement.

This series is intended to provide a vehicle to foster interaction of the elements of the modern approach to quality, including statistical applications, quality and reliability engineering, management, and motivational aspects. It is a forum in which the subject matter of these various areas can be brought together to allow for effective integration of appropriate techniques. This will promote the true benefit of each, which can be achieved only through their interaction. In this sense, the whole of quality and reliability is greater than the sum of its parts, as each element augments the others.

The contributors to this series have been encouraged to discuss fundamental concepts as well as methodology, technology, and procedures at the leading edge of the discipline. Thus, new concepts are placed in proper perspective in these evolving disciplines. The series is intended for those in manufacturing, engineering, and marketing and management, as well as the consuming public, all of whom have an interest and stake in the improvement and maintenance of quality and reliability in the products and services that are the lifeblood of the economic system.

The modern approach to quality and reliability concerns excellence: excellence when the product is designed, excellence when the product is made, excellence as the product is used, and excellence throughout its lifetime. But excellence does not result without effort, and products and services of superior quality and reliability require an appropriate combination of statistical, engineering, management, and motivational effort. This effort can be directed for maximum benefit only in light of timely knowledge of approaches and methods that have been developed and are available in these areas of expertise. Within the volumes of this series, the reader will find the means to create, control, correct, and improve quality and reliability in ways that are cost effective, that enhance productivity, and that create a motivational atmosphere that is harmonious and constructive. It is dedicated to that end and to the readers whose study of quality and reliability will lead to greater understanding of their products, their processes, their workplaces, and themselves.

Edward G. Schilling

Preface

The role of the human being in achieving quality has been seriously underrated by both quality professionals and management for decades. Only recently, with the impact that Japanese efforts have had on the competitive environment worldwide, has the concept of the individual worker as the most fundamental resource in business and industry been recognized. Indeed, the notion is becoming popularized in American society due to NBC White Papers, books such as Peters and Austin's *In Search of Excellence*, and the statements of leaders such as:

—W. E. Deming: "Only two in 100 people have a chance to work with pride." (1986 Annual Quality Congress)
—Harold Geneen: "... in business, with all its automation, it is still the people, with all their faults and frailties,

that provide the mortar which holds together the building blocks and bricks of business enterprise." *(Managing)*
—William Ouchi: "It is clear that the focus [for quality] must be on people." (1986 Annual Quality Congress)
—Lee Iacocca: "How did Japan's cars get so good? It starts with the workers." *(Iacocca: An Autobiography)*

The intent of this book is to provide quality professionals as well as all levels of management with an overview of some of the most important tools being used today to optimize the effect of that most critical (and difficult) resource: people. In the process, we also hope to provide readers with a sense of excitement about the possibilities inherent in the use of these tools. Only if we can motivate *you* to action will this book have accomplished its objective.

The book is organized in a sequence that moves through typical stages of awareness of human potential in an organization. We take special pride in the chapter of case studies, for it represents a group learning effort with the creation of a valuable product as its goal—as well as being a look into our own future.

When dealing with human beings, though we may seem to have made some progress over the years as documented here, we might do well to remember one of the oldest maxims on record:

Do unto others as you would have others do unto you.

A good business rule? Yes! Why do you think it's called the *golden* rule?

We hope you will take our message to heart, for it comes straight from each of our own. And, after you have taken it to heart, please take it to work.

Acknowledgments

The Human Resources Division of the American Society for Quality Control would like to thank each of the authors for their considerable labor in developing both their own sections and the

PREFACE

overall framework of this book. In addition, special thanks go to Jeanine Lau for her timely assistance in bringing the book to reality through the ASQC Quality Press.

Jill P. Kern	C. B. (Kip) Rogers
Chairwoman	Chairman
Human Resources Division	Human Resources Division
1985-86	1986-87

Contents

About the Series	*iii*
Preface	*vii*
Contributors	*xiii*
1. Human Resource Development: An Overview John J. Riley	1
2. Preparing an Organization for Change Louis N. Jones	15
3. Human Factors Engineering C. B. Rogers	49

4.	Quality Circles Promote Quality Performance Robert Amsden and Davida Amsden	77
5.	Leadership and Management Training and Development Barbara Affourtit and Thomas D. Affourtit	91
6.	Participative Management Jill P. Kern	139
7.	The Art of Statistics William G. Barnard	151
8.	Developing a Quality Selection System John A. Berger	173
9.	Strategic Quality Planning William A. Golomski	189
10.	New Organizational Structures and New Quality Systems Phil Alexander, Michael Biro, Everett G. Garry, Dale Seamon, Tom Slaughter, and Duane Valerio	203

Index   *269*

Contributors

Barbara Affourtit Interaction Research Institute, Inc., Fairfax, Virginia

Thomas D. Affourtit Interaction Research Institute, Inc., Fairfax, Virginia

Phil Alexander Ann Arbor Associates, Ann Arbor, Michigan

Davida Amsden Consultant, Dayton, Ohio

Robert Amsden University of Dayton, Dayton, Ohio

William G. Barnard Vita-Mix Corporation, Cleveland, Ohio

John A. Berger RIMS, Oak Brook, Illinois

Michael Biro SARNS/3M, Ann Arbor, Michigan

Everett G. Garry L&W Engineering, Belleville, Michigan

William A. Golomski   W. A. Golomski and Associates, Chicago, Illinois

Louis N. Jones   Quality Technics, Olean, New York

Jill P. Kern   Digital Equipment Corporation, Stow, Massachusetts

John J. Riley   Jack Riley and Associates, Ardmore, Pennsylvania

C. B. Rogers   Digital Equipment Corporation, Stow, Massachusetts

Dale Seamon   SARNS/3M, Ann Arbor, Michigan

Tom Slaughter   International Foam and Trim, Jackson, Michigan

Duane Valerio   Hydra Matic Division GM, Ypsilanti, Michigan

HUMAN RESOURCES MANAGEMENT

1
Human Resource Development: An Overview

JOHN J. RILEY Jack Riley and Associates, Ardmore, Pennsylvania

Although we are constantly aware of the need to develop more productive technology in order to find substitutes for depleted resources, we are missing the trees for the forest. Perhaps the most significant of our natural resources is the readily available human resource. It is the "sleeping giant" of business.

The potential for human relations development was best expressed by Roger Kelley, retired vice president of Caterpillar Tractor Company, as follows:

> How important are human resources to business? Peter Drucker has written that the productive capacity of all businesses depends on three factors—the human resource, the capital resource, and the physical resource. It is interesting to note that the human resource is the only produc-

tive resource of business which can synergize; that is, produce a result (output) greater than the sum of its parts. Also, the human resource is the only resource with a capacity to produce, whose upper limits cannot be defined.

The ability of humans to maximize their contribution to their own welfare and that of their employers is the subject of this book. One might ask, "Why should this be a problem? We all know people who love their work and are highly motivated by it." Conversely, however, there are many others who dislike their work, will do just the minimum to retain their position, or, as former General Motors executive "Dutch" Landon says, "are required to leave their brains at the factory gate and pick them up on the way home." It is to this group and their managers that we wish to address the message of this book.

Why Is Human Resource Development Difficult?

The enormous diversity of humans' reactions to their environment, based on genetic and learned-experience backgrounds, makes it difficult to determine the environmental conditions most productive to motivating people in the world of work. American management, once recognized the world over as the most effective, innovative, and imitated, is also known as the least patient with the time it takes to get things done. Working with people is a time-consuming job, requiring patience, empathy, and a level of tolerance for differences that the hard-driving, results-oriented American management is not renowned for. If they can obtain the necessary productivity increases with improved machines, better tooling, and better processes—which are clearly quantifiable to the financial men who supply the money—why count on people who are renowned for being difficult to handle, uncooperative, and forever filing grievances? Interestingly, however, there are many common denominators that seem to transcend nationalities, cultures, and even learned experience. The major elements appear to be recognition of work results, a feeling of teamwork, mutual trust, and respect, knowing and being a part of what is going on—in a sense, being able to contribute and be recognized for their contribution even though it be only a small part of the whole picture.

The Japanese worker is regarded as a highly motivated contributor to his work. This is usually credited to his cultural background. If this is so, why did Japanese management study and then implement the recommendations of American behavioral scientists? The answer must be that there is a thread of behavioral attitude that lies below the culture, language, and traditions that separate different peoples and nationalities. The following quotation seems to indicate that the desire to be a contributor to an enterprise is not new or even modern. Around 100 A.D., a Roman landowner wrote of his approach to managing workers on his estate:

—Nowadays I make it a practice to call them into consultation on any new work—I observe that they are more willing to set about a piece of work on which their opinions have been asked and their advice followed.

Columella, *On Agriculture I*

The real question is how to convince both management and labor that the confrontation politics of over 100 years, in this country, can and must be changed. We will find that education on what is possible, through the proper application of modern (really very old) human resources and motivation techniques, will be bought by these two basic elements of both the business and social structure if we know what to do and how to do it. We must inform, educate, motivate, train, and orient all functions in the business sector to the proper and effective use of the human resource, not only to improve the quality and productivity of our nation's economic base but also to improve the quality of working life of the people who man the factories, stores, offices, and transportation systems of this, the most productive nation on earth.

In the quality function, the cooperative responses on common objectives of management, workers, staff, and all others create an environment where high-quality products and services are most easily produced. As we will show shortly, regard for the thoughts and motivation of workers has not always played an important part in management planning and organization. Management has traditionally concerned itself with the technical means of production, considering the workers as another, often inanimate element of the production unit. Let's try a little test to place our proposition for human resources on a more personal basis. Think about the best boss you ever had. Did he inspire mutual trust, communicate much of what was going on, supply the necessary elements to get the job done, and recognize whether or not the job was done well? In a word, the good boss usually supplied what is called "positive reinforcement." This is a reaction that clearly recognizes good performance and does not dwell on poor performance, though it does caution against repeat of a poor performance.

The Pioneers in Human Resources Development

We indicated earlier that much work and many studies have been accomplished by industrial psychologists in this country and abroad to find the environmental elements most conducive to motivating employees to be productive. Early in this century F. W. Taylor, the Father of Scientific Managment, advanced, among other ideas, the concept that management was a science of numbers—an excellent contribution to improved business efficiency. However, he also felt that productivity was best served by breaking jobs down into simple elements, requiring little training and leaving all production decisions to "technicians and supervisors." He further believed that human problems stood in the way of production and so should be removed; the worker was best served by being closely supervised and paid in some proportion to his production.

The work of Gilbreth, Emerson, Bedoux, and others in the 1920s further advanced the idea that people were only productive when paid an incentive to produce. With the largely immigrant work force of the day, this seemed satisfactory. These movements also led to the encouragement of union organization to help improve the worker's status. Such concepts are not productive with today's better educated worker who wants to be involved, recognized as an individual, and trusted as responsible for his work.

To simplify a look at some of the behavioral research in motivation over the past 50 years we shall treat the specialists and their theories individually. Reference will be made to these researchers in other areas of this book. However, these short explanations of their work will serve as a base for further development of their ideas.*

Chris Argyris

1. The argument that much counterproductive employee behavior (poor productivity and quality, high absence, turnover, and lateness) is a result of the organization's failure to meet individual growth needs rather than an indicator of something wrong with the employees themselves
2. The thesis that interpersonal rather than technical incompetence is at the root of most organizational difficulties.

Frederick Herzberg

1. The concept of man as having two sets of needs, which are independently met. One is for avoiding pain and discomfort through one's environment (or the conditions that surround what we do); the other is the need for psychological growth through what one does in work or other activities.
2. The suggestion that well-designed, interesting work can be a motivator in and of itself.

---

*Acknowledgment for most of these descriptions is given to the American Management Association for use of David A. Whitsett's comprehensive article on the subject (16).

Rensis Likert

1. The descriptions of four basic approaches to, or systems of, management ranging from the least desirable, System I—which he describes as autocratic and explosive—to System IV—which he suggests is characterized by strong work groups, participatively managed and linked together by overlapping membership.

2. The concept of human resources being of value in an economic (specifically, an accounting) sense and that activities undertaken by an organization that ultimately diminish the value of this (human) asset thereby diminish the economic value of the organization.

Abraham Maslow

1. The idea that man's motivations operate according to a hierarchy of five important needs—physiological, security, belongingness, self-esteem, and self-actualization. Most people achieve the first three. An objective of human resource development is to create conditions conducive to bringing employees to the fourth and fifth stages.

2. Development of our awareness of the concept of growth (or self-actualization) of motivation in man.

Elton Mayo

1. Working in a Philadelphia textile mill from 1923 to 1924, he discovered that people were more productive when organized into groups he called "families"—an early approximation of (autonomous) work groups. Mayo and his followers sought to increase production by humanizing it.

2. He began, and Roethlisberger finished, one of the most highly regarded human resources productivity studies at the Chicago Hawthorne Works of Western Electric. The basic thrust was to

determine how production output could be changed as a function of such external factors as length of time at work, the number of rest periods, etc. Almost always, regardless of changes in working conditions, production generally improved. In summary, "only one thing seemed to show a continuous relationship with this improved output. This was the mental attitude of the operators."

Douglas McGregor

1. The suggestion that any manager's style or way of operating with his people is based on his or her set of beliefs about man's basic nature.
2. The notion that these sets of beliefs can be thought of as falling into one of two categories: One, which he calls "Theory X," conceives of man as inherently lazy, desiring to avoid responsibility, and requiring strong external control; the other, Theory Y, conceives of man as desiring to work and use his skills, to make decisions for himself, and operating heavily on internal controls.
3. The suggestion that most business and industrial organizations are managed using Theory X. This then means that most managers perceive their employees as requiring strong external control.

William Ouchi

This American researcher, of Japanese origin, expanded on and modified McGregor's work with his Theory Z. His ideal organization is egalitarian, engages fully the participation of employees in running the company, and emphasizes subtle concern in interpersonal relations. It is characterized by employee cooperation with the objectives of the company.

Background of Human Resources Application in Business and Industry

The earliest manufacturing facility, before the dawn of the Industrial Revolution, was the home of the worker. The "cottage industry" had all of the elements of personal concern for quality, since the worker performed all or most of the operations and felt a personal responsibility for product quality. This, with his productivity, determined the style of life he could afford. With the establishment of factories, this internal feeling of responsibility was lost to machines, engineers, supervisors, and managers.

We can easily follow the development of technology over the last two centuries since the advent of the Industrial Revolution in England. The high points of steam power, electrical development, improved transportation, and the growth of technology in all fields following wars are well documented. This progress continues in most fields, including the almost explosive development of new machines, methods, and materials. However, if we look for a similar progression in the application of human resources to business and industry, we find little or no information. The usual answer is "Look how much better off we are than our fathers and grandfathers in the ownership of goods and the availability of services." Could we say this about the relationship to our work, to the way we operate and feel in the factory or the office? We doubt it.

Much of Taylor's autocratic approach to management remains the American style. We notice, however, the lead developed by the auto companies, and some early human resource believers in "search for excellence" are beginning to penetrate the industrial establishment with the concept that there is "gold in them 'thar' human resources hills."

What's in a Name?

Perhaps the most confusing aspect of human resources development is the "name game." Though later chapters will develop these terms, some listing is appropriate here to be used as a road

HUMAN RESOURCE DEVELOPMENT: OVERVIEW

map through the semantic wilderness. These terms are randomly listed.

1. *Human resources development* is the umbrella term covering the many forms and techniques to maximize the contribution of the human resource of the enterprise toward the joint objective of meeting the business goals of management and satisfying the overall human needs of the people who work in the company at all levels.

2. *Quality of work life* is the term coined by General Motors and the United Auto Workers to describe their approach to human resources development. It is a state of being, not a program or procedure. It defines the degree of satisfaction one has with work processes involved with earning a living. If one is satisfied and interested in his work, he is usually motivated to perform well, and this satisfaction builds on itself, creating a self-actualization, as defined by A. H. Maslow. This is a satisfactory quality of work life. The reverse attitude, dissatisfaction and lack of interest, provides a poor quality of work life accompanied by poor productivity and quality of work.

3. *Participative management* is a system in which subordinates are involved in making operations or business decisions with guidance from their supervisors.

4. *Quality circles* are groups of people who meet on a regular basis to identify, analyze, and solve quality and other problems in their areas.

5. *Employee involvement* is another name for participative management and sometimes used as a way to avoid using the term quality circles.

6. *Autonomous work groups* operate without direct supervision; peer pressure accomplishes high outputs, high quality, good shop discipline, and low absenteeism.

7. *Elimination of time clocks* is a reinforcement of trust and a statement by management of their people's honesty.

8. *All-salary work force*, with no time clocks and everyone treated equally reinforces trust and teamwork.

9. *Productivity gain sharing* replaces outmoded individual financial incentives and promotes productivity and quality by peer pressure.

10. *Job enrichment* is improvement of jobs in a manner that provides increased motivation, to keep the maintenance (Herzberg) factors constant or higher while increasing motivation factors.

11. *Organization development* is an educational strategy that focuses on the whole culture of the organization in order to bring about planned change. It seeks to change beliefs, attitudes, values, and structures, in fact, the entire culture of the organization, to allow better adaptation to technology and to keep up with the fast pace of change.

Means of Achieving Improved Human Resource Application

Learning why we should try to change old habits is almost as important as the change agent or the technique we will use for the change. This country has been facing a lack of productivity growth crisis, unparalleled in our history. The traditional manager will usually respond by saying, "Pay them more money and they will work harder." The day when this approach worked is almost over. Many of today's workers have their own homes, cars, boats, and other extras that only wealthy executives of their fathers' day could afford. To use an old phrase, "Money can't buy happiness." The contemporary American worker has a new set of values quite different from the traditional worker.

Mark Mindell and William Gorden expressed these changing values in the American Management Association's "employee values in a changing society" (AMA Management Briefing, 1981). No more than a decade ago, the work force generally held the following values:

HUMAN RESOURCE DEVELOPMENT: OVERVIEW

1. Strong loyalty to the company
2. Strong desire for money and status
3. Strong desire for promotions up to the management hierarchy
4. Critical concern about job security and stability
5. Strong identification with work roles rather than personal roles

To some extent, these values were shaped in response to actions by the company itself. Employees often learned their skills at the employer's expense, and the training and promotion opportunities forged strong links between the worker and his company. Loyalty to the company made personal initiative pay off in terms of greater opportunity, personal freedom, and life satisfaction.

But a majority of employees today acquire their skills and specialized knowledge outside the corporation. More employees now enter the corporation at a higher level, and upward mobility often comes through a change in employers, rather than by promotion from within. In other words, the values of opportunity, personal freedom, and life satisfaction are fulfilled by what the individual is and does, rather than what he believes the company has done for him. This same personal focus is seen in other values that characterize the contemporary employee:

1. Low loyalty or commitment to the organization
2. A need for rewards geared to accomplishments
3. A need for organizational recognition for contributions
4. Decreasing concern for job security and stability
5. A view of leisure as being more important than work
6. A need to perform work that is challenging and worthwhile
7. A need to participate in decisions that ultimately affect the employee
8. Stronger identification with a personal role than with a work role

9. A need for communication from management regarding what is going on in the company
10. A need to rise above the routine and approach tasks creatively
11. A need for personal growth

The new breed of employee wants recognition for accomplishment and the freedom to find new and better ways of approaching problems. They do not rely on their jobs for feelings of self-esteem, but they do desire to be recognized as persons. That is, they prefer to think of themselves as individuals and not as members of a highly structured organizational hierarchy.

The first step in the change process is for top management to acknowledge that a change in style and culture is significant to the future financial health and market share of the organization. This must be a real feeling and understanding; no posturing will suffice, since employees seem to have a form of infrared vision that sees through a posturing management.

Next, obtain an objective assessment of your employees' thoughts on work and the workplace, with an attitude assessment planned and conducted by a professional. You now have a point of departure about which to plan the steps necessary to create an environment for mutual trust and understanding, which will be an unusual WIN-WIN situation where both management and labor can profit. Above all, make sure the union is involved and hopefully cooperative in all plans and actions.

Finally, be patient. It required over a hundred years of ignoring the employees' real needs, other than money and fringe benefits, to get into this situation. If it is turned around in 3-5 years of honest, dedicated work on both sides, you will be lucky. The following quotes may help your resolve in the trying days ahead.

> The ingenuity and the perseverance of industrial management in the pursuit of economic ends have changed many scientific and technological dreams into common place realities. It is now becoming clear that the application of these

same talents to the human side of enterprise will not only enhance substantially these materialistic achievements but will bring us one step closer to the good society. Shall we get on with the job?

—Douglas McGregor, *Leadership and Motivation*

There is nothing more difficult to take in hand, more perilous to conduct, or more uncertain in its success, than to take the lead in the introduction of a new order of things.

—Niccolo Machiavelli

Selected Readings

1. Crosby, P. B., *Quality Is Free*, McGraw-Hill, New York, 1979.
2. Riley, J. J., Origin, methods and problems to achieving quality of work life, *SME Technical Paper IQ82-251*, May 1982.
3. Maslow, A. H., *Motivation and Personality*, Harper & Row, New York, 1954.
4. Deming, W. E., *Quality, Productivity and Competitive Position*, M.I.T., Center for Advanced Engineering Study, Cambridge, MA, 1982.
5. Marsh, W. A., Management theories: Comparing X, Y, Z, *Quality Progress*, December 1982.
6. Schmidt, J. L., Participative management—Challenge to competition, *ASQC Tech. Conference Transactions*, Atlanta, 1980.
7. Juran, J. M., Management interface, *Quality Progress*, July 1973.
8. Berry, B. H., Can GM redesign the manager-worker relationship?, *Iron Age*, March 10, 1982.
9. Taylor, F. W., *The Principles of Scientific Management*, Harper & Brothers, New York, 1911.
10. Fotilas, P. N., Semi-autonomous work groups: An alternative organizing production work, *Management Review*, AMA Publication, July 1981.
11. Nelson-Horchler, J., Paying for productivity, *Industry Week*, April 4, 1981.

12. Ozley, L. M. and Ball, J. S., QWL: Initiating successful efforts in labor-management organizations, *Personnel Administrator*, May 1982.
13. Guest, R. H., Quality of work life—Learning from Tarrytown, *Harvard Business Review*, July-August 1979.
14. Herzberg, F., One more time—How do you motivate employees? *Harvard Business Review*, January-February 1968.
15. Cox, M. G. and Brown, J. C., QWL: Another fad or a real benefit? *Personnel Administrator*, May 1982.
16. Whitsett, D. A., Making sense of management theories, *Personnel*, American Management Association, May-June 1975.
17. Nadler, D. A. and Lawler, E. E., *Quality of Work Life: Perspectives and Directions*, Organizational dynamics, AMACOM (American Management Association) Periodical Division, Winter 1983.
18. Mindell, M. G. and Gorden, W. I., Employee values in a changing society, *Management Briefing*, American Management Association, 1981.
19. Carlson, H. C., GM's quality-work life efforts, *Personnel*, AMA Publication, July-August 1978.
20. Proham, J., What's wrong with management? *Dun's Business Monthly*, April 1982.
21. Rubinstein, S. P., Quality control requires a social and technical system, *Quality Progress*, August 1984.
22. Riley, J. J., The effect of improved quality of work life on quality assurance organizations, *Quality Circle Digest*, July 1984.
23. Tribett, C. W. and Rush, R. J., Theories of motivation: A broader perspective, *Quality Progress*, April 1984.
24. McGregor, D., *The Human Side of Enterprise*, McGraw-Hill, New York, 1960.
25. McGregor, D., *Leadership and Motivation*, M.I.T. Press, Cambridge, MA, 1966.

2

Preparing an Organization for Change

LOUIS N. JONES Quality Technics, Olean, New York

> Change is the process by which the future invades our lives.
>
> —Toffler, *Future Shock* (1)

Introduction

The manner in which human resources are utilized in improving quality has caused an accelerated rate of change in the basic life and structure of many organizations. Change means not only the implementation of many different programs and systems, but it also means a cultural alteration for the people involved. Alvin Toffler, in his classic book (1) on change, recognized this human involvement:

It is important to look at it (change) closely, not merely from the grand perspective of history, but also from the vantage point of the living, breathing individual who experiences it (1).

When change is implemented into an organization, individuals react to it in several ways. Dr. Robert Schuler (2), in a dissertation about change, noted the following reactions to change:

1. Some resist it.
2. Some fear it.
3. Some deny it.
4. Some react negatively to it.
5. Some believe in it and accept it.

I have personally encountered all of these reactions as I was involved in the implementation of a total quality program into the Hysol Division of the Dexter Corporation. I would like to share with you, as a case study, the initial effort that was employed to prepare this organization for cultural and systematic change.

My first step after being assigned to this project was to reread *Future Shock* and try to interpret it in terms of the assigned project and the desired end results. It is thus no surprise that I believe that books about change, such as *Future Shock* (1), *Megatrends* (3), *In Search of Excellence* (4), etc., are must reading for anyone planning to implement change, especially change that affects people.

As I began to plan for this project, I realized that it was difficult, if not impossible, to plan with precision and certainty about the future, but by accepting the following reservations, I was able to warrant my future planning:

The inability to speak with precision and certainty about the future, however, is no excuse for silence. Where "hard data" are available, of course, they ought to be taken into

PREPARING FOR CHANGE 17

account. But where they are lacking, the responsible writer—even the scientist—has both a right and an obligation to rely on other kinds of evidence, including impressionistic or anecdotal data and opinions of well informed people. I have done so throughout and offer no apology for it.

In dealing with the future, at least for the purpose at hand, it is more important to be imaginative and insightful than to be one hundred percent "right" (1).

Let's use our imagination!

Imagine that you are lying on a white-sheet-covered cart in the tiled corridor of a modern hospital. You are scheduled for heart transplant surgery. Your life and life-style are about to encounter a massive change. You have already received the preoperative sedative and you are beginning to become drowsy. As the burly orderly pushes your cart into the operating room for what you hope and believe will be a lifesaving experience, you begin to sum up the factors that make up your expectations. The surgeons in their green-paper throwaway uniforms and masks stand around the irregularly illuminated table while a myriad of modern machines blink their colored light like overpriced video games emitting weird sounds that bring back memories of old Frankenstein movies.

The smells of anesthetic and disinfectant attack your senses as the anesthetist begins the sodium pentathol drip into your system and whispers for you to start counting backward from 100. As you slowly drift into unconsciousness, your mind begins to recall and sum up the many expectations you have accepted for this "change experience."

Certainly, you would expect or demand that the surgeon who will cut and probe into your body would have had the necessary training and experience to accomplish this operation. You expect that his support staff are also adequately trained and experienced to aid in this change. You would expect that the instruments, equipment, drugs, and whatever else is needed have met the quality and reliability requirements that are needed to maximize your chance of success. What doctor would dare perform major surgery without an extensive medical workup and historical background that included testing to determine facts about the patient's physical, mental, and emotional states?

You would expect that the entire staff had prepared not only for the "routine" of the normal operation, but that they were prepared for most emergencies that could occur. Your expectations would demand that possible side effects would have been considered, and whenever possible, harmful ones would be minimized. And finally, you would expect that when your heart had been removed and a "new" one replaced, adequate follow-up, checkup, and recovery procedures would be conducted to make your overall quality of life equal to or greater than what it was prior to this lifesaving experience.

If these expectations exist for medical changes, why not for major change of an organization, which is a living, breathing, "human-containing" organism. I see the above-imaged surgical example not just as an analogy, but rather as a point of view—a point of reference that could be, and in this case study was, used in the planning phase for the organization "change."

Background on Case Study

Before any effort is made to create, develop, and implement a specific program for an organization, it is beneficial to ascertain the historical environment that has created the present system. Thus, in this case study it was necessary to research the Dexter Corporation.

The Dexter Corporation, a Windsor Locks, Connecticut-based specialty material maker, is the oldest company presently listed on the New York Stock Exchange. It was founded in 1767, almost a decade before the United States was founded. But although Dexter is an old company, it does not equate "old" with "old-fashioned." As David L. Coffin, Chairman of the Board of the Dexter Corporation, has stated, "We all talk future around here" (5).

Although the Dexter Corporation's past history and performance may not meet all the criteria to be listed as a "Z"-type company by Ouchi in his best-selling book *Theory Z* (6), it certainly contains many of the Z-type characteristics. For example, Ouchi states, "The bedrock of any Z company is its philosophy" (6). Dexter's President, Worth Loomis, gave an insight into the corporation's philosophy about business ethics when he told the entire corporation "If a practice cannot be discussed openly, it must be wrong.... Dexter has enjoyed a reputation based on integrity for over two centuries. We are guardians of that reputation, and that responsibility requires vigilance" (7). Another Z-type criterion exhibited by Dexter is that for many years they have allowed employees to share directly in the company's business success through profit-sharing-type programs.

Dexter prides itself on its decentralized management structure and believes it has the following advantages:

1. It allows decisions to be made closer to the market.
2. "It makes life a hell of a lot more interesting for people in the divisions because it allows them to run their own shows," states Dexter's CEO (5).

With the above attitude it is easy to discern why Dexter, rather than imposing a single, corporate-wide program for change to participative management, has encouraged each division and operational unit to develop its own specific program within corporate guidelines. Corporate involvement was restricted to such areas as the following:

1. Establishing corporate-wide training programs in conjunction with the Hartford Graduate Center in areas such as management training, quality circle leadership, etc.
2. Stating its position to stockholders, management, and employees by feature articles in its *Annual Report* (7).
3. Presenting this change as an "invitation" to its operational units that the corporation would support and nurture as a long-term corporate goal to help meet the challenges of the future.

With this background in mind, it became clear that any program of participative total quality control would not only have to meet the guidelines established by the corporate body, but would have to take into account the historical and environmental background of all its employees.

Thus, to achieve a high degree of success for any proposed change, it is imperative to know certain facts about the environmental background of the organization, and to use these factors in the preparatory step of the program.

IQ Triangle

To illustrate how our organization prepared for change, I will present some of the preparatory steps taken as I was involved in implementing a "total-quality" program into the Hysol Division of the Dexter Corporation. This particular program was named the Improved Quality Program and was usually referred to as the "IQ Program." This program was devised to create an invisible integrated chain that would provide a means of merging the new participative programs with the existing management systems to improve the overall organization quality and profitability.

The concept of "IQ" can be described by the following simple equation:

$$IQ = \underbrace{\frac{\text{Natural and produced}}{\text{resources utilization}}}_{A} \times \underbrace{\frac{\text{Tool and equipment}}{\text{utilization}}}_{B} \times \underbrace{\left(\frac{\text{Human effort}}{\text{Work system}}\right)^M}_{C}$$

where M = motivational factor.

This equation is, of course, simply another way of showing the relationship of the three "P's," product, process, and people, and how they relate to the process of improving overall quality. The "people" or human resource factor in the above equation is defined as "human effort" divided by the "work system" in which that effort is expended. This was done to account for those instances where negativity occurs because human effort is reduced

PREPARING FOR CHANGE

by the work environment. The "M" power factor is employed to cover the exponential effect that programs such as quality circles, quality of work life (QWL), etc., can have on the people factor when properly utilized.

The relationship of the three interrelated "success factors" shown in Figure 1 is the IQ triangle. This was devised as a triangle because all three factors are equally important and interrelated. Although all factors need preparation for change, we will concentrate on the human resource or people factor, with the understanding that similar planning would be required for the other phases.

The following concepts were formulated to form the foundation of the IQ system philosophy:

1. Creation and promotion of specific pathways to increase the employee's individual growth

2. Creation and channeling of employee effort by teams, circles, and task forces to improve organizational "togetherness"

3. Integration of concepts and programs into the existing company system to merge, integrate, and grow to form the nucleus of a new system

An adaptation of the Rudge plan for increasing business credibility, as suggested in the book *The Keys to Increased Productivity* (8), provided the following five-prong attack force for the IQ Program:

1. Factfinding

2. Feedback of findings

3. Development of indices to measure program effects

4. Organized action plan

5. Auditing and evaluation system to ensure long-term corrective action results

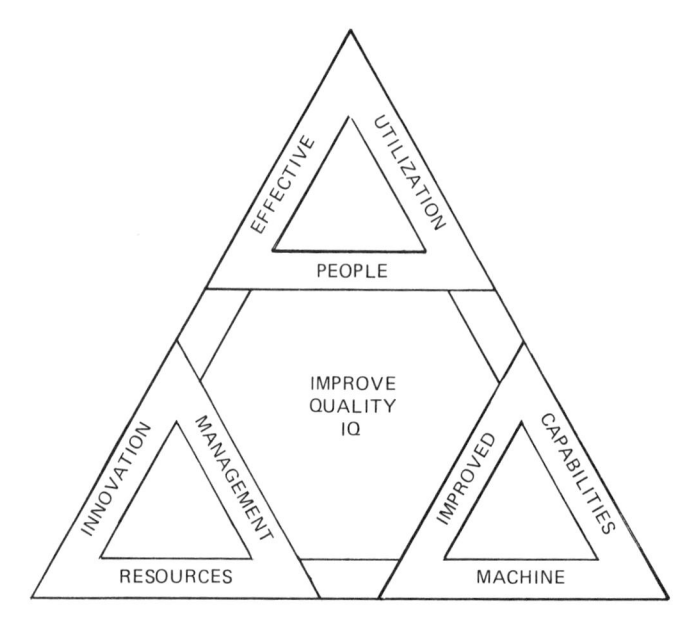

Figure 1 IQ triangle.

To further clarify the above concepts and plan, let me relate actual factors that were explored in the preparatory stage for implementation of the IQ Program.

Perspective

Many different perspectives could have been selected; the one used was entitled Directed Total Participation, "DTP." In this approach, once a program has been created, tested, and accepted by management, it is introduced to the total organization as a program for everyone, just like a medical insurance or profit-sharing plan. It is participative in that each person can elect to be *active* or *nonactive*, but it is directive because it is a top-down program that dictates that everyone will in some way be involved in the actions and results of the program.

Let me illustrate this further by describing how DTP was applied to the introduction of quality circles into our organization.

PREPARING FOR CHANGE

One of the basic elements of the classic quality-circle methodology as it evolves from the Japanese-created program is that participation in circles is "voluntary." And although this is both necessary and meaningful, what it tends to do in many cases is to further increase the gap between employee and employee, and the gap between employee and management.

In DTP, when the circle program was introduced, it was presented as a part of the organization's structure—everyone from top management through middle management to janitorial staff was to be part of it. Those who elected to be "active" became involved in the traditional circle training, meetings, and problem-solving modes, but were constantly reminded that their actions, both successes and failures, would be shared by everyone, active and inactive.

Under DTP no one ever joins or quits a quality circle; he simply moves from active to nonactive status, or vice versa. Every solution suggested by a circle must take into account the effects of that solution on all related areas, and whenever possible, those affected must be actively involved in the solution.

Lack of middle-management support and commitment has been listed (9,10) often as one of the main stumbling blocks or reasons for circle failure. This occurs because in most cases middle management perceives circles as an "artificial-organ inplant." That is, even though this foreign article may be doing good and even saving the total life, it is still not part of the "natural" system, and rejection mechanisms are created to destroy the intruder.

To return to my surgery analogy, every doctor today realizes that a rejection phase is going to occur at some time in the patient's recovery, and preparative steps are taken to minimize this by using certain drugs which, in fact, are designed to "disguise" the organ until the body will accept it. Similarly, when changes such as circles are instituted, it must be realized that middle management is almost certainly going to "reject" this threatening intrusion, and means and methods must be planned and implemented to counteract this expected phenomenon.

The mechanism we used to ensure middle-management involvement was training and communication. Prior to the start-up of the first circle, middle managers were required to attend a 2-day training session in which they were not only made aware of circle tactics and methodology, but were also made aware of how circles would interface with their particular areas. Emphasis was on blending the circle program into the current structure so that managers would share in the "success" and "failures" of the circle program.

Just like the "rejection drugs," our solution has some side effects, and not all are good, but if this planned diversion can be carried out long enough, the organizational body, like the human body, will eventually accept the "foreign article" as its own. This is the end goal.

Although the directed total participative approach is different and somewhat controversial, it is my belief that in creating "change" for an organization, tools such as quality-circle programs should be revised and stylized to meet the needs of the organization in question. It is not suggested that this approach should be universally applied, but it was an approach that was planned and utilized to meet a specific problem that was almost certain to occur, and preparation for possible side effects is the important point to be made here.

Policy

Since an organization's "quality policy" is the foundation for all activities related to the quality system, it is one of the factors that should be considered during the planning stage. General and specific information, descriptions, and examples of quality policy statements have been adequately covered by Juran (11), Caplan (12), and others (13,14).

Like many organizations, we had a policy statement, but it was buried in the QC Manual and similar documents. It was known to only a few and understood by even fewer. Policy making should remain a top management decision, but it should be arrived at with the involvement and consensus of other levels. The policy statement should also not be a hidden, static document, but a dynamic, open one.

Our plan concerning this factor was to ensure that:

1. It would be a dynamic instrument subject to review and modification to meet the current needs.
2. It would be adequately publicized and displayed for the information and knowledge of suppliers and customers, as well as employees.

Participative actions from many levels of management were utilized in our organization within the management system to develop and publicize the Hysol Quality Policy which is shown in Figure 2.

Planning for this factor of change ensures that a meaningful, well understood quality policy exists and that it is utilized as a guiding principle for the planned organizational change.

Pressures

One of the factors that was certain to develop within our total-quality program was dealing with pressures. One possible approach was to simply react to the various pressures as they surfaced. Our approach, however, was to try to anticipate this factor and plan to either eliminate or at least minimize the effect of it on our overall program.

External Pressures

With the wave of "quality awareness" sweeping the country, many companies are not only rushing to improve their own quality, but are taking definite steps to pressure their suppliers into improving their quality programs.

For example, organizations that have accepted the Deming statistical approach are conducting seminars on statistical process control and "inviting" their suppliers to attend in a Godfather-like "deal they can't resist." In many cases, it seems not to matter whether the supplier is ready for or wants the process; it is just a

HYSOL DIVISION
THE DEXTER CORPORATION

QUALITY POLICY

It is Hysol's policy that
for every product we supply
we shall define quality requirements
to meet the customer's needs
and we shall conform exactly to
those requirements without exception.

K. Grahame Walker
President

Cal Cialdella
Senior Vice President

Allen Sheals
Vice President, Marketing

Ronald Benham
*Vice President,
International Marketing*

David Woodhead
Vice President, Finance

Dan Clark
Vice President, Operations

Nancy Layman
*Vice President and President,
Frekote Inc.*

Richard Dauksys
*Marketing Manager,
Aerospace and Structural
Materials*

Lester Hicks
*Division Manager,
Industrial Relations*

Figure 2

PREPARING FOR CHANGE

matter of either being "saved" or not belonging to the right crowd. The unspoken message is that if the supplier does not join in or at least put on the facade of joining, they will be in danger of no longer being considered as a supplier. In some cases, vendor rating systems are used as a means of punishing or eliminating suppliers who fail to conform.

Those companies that are using Philip Crosby's 14-step *Quality Is Free* (15) approach are trained to make their suppliers a part of their quality-improvement program. Philip Crosby has said, "The first step in any drive to improve quality is to demand defect-free products and services from your suppliers" (16).

There is nothing wrong with the thrusts by those embracing either Deming or Crosby in bringing suppliers in line with their concepts, but for many vendors this has meant being bombarded by pressures from many sources. Each major customer may have his own particular brand or adaptation of a quality-improvement program and in many instances is forcing the supplier to conform not just to a good improvement system, but to "his desired" brand.

As a company whose major customers were the Motorolas, the Texas Instruments, the Mitisubuta, etc., who had embraced one of the above-mentioned improvement programs or had their own brand of program, it was almost certain that we would feel the pressure of the "accept our program" movement.

Our approach was to study and fully understand as many of the major quality-improvement programs as possible, and to ensure that our program contained the critical elements that matched or surpassed those of the outside programs. In this manner we could withstand the pressures and maintain the integrity of our own program.

Internal Pressures

Even when top management supports and authorizes "change," internal pressures often occur. American management is still goal oriented, and even when they seem to agree when informed that many programs are long-term programs, they are still pushing for immediate results and visible short-term profits. Much of this pressure will continue until a complete change of business philosophy occurs. At this stage, our approach was to recognize this factor and by continuing, dynamic communication to minimize its effects.

Planning

Planning for a major change will almost certainly involve the use of planning aids such as PERT, Critical Path Analysis, and other similar project-controlling plans. However, the amount of planning should be related to the needs and conditions of the organization and the projects.

Organizational Change—Integral Management

To provide backbone for the proposed participative total-quality system, a new type of organizational structure was required. This organizational factor was provided by Hysol's President, K. Grahame Walker. Mr. Walker had previously built Hysol's Munich-based European operation into a thriving profit center by using "an autocratic European style" (17), but when he assumed the reins of the Industry, California-based Dexter Division, he changed the environment by "injecting a freewheeling participatory management style which forced decision-making down the management ladder" (17). Walker's management system, which was named "Integral Management," was the organizational skeleton utilized for preparing for change.

The classic functional management chart for the Hysol Division is shown in Figure 3. Walker has taken this system and "added a dash of Theory Z, a dollop of matrix management, and doses of participatory and consensus management styles" (17) to create a "shadow" organizational structure called Integral Management. The Integral Management structure, as shown in Figure 4, has the outline of a broad-based, but short cone made up from three layers of horizontal interlocking rings. Each of these rings represents a team. Each team makes decisions or, where limited by

PREPARING FOR CHANGE

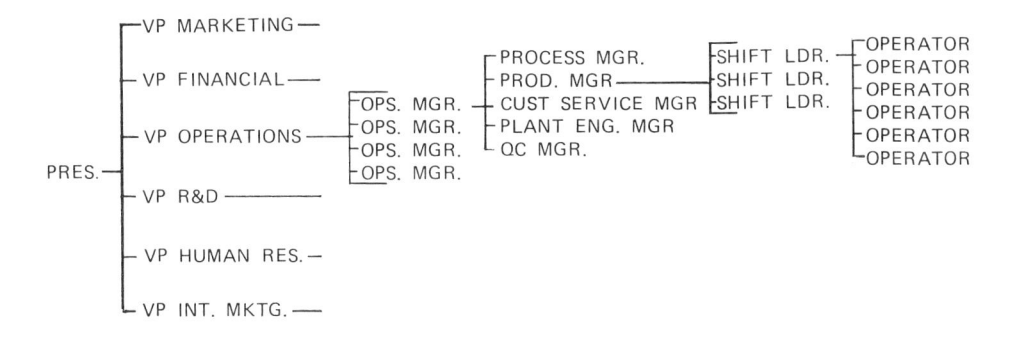

Figure 3 Functional management chart.

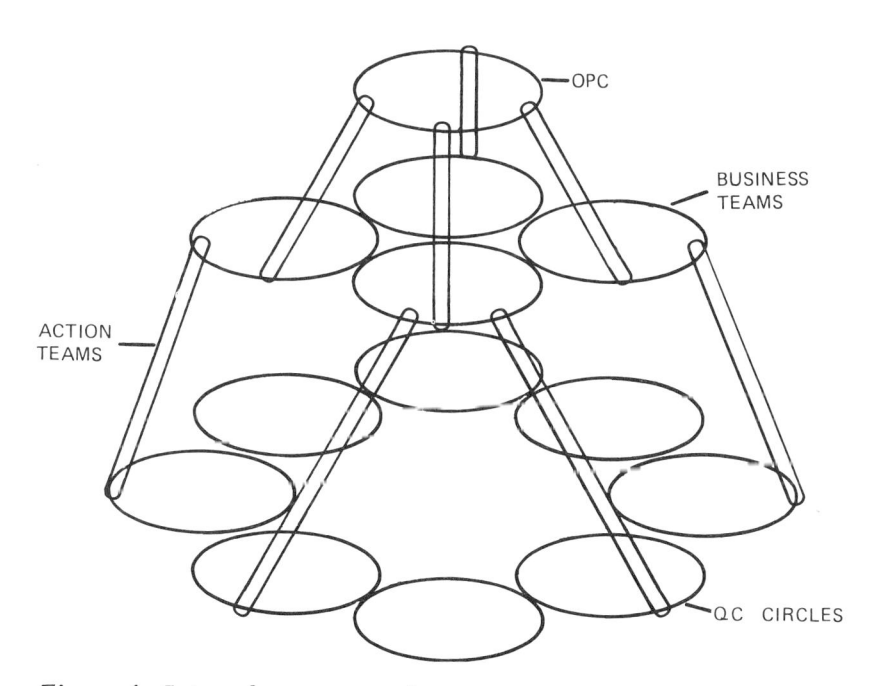

Figure 4 Integral management.

authority, makes recommendations of actions needed to improve overall business.

The three horizontal layers are composed of:

1. *The operating policy committee.* Comprised of top management personnel and chaired by the divisional president.
2. *Business teams.* Include appropriate management personnel from manufacturing, finance, quality, customer service, etc., led by the appropriate product manager.
3. *Quality circles.* Groups of employees from various levels who perform similar work and are trained and organized to improve the company and the employee's work life quality.

The vertical rings in the integral management diagram are action teams.

4. *Action teams.* Groups of various specialists chosen and geared to accomplish specific problem-solving projects. These teams also provide coordination and consultation for all the horizontally aligned management elements.

Although integral management certainly suffers from many of the disadvantages of matrix-type systems, it does provide the following very positive factors for the proposed participative total-quality program:

1. It merges innovative new structures like quality circles into the prime organizational structure rather than maintaining them as a separate entity.
2. It provides a formal structured environment in which people at various levels can communicate with each other, i.e., from employee quality circles through appropriate management presentations to top management.
3. It provides the opportunity to make "every employee a mana-

ger" (18) in a manner similar to the process described in M. Scott Myers' book. Employees at every level not only are able to uncover problems, but are able to solve and to make certain definitive decisions about those problems.

Although integral management is certainly not suggested as a general organizational system, it is believed that in preparing an organization for change, it is often necessary to provide a new or revised management system to increase the probability of successful change.

Invisible Organization

The theory, methods, and procedures of introducing organizational change into companies that have unions are covered in Chapter 5 by Rubenstein and in various other current publications (19,20).

However, our organization was nonunion, and in many instances the invisible organization that exists in many nonunion shops must be considered, treated, and involved in the change process in a manner similar to those used for unions, if we are to maximize the chances for success.

One of the major problems is that the "invisible organization" is more difficult to define and thus to include in implementation plans. It is somewhat similar to the problems encountered in fighting the Vietnam battles when, rather than having known battle lines and well-defined adversaries, the enemy was everywhere and sometime changed sides dependent on conditions.

One of the side benefits of conducting a quality-attitude survey and feeding back the information to small groups was that it allowed for location and definition of these internal influence groups. Once the groups were defined, the leaders of these "invisible unions" were involved at an early stage and treated and handled in a manner similar to traditional union representatives.

Unless this "invisible organization" factor is recognized and planned for prior to implementing a major change in an organization, it could become an important factor in the failure to implement such change.

Evaluation—The Quality of Work Life Survey

To Do or Not To Do: That Is The Question

Suggestions to conduct attitude surveys usually are met with mixed emotions, and this was certainly the case when it was suggested as a tool to determine the current status of the Hysol work life quality. Following the suggestions in the Bureau of Business Practice *Special Report* (21) the following questions were discussed with top management before making the final decision:

1. Can we afford it?
2. Do we have the necessary expertise?
3. Will this survey be used to change our operating or corporate policy?
4. Are we certain that there are no better sources of these data available?
5. Do we have adequate facilities to collect and analyze the requested data?
6. Are we prepared to act on the basis of the survey's results?

When these questions were answered affirmatively and satisfactorily, the consensus was to conduct the survey.

Finding the Appropriate Survey

There are many sources that will provide standard attitude/opinion surveys or modified ones, or will construct, usually at very high cost, a specific survey. All of these options were explored and discarded. To meet our particular needs, it was decided to develop a survey by joint participation of our internal staff and local university personnel.

Historical Background of HIQWL Survey (22)

The HIQWL Surveys were developed by a team led by Dr. K. Murrell, Assistant Professor, School of Management, Saint Bonaventure University, Saint Bonaventure, New York, and myself. The basic survey had a statistical factorial-designed format, which used 45 questions to analyze 15 QWL factors arranged in three major concern groups (individual, group, and organization). Over 400 questions were obtained from interviews conducted with all levels of company employees, and from standard attitude surveys. The questions selected for use came from a joint consensus agreement of a selection team made up of university and company personnel. Specialized surveys were also created to gain additional information from specific groups. Specific surveys were given in the following areas: scientists and engineers; managers and supervisors; office and service personnel; sales and field personnel.

The surveys were conducted in small groups by a team made up jointly of company and university personnel. All initial data were compiled by university personnel, and only the coded averages were evaluated by the joint company/university team using various statistical evaluation methods.

Besides providing reports to all levels of management, the condensed results of the surveys were fed back directly to the employees in the same small groups (8-15) in which the survey was taken to accomplish the following objectives:

1. To inform all employees what their group had said, and how it agreed with and related to the total organization

2. To convince employees that upper management had listened to what had been said with deep interest

3. To allow employees the opportunity to comment on or clarify results and interpretation of results

4. To prepare the groups for actions designed to alter some conditions, and whenever possible to provide for the employees' active commitment and involvement in the corrective-action phase of the program

An example of survey results and action taken to correct conditions is described later under the communication factor.

What Was Accomplished?

It cannot be denied that surveys do require expenditure of time and dollars, but in this instance the following objectives were accomplished:

1. It provided a baseline workmark that indicated where the organization was at, at that particular time. These data also serve as a monitoring tool for determining the magnitude of future change.
2. It involved all Hysol employees in the program using small teams to determine the area of QWL that needed attention and revision. An additional result was that we gained the active commitment and involvement of all employees early in the program.
3. It provided an internal research tool to show relationships of QWL to other organizational systems.
4. It provided input for strategic planning and development.
5. It provided specific information about areas needing improvement, so that an action plan could be established.

Employee/Management Gap

In our organization, as in many companies, an employee/management gap existed. The job function of management commonly is defined in business schools as planning, organizing, leading, and controlling, as shown in Figure 5. Many managers will agree to delegate some of the leading and controlling to their first-line supervisors, but the prime task of doing belongs to the workers. This is depicted in Figure 6. This type of management thinking creates a management-labor dichotomy (18), which deliberately or otherwise portrays workers as dumb, uninformed, noncreative,

PREPARING FOR CHANGE

1 — *Planning*: objectives, goals, strategies, programs, systems, policies, forecasts.
2 — *Organizing*: manpower, money, machines, materials, methods.
3 — *Leading*: communicating, motivating, instructing, delegating, mediating.
4 — *Controlling*: auditing, measuring, evaluating, correcting.

Figure 5 The functions of management.

irresponsible people who must be closely directed and controlled to achieve desired results. These beliefs produce a "we/they" society, and work and social alienation between the two groups. This management-labor dichotomy is depicted in Figure 7.

This gap could be observed at lunchtime in the company cafeteria. Plant workers sat, talked, and played cards with plant workers, and those of management who frequented the lunchroom tended to sit at separate tables.

Our two goals concerning the employee-management gap were (1) to find a method to measure it, and (2) to plan ways to improve or minimize the effect of this factor on our program.

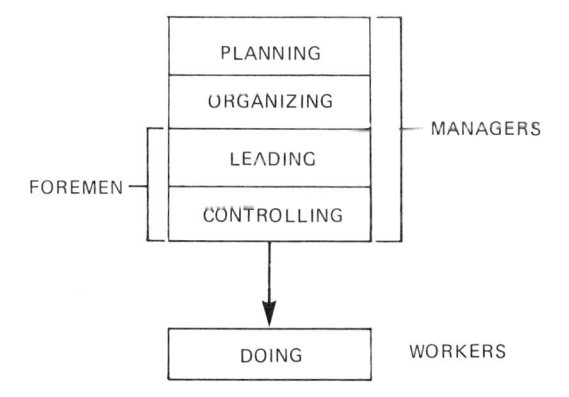

Figure 6 The manager's traditional perception of his job.

```
    PLANNING
    ORGANIZING
    LEADING
    CONTROLLING        MANAGEMENT
         |          ─ ─ ─ ─↑─ ─ ─ ─
         |             SOCIAL DISTANCE
         |              ALIENATION
         ↓          ─ ─ ─ ─↓─ ─ ─ ─
      DOING              LABOR
```

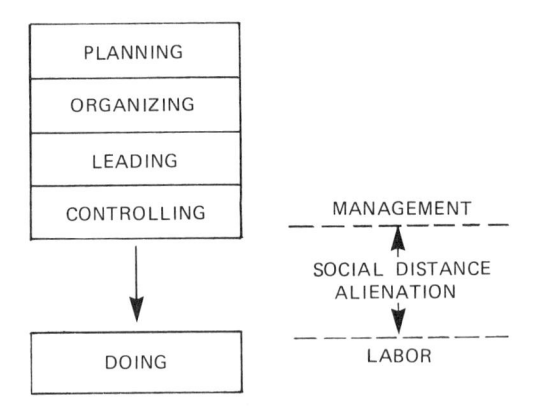

Figure 7 The management-labor dichotomy.

The measurement of this factor came as a side result of the quality of work life survey explained earlier. Figure 8 shows the results of the attitudes of Hysol hourly employees in contrast to those of Hysol management concerning the 14 elements of the QWL survey. Although this gap varied from operating plant to operating plant, it provided an index that showed the current gap and also could be used to show improvement as positive corrective action steps were completed.

Programs such as quality circles, QWL, and integral management were planned to improve the socioeconomic status and the aspiration of the workers. To reduce the gap from the management side, training about the awareness of management's new role in a participative organization was the prime thrust.

Training

If a total-quality management program was to have any chance at all of succeeding, massive and extensive training had to be planned for and implemented. This need for training was realized and pinpointed during the quality survey and was the number one corrective action suggested to top management for implementation.

Since the organization at that time had no formalized training department, steps were taken to create and staff one. The training

PREPARING FOR CHANGE

EMPLOYEE CONSIDERATION

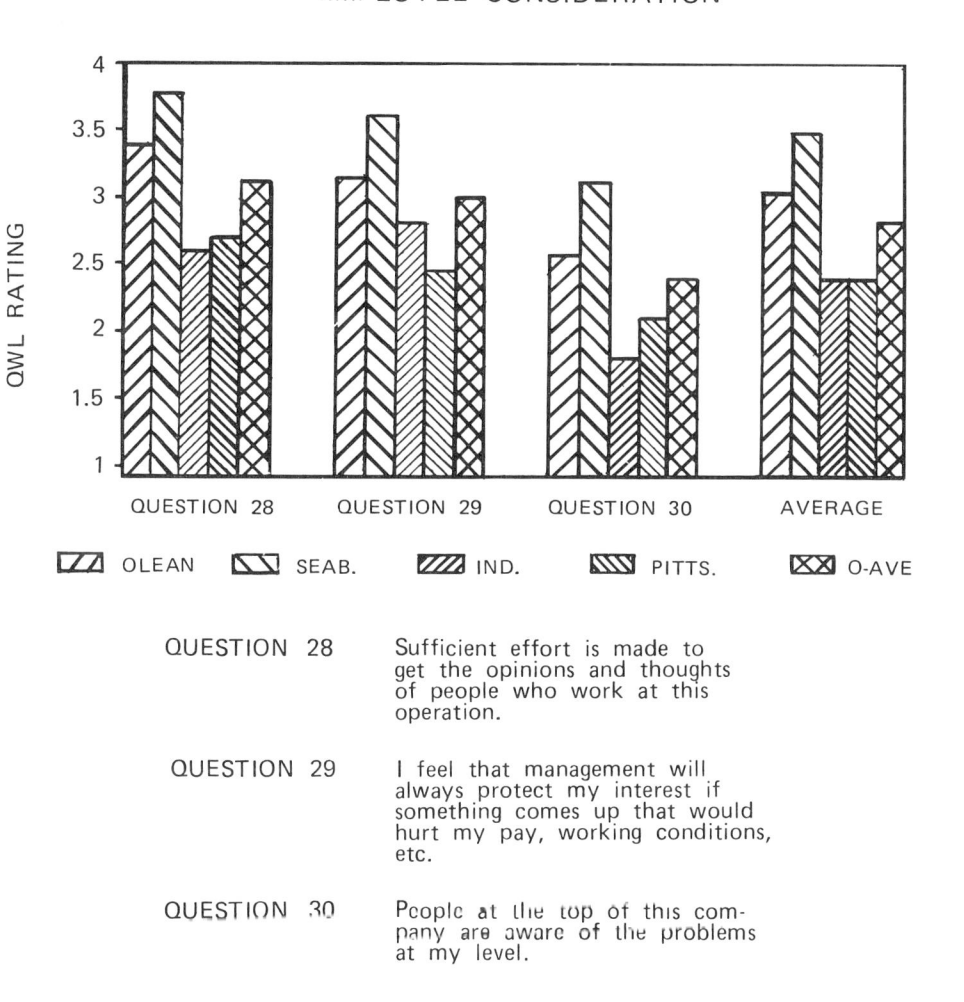

QUESTION 28	Sufficient effort is made to get the opinions and thoughts of people who work at this operation.
QUESTION 29	I feel that management will always protect my interest if something comes up that would hurt my pay, working conditions, etc.
QUESTION 30	People at the top of this company are aware of the problems at my level.

Figure 8 Hysol improved quality of work life survey: organizational concerns, Hysol division.

program was planned to involve employees from top management down to the factory floor.

Managers were trained in such things as: (1) statistical techniques; (2) setting program goals and workmarks; and (3) establishing and utilizing quality cost systems.

Technical, quality, and engineering personnel were trained in: (1) how to support the project; (2) statistical process control; (3) utilization and measurement of resources.

Supervisors were trained in: (1) leadership and communication skills; (2) statistical and creativity problem-solving skills; and (3) team-building methodology.

Employees were trained in subjects such as: (1) quality awareness; (2) teamwork; and (3) statistical techniques.

Some of the training was conducted externally at ASQC, AMA, Crosby College, and other appropriate workshops and seminars. Whenever possible, however, local community colleges and universities were used for training because of economic and/or logistic consideration. Extensive utilization of community colleges in providing quality training is currently being fostered by the Transformation of American Industry program in conjunction with ASQC (23).

Well-trained employees are an essential element in any organization change program. This factor requires the expenditure of resources and time, and thus must be incorporated into a program during the planning stage.

Incentives

When workers are invited and allowed to become involved in teams, circles, and other participative groups, one question that is sure to arise is, "How are the workers to be compensated?" It has been shown (24) that companies that have formal incentive plans for their top executives earned, on the average, 43.6% more pretax profit than did the nonincentive companies. If incentives help to increase the involvement and commitment of top managers, why shouldn't this method be applicable to all workers who are involved in improvement programs? Edward J.

PREPARING FOR CHANGE

Feeney, consultant, believes that "if you want to get more out of your employees, reward them" (24). He goes on to state, "Money, I firmly believe is the single most powerful reinforcer. It's a myth held by some management people that money isn't a strong reinforcer. What makes money so powerful is the multitude of reinforcers you can buy with it" (24).

Most quality circles, QWL programs, and other participative authorities (25) have strongly advised against monetary incentives. Many have stated that the only incentive or reward workers require is a feeling of satisfaction from having done a good job and having helped the company. Workers, however, recognize this dichotomy, and it becomes another factor in widening the employee-management gap.

For our program, it was decided to investigate ways of allowing all members of the organization to share monetarily in cost reductions that occurred due to direct quality improvement. Productivity improvement plans such as the Scanlon Plan (26) were developed as early as 1930, and some, such as the plan at Herman Miller, Inc. started in 1934, are still active and considered successful by the existing management (27).

After investigation of Scanlon type plans, Rucker Plans (28), Improshare Plans (29), and other bonus and profit-sharing plans, we decided to utilize the existing profit-sharing plan, but to tie it in with the new improvement program. An advantage of this decision was that the plan was already in existence, and it was compatible with the "perspective" we were promoting in that everyone, both active and inactive employees, shared in the profits. It was thus just a matter of aligning the structure, making employees aware, and trying to develop a family-sharing environment, which was needed to provide a monetary incentive for our improvement program.

Innovation

One of the prime reasons for introducing quality circles and similar participative groups into an organization is to tap the creativity and innovative abilities of workers. When we looked at our group of volunteers, many of whom had little or no experience or training in innovative processes, many questions came to mind, such as:

Which individuals or groups are innovative?

What forces promote innovation?

Which forces inhibit innovation?

Does the group have sufficient innovation to successfully solve its selected problem?

If we define "innovation" as the process of making something that has intrinsic value—economic, scientific, motivational—into something new, then it becomes desirable to have a means of forecasting this property in circles or other groups to reduce the frustration and possible failure related to selecting and attempting to solve problems without the required essential attributes.

A Northwestern University group (30) has studied the innovation process in U.S. industrial organization and isolated the following elements as positive or negative influences on the innovation process in U.S. industrial organizations and isolated the folstimulants.

Milton A. Glaser, a former Vice President of R&D for the Dexter Corporation, developed an "innovation index" to provide a method of measuring and enhancing the chances of success of R&D groups by looking at certain key elements, which embodies the five influences outlined by the Northwestern University group (31,32). This index was revised and used to aid in improving the probability of selecting quality-circle problems that ensure a high degree of success, completion, and satisfaction for the circle and the company.

When the group of workers who perform similar work decides to establish a quality circle to identify and solve problems, it is typical for them to suggest from 30 to 100 possible problems concerning their immediate work area. Selecting the problems that have the best chance of establishing a "win-win" success pattern

Table 1 Jones-Glaser Innovation Index: Quality Circle Model

| Element | Weight | Rating of Project ||||
		A	B	C	D
1. Effectiveness of communications composed of:	20				
a. CM-Circle/management interface (10)		14	18	18	15
b. CC-Circle circle interface (5)					
c. CP-Circle production interface (5)					
2. Technical competence	15	14	12	15	11
3. Effectiveness of a champion	15	12	15	14	12
4. Improvement of work life	15	15	15	13	14
5. Improvement of quality	15	11	15	12	12
6. Cost saving	10	6	4	10	6
7. Timing	10	6	8	10	10
Innovation potential	100	78	72	92	80

Project descriptions:
   A. Master keys for leadmen to tool and supply locker.
   B. Establishment of system for broken tool compensation.
   C. Regular shop meetings with management.
   D. System for updating and obtaining new tools and equipment.

tern for the circle and the company is difficult. Typically, the selection has been achieved by group consensus using a democratic voting process, but in many cases, the problem selected not only does not meet the criteria desired, but actually becomes a factor that is detrimental to the circle's progress and development.

The Jones-Glaser Innovation Index (JGII) was adapted from the Glaser Innovation Index (GII) to provide a numerical method for evaluating and monitoring the selection and results of problems selected by small participative teams.

Table 1 shows the original innovation potential results for the top four projects selected from the brainstorming list of a Dexter-

Table 2 Quality of Work Life Evaluation Sheet

Project name_____

Instruction: Rate each quality of work life (QWL) factor on a scale of from 0 to 10 depending on how you feel the completed project will affect you and your particular work area and situation.

Factor	Rating of project			
	A	B	C	D
1. Economic well-being	6.6	9.7	9.0	6.5
2. Physical working environment	9.0	9.2	8.1	9.0
3. Recognition of performance	8.4	7.4	9.8	8.2
4. Employee involvement and influence	6.4	8.2	9.0	7.2
5. Job stress	6.5	8.8	7.1	8.3
6. Skill development and utilization	6.2	5.5	7.2	7.8
7. Employee management relations	4.8	8.2	9.7	5.4
8. Intergroup relations	8.2	5.5	9.1	4.7
9. Job progress	8.1	9.6	8.2	8.9
10. Communications	6.2	4.7	9.9	2.4
11. Employee loyalty	5.5	7.2	7.7	4.5
12. Employee state of mind	8.2	9.8	9.8	7.4
13. Job interest	9.1	8.5	9.9	9.6
14. Job satisfaction	7.8	8.2	8.8	8.8
15. Respect for the individual	6.0	7.0	8.2	4.2
Grand total	107	117.5	131.5	102.9
QWL index	71.3	78.3	87.7	68.6

$$\text{QWL index} = \frac{\text{Grand total}}{150} \times 100$$

Project descriptions:
A. Master keys for leadmen to tool and supply locker.
B. Establishment of system for broken tool compensation.
C. Regular shop meetings with management.
D. System for updating and obtaining new tools and equipment.

PREPARING FOR CHANGE 43

Hysol quality circle composed of maintenance department employees. After the projects were completed by the circle, they were rated by circle members and management as to how they believed the end results affected the quality of the group's work life. The results of the rating of the projects are shown in Table 2.

By utilizing the Jones-Glaser Innovation Index, we were able to break the suggested projects into certain elements and place measurements on the elements and on the overall projects. Projects that obtained an innovation potential below 70 were either rejected as possible problems, or the innovation potential was raised by providing additional emphasis or expertise for that element, as needed. The opinions and attitudes of the workers and management about the projects were measured to provide an index of the workers' satisfaction.

Participative group activities were a "new change" for our workers. Rather than allow them to stagger through this change, early in the planning stage we took steps to aid the change by creating and planning innovative procedures.

Communication

Planning for improved communication at all levels must certainly be one of the change factors included in a successful program. Lack of communication was the most negatively rated factor in our quality survey. As an example, Figure 9 presents the results obtained in reply to the following question, "Do you believe top management understands your problems?"

Our planned approach was based on the communication matrix as described by Level and Galle (33). However, some adaptation was needed.

The communication matrix was structured to include the tasks and tools for communication among staff/professionals, front-line managers, middle managers, and top managers. For our use, this matrix was extended to include supervisors and line workers, since our program goal was to include all employees, not just managers and professionals.

The following list describes some of the communication tools planned to help improve Hysol Division communication:

––– Employee QWL Survey Response

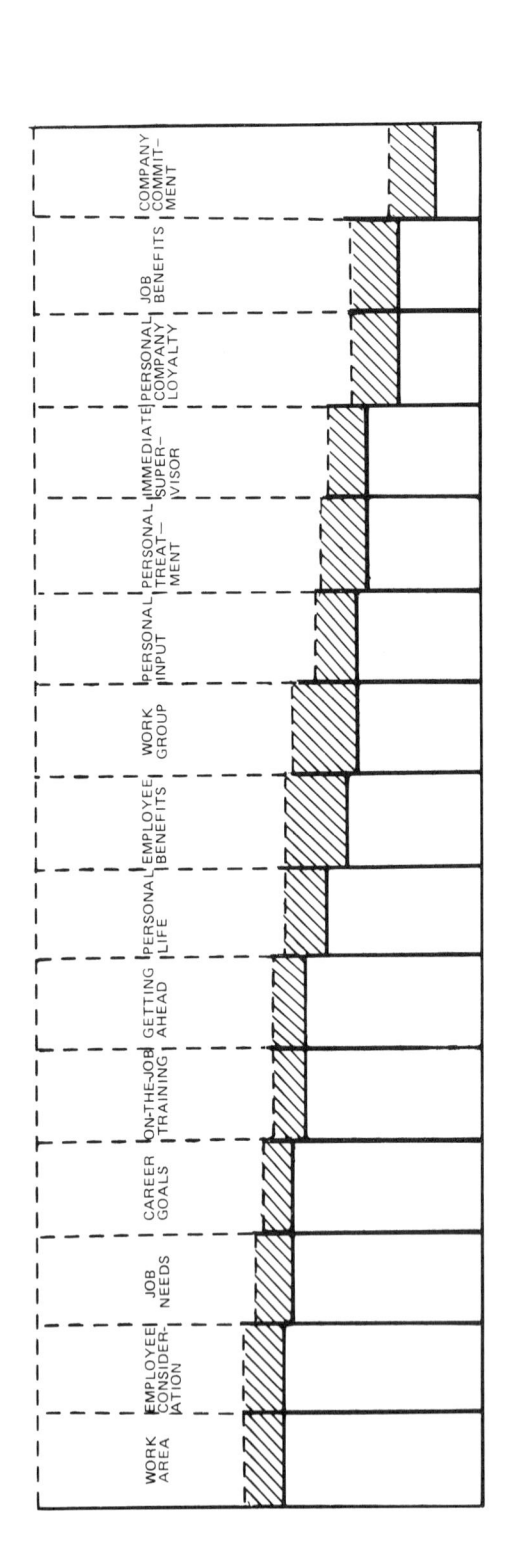

––– Management QWL Survey Response

▨ Employee / Management Gap

Figure 9 Employee/management gap.

1. Top-management letters—The divisional president instituted a periodic informative letter to all employees to increase awareness of developments that affected the employees.
2. Division newsletter—A division newsletter was established and structured to maximize employee participation.
3. Quality-circle newsletter—Individual teams were provided with a means of communicating with both the active and nonactive members.
4. Special publications—One of the quality circles, The Golden You, dedicated its entire program to improving communication. It published people-oriented articles with special emphasis on employee's nonwork life as well as their work life.
5. Toastmaster International—Special inhouse Toastmaster Clubs were established and subsidized by the company to allow workers to independently improve their communication skills.

Improvement of communication is a never-ending program, but is certainly one of the factors that must be planned to aid a people-oriented program.

Putting the Factors Together

By putting together the initial letters of our program factors, the acronym, POETIC is spelled out. In addition to providing a means of structuring and remembering the elements of our plan, the acronym POETIC was utilized for another special reason. Poetic is defined as the art of creating a language of imagination expressed in verse. Good or bad poetry cannot be adequately defined as the putting together of certain metered lines, since there are additional undefinable properties that distinguish the good from the bad.

Peters and Waterman, in their book *In Search of Excellence* (4), alluded to the emotional and idealistic properties that seemed to permeate those excellent companies. This attribute was provided at IBM by Thomas Watson, Jr., at McDonalds by Raymond

Kroc, and at Disney Productions by Walt Disney. In a like manner, it is my belief that every good program must try to foster this undefined emotional aspect, to improve the opportunity for success.

Planning for change is only part of the game. These plans must be implemented, audited, revised, and nurtured to obtain success. But without the thought, insight, and creativity that go into a good planning stage, the chance of final success in introducing CHANGE into an organization is drastically diminished. For, as Naisbitt remarks in his book *Megatrends* (3):

> Change occurs when there is a confluence of both changing values and economic necessity, not before.

Selected Readings

1. Toffler, Alvin, *Future Shock*, Random House, New York, 1970.
2. Schuler, Robert H., *Tough Minded Faith for Tender Hearted People*, Bantam Books, New York, 1983.
3. Naisbitt, John, *Megatrends*, Warner Books Inc., New York, 1982.
4. Peters, T. and Waterman, R. H., *In Search of Excellence*, Warner Books Inc., New York, 1982.
5. Gibson, David W., Dexter, rooted in the past, looks to the future, *Chem. Week*, April 1977, pp. 25-29.
6. Ouchi, W. G., *Theory Z*, Addison-Wesley Publishing Co., Reading, MA, 1981.
7. *The Dexter Company Annual Report*, Windsor Locks, CT, 1981.
8. Rudge, Fred, *The Keys to Increased Productivity*, Bureau of National Affairs, Washington, DC, 1977.
9. Ingle, Sud, How to avoid quality circle failure in your company, *Training and Development Journal*, June 1982.
10. Werther, William B., Quality circles and corporate culture, *National Productivity Review*, Summer 1982.
11. Juran, J. M., *Quality Control Handbook*, McGraw-Hill, New York, 1978.

12. Caplan, Frank, *The Quality System*, Chilton Book Co., Radnor, PA, 1980.
13. Hayes, G. E. and Romig, H. G., *Modern Quality Control*, BRUCE, Encino, CA, 1977.
14. Higginson, M. Valliant, *Management Policies II*, American Management Association, Inc., 1966.
15. Crosby, Philip B., *Quality Is Free*, McGraw-Hill, New York, 1979.
16. Crosby, Philip B., How to stem the tide of shoddy materials, *Purchasing*, May 1982.
17. Executives in action, *The Executive of Los Angeles*, Vol. 5, No. 13, Nov. 1981.
18. Myers, M. Scott, *Every Employee a Manager*, McGraw-Hill, New York, 1970.
19. Brower, Michael J., Growth in union support, *QWL Focus*, Ontario QWL Centre, Ontario, Canada, Feb. 1983.
20. Bluestone, Irving, Human dignity is what it's all about, *Viewpoint*, Vol 8, No. 3, 3rd Quar. 1978.
21. Bureau of Business Practice, *"Special Report: Attitude Surveys,"* Waterford, CT, 1981.
22. Jones, Louis N., *IQ Surveys*, 1364 Windfall Rd, Olean, New York.
23. Hannan, C. J. and Leddick, A. Susan, Industrial reform, *Community and Jr. College Journal*, Feb. 1984.
24. How to get more from your employees, *INC*, Nov. 1981.
25. Dewar, Donald L., *The Quality Circle Handbook*, Quality Circle Institute, Red Bluff, CA, 1980.
26. Cartin, Thomas J., Quality circles concept—An American invention, 1981 ASQC Quality Congress Transactions, Milwaukee, WI, 1981.
27. Zager, R. and Rosow, M. P., *The Innovation Organization*, Chap. 4 in C. F. Frost, *The Scanlon Plan at Herman Miller, Inc.*, Pergamon Press, Elmsford, NY 1982.
28. Schuster, M. H. and Miller, C. S., Integrating gain sharing and quality circles, *Quality Circles Journal*, Vol. 7-3, Sept. 1984.
29. Fein, M. *Improshare: An Alternative to Traditional Managing*, Institute of Industrial Engineers, Norcross, GA, 1981.
30. Rubenstein, A. H. and Chakrabarti, A. K., *Third Progress*

Report of Field Studies of Technical Innovation Process, Northwestern University, Evanston, IL, 1974.
31. Glaser, Milton A., The innovation index, *Chem Tech.* Vol. 6, March 1976, pp. 182-187.
32. Glaser, Milton A., Managing for innovation in coatings, *American Paint & Coating Journal*, March 1980, pp. 50-58.
33. Level, Dale A., Jr. and Galle, W. P., *Business Communication—Theory and Practice*, Business Publication, Dallas, TX, 1980.

3
Human Factors Engineering

C. B. ROGERS   Digital Equipment Corporation, Stow, Massachusetts

The study of human factors involves learning how to substantially improve the ways in which each of us performs our daily tasks and how we interact with others. Early caveman quickly discovered that the length, diameter, and roughness of the branch he was fashioning into a spear affected how well he was able to stop the charge of a saber-toothed tiger. Although the conditions have changed (some would say just slightly), each of us has the ability to improve our effectiveness and comfort by learning how to make positive adaptations between ourselves and the rest of the world. This chapter deals with scientific ways in which all of us, whether president, engineer, or quality-circle member, can make QUANTUM leaps in performance and effectiveness by application of some of the simple tools of human factors.

We are part of several systems: the world, our company, the state we live in, and our family, and our circle of friends. In each we interact with others, use tools and/or machines, and in one way or another affect the environment around us. In another sense, each of us is a separate, highly complex, and unique system and, as we shall see, much more unique than we probably thought. For most of us, our visual and auditory systems (eyes and ears) are the major sources of information input. The manner in which signals are presented to these systems can greatly impact whether or not they are perceived and understood. Moving out from these inner systems, we will look at how our immediate surroundings (the work station) can affect our performance and how to make it work for us rather than against us. We will also study yet another type of system, the human/computer interface. From the panel of a microwave oven, to electronic banktellers, to the keyboard of a word processor, application of human factors principles can help to guide us in the selection and use of these devices. How we approach this task both separately and collectively will have a major impact on our life-style and productivity in the months and years ahead. To take advantage of this, we need to understand what "user friendly" means in more than a casual manner. Both hardware (keyboards, CRTs, etc.) as well as software will be examined in the light of individual needs.

In one respect this chapter will depart from traditional human factors literature, which for the most part describes the results of studies and serves to document *what was*. A more proactive approach is needed to find out *what can be*, and it is here that work sampling and design of experiments can play an important role. Both these techniques can be used to help each of us achieve more with less effort and come to better understand the amazingly complex and variable electrochemical system each of us calls "me."

Visual Systems

The study of a system is aided by subdividing the process into at least three parts: input, processing, and output, as shown in Figure 1.

HUMAN FACTORS ENGINEERING

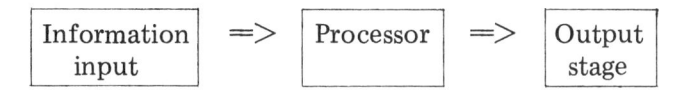

```
┌─────────────┐      ┌───────────┐      ┌──────────┐
│ Information │ =>   │ Processor │ =>   │  Output  │
│    input    │      │           │      │   stage  │
└─────────────┘      └───────────┘      └──────────┘
```

Figure 1 Systems subdivision.

The input to the visual system is capable of an enormous range of sensory stimuli. At the low end of visual sensing, the eye can detect the light from a candle flame at a distance of 30 miles on a dark night, while at the other extreme, it can also see objects illuminated by direct sunlight at a level 10,000,000,000 times greater. Despite the great capability of the human eye, performance can be significantly affected by the illumination provided for the task at hand. Fortunately, a great deal of effort has gone into the study of the effects of lighting over the years, and these data are now available in a form that can be converted into practical use. What is especially important is the recognition that for a given task, the lighting requirements need to be modified according to the age of the viewer, the criticality of the task, and the reflectance of the task background (Tables 1 and 2).

Thus, a younger supervisor setting up an inspection task for an older worker could easily misjudge the light level necessary to allow the worker to perform at optimum. In applying Tables 1 and 2 multiply the minimum illumination levels by the weighting factors to obtain the recommended value. Not only is the amount of light important, the manner in which it is presented should also be considered. Here, glare can influence the discomfort a worker experiences. In this category it should be noted that blue-eyed and older people are significantly more sensitive to glare than brown-eyed and younger people. Once again, this is of importance to those of us who are setting up work areas for others to use.

Information Presentation

It has been said that the United States is data rich and information poor. In recent years, we have seen a great increase in our ability to pump out vast amounts of printed material. At the push of a

Table 1 Recommended Minimum Indoor Illumination Levels

Minimum illum. (foot candles)	Activity/reference
0.01 REF	Full moon
20	Public streets with dark surroundings
50	Simple orientation
100 REF	Overcast day
200	Simple visual tasks—reading large print with good contrast, general assembly, simple inspection
500	Visual tasks with medium contrast—medium-pencil writing, medium assembly and inspection work
1000	Low-contrast or small-size visual tasks—hard-pencil writing on poor-quality paper, difficult inspection
2000	Low-contrast and very small size continuous visual tasks—fine assembly work, very difficult inspection
5000	Very prolonged and exacting visual tasks—extra-fine assembly work, most difficult inspection
9000 REF	Direct sunlight

Source: Adapted from Ref. 3 and Ref. 5 (Figure 6.6).

Table 2 Recommended Multipliers for Illumination Levels

	Multipliers		
Factor	×100%	×150%	×200%
Age	Under 40	40-55	Over 55
Speed or accuracy	Unimportant	Important	Critical
Reflectance of task or background	Over 70%	30-70%	Under 30%

HUMAN FACTORS ENGINEERING

button, many of us can now create tabular and written reports thousands of pages long. It is only very recently that we have been able to convert this vast amount of numerical data into pictorial format with the same ease. As we gain more understanding about how we humans process information, it is becoming clear that most of us remember and understand graphical forms of data presentation much better than plain tables or numbers. The application of human factors information can often aid in the process of information transfer. For example, most people expect values to increase as the graph goes from left to right and from bottom to top. In addition, the form of the presentation can greatly affect the accuracy and speed with which graphical information is interpreted, as shown in Figure 2.

The effective use of color has been recognized and taken advantage of in both work and nonwork situations for countless years. Red, for instance, is associated with STOP and DANGER and LOSS. Yellow is used to connote CAUTION, and green is used for

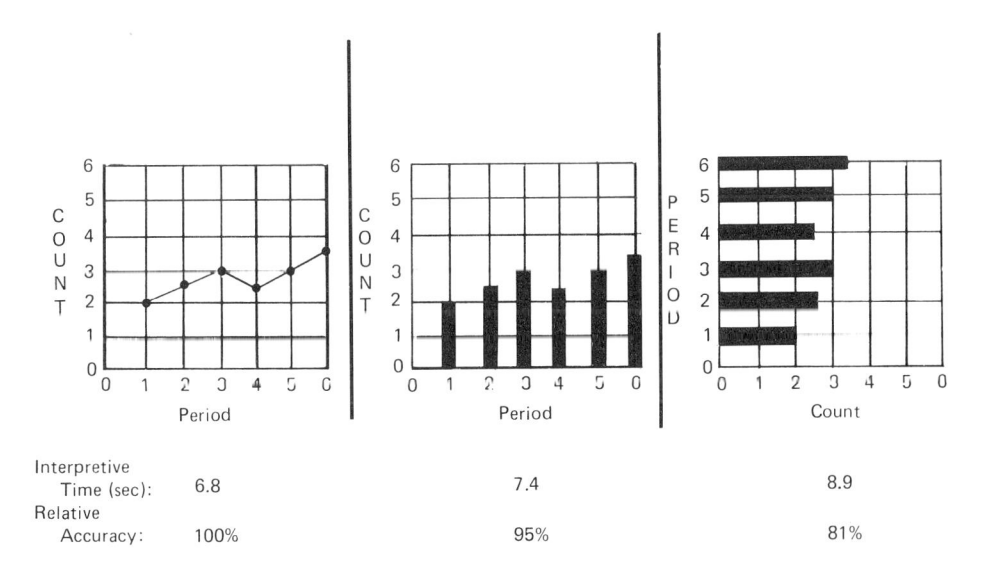

Interpretive Time (sec):	6.8	7.4	8.9
Relative Accuracy:	100%	95%	81%

Figure 2 Time and accuracy in graph interpretation. (Adapted from Ref. 3, Figure 4.20.)

GO, OK, and PROFIT. In information presentation we can liken the use of color to the use of a third dimension which can add to the quality of the information transfer. Here again, good human factors knowledge can be put to use as we realize that 6-8% of the male population and 0.5% of the female population suffers from some partial color blindness. Thus, the use of color as a sole identifier is not a wise decision. The most common color dysfunction is red/green; so graphics and markings that use this combination should be carefully annotated. It might be of interest to note, however, that only 0.003% of the population see no color at all; so the significant value of color coding should always be considered.

Printed Materials

The use of printed material to communicate is so common that we often overlook the application of human factors in this area. The ease with which we are able to read various documents often dictates which ones we read and how well the material is understood. Human factors studies show that the readability of printed matter can be influenced by many factors, including type style (font), type form (capital, lowercase, italics, boldface, etc.), spacing between lines, size of type, and width of lines. Readability is improved if the text contains upper- and lower-case letters RATHER THAN BEING ALL UPPER CASE. Readability is also better when the lower-case letters have true descenders (i.e., extensions below the line), such as with y, g, and q. Use of **boldface** is preferable to *italics* for emphasis, especially when the message is lengthy. Line length also tends to influence comprehension; the two-column style is preferable. Finally, in dim lighting conditions, a plain typeface, such as Gothic, is preferred together with larger print.

The preceding guidelines clearly have practical applications if we take the time to consider how the material is going to be used. It is not unusual to find a poorly reproduced copy of instructions printed in small, low-quality type, being used in dim light; the text covers a full 8.5 × 11 page with no illustrations and is written in a style that would put even an insomniac to sleep. The answer

HUMAN FACTORS ENGINEERING

(which can save your company tens of thousands of dollars of scrap, rework, and errors) is to provide every writer of instructions with a copy of *Popular Science*. This excellently written magazine is a near-perfect example of how to clearly and interestingly package technical information so as to appeal to a broad audience. By studying its style, layout, and use of graphics, writers can go a long way toward minimizing the high costs of (mis)understanding. (You might even start a *Popular Science* Challenge Campaign, awarding annual free subscriptions to the writers of the most readable instructions and/or procedures.)

As a final comment on written instructions, the old KISS (Keep It Simple, Stupid) motto can apply to warnings as well. A military manual was found with the following note:

> WARNING: The batteries in the AN/MSQ could be a lethal source of electrical power under certain conditions.

Fortunately, some clear-thinking soldier had printed next to the lethal terminals in large red letters:

LOOK OUT!
THIS CAN KILL YOU

In six words, the soldier not only got the message across, he did it in a fashion most everyone could relate to (2, p. 406).

Dials, Scales, and Displays

Few of us pass a day without using or being affected by the setting on a dial or display of one sort or another. From the speedometer in our car to a dial indicator in an inspection department, from the knob on an electric range to the altimeter being used by the pilot in a jet plane we are riding in, our lives and the products of our work can be influenced by how well and how quickly the meaning of a dial or display is interpreted.

In minimizing errors, a good human factors principle is to take advantage of peoples' familiarity with common items. A simple example is the clock. Most of us are conditioned to a clockwise (note the terminology) movement of a pointer as representing an increase. In some of my early work in the quality field I encountered several inspection gages with dials reading positive values in the opposite (counterclockwise) direction. The supervisor blamed the errors on 'people don't try hard enough' until one day, while instructing a new operator, the supervisor also misread the gage several times. Fortunately, in this case the supervisor recognized the human factors principle being violated, and shortly thereafter the gage was replaced with one that had positive values going in the 'right' direction (Figure 3).

Misreading is a common problem with displays that contain multiple scales. Even with correct pointer movement, it is common for persons to make errors when reading this type of scale. One manufacturer's solution was to place the scale factors in a window so that when the meter was switched from one setting to another, the correct scale value appeared in the window and all other (incorrect) scales were hidden. The advent of digital readouts has provided some relief in this area, but again, it has taken a while for the human factors influence to catch up. Some early electronic meters, when presented with a dangerous overload, would merely go blank. This frequently left the user assuming that there was *no* voltage present! Newer versions now contain both an analog display showing an offscale indication >>>>> as well as a digital readout.

Good (Clockwise)   Poor (Counterclockwise)

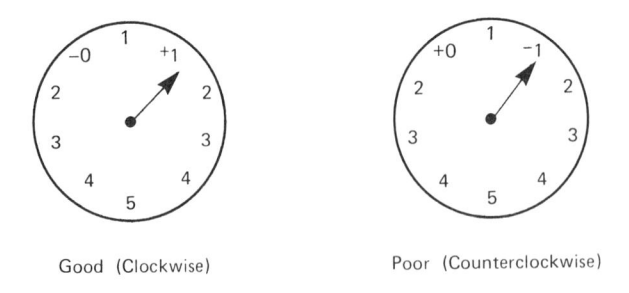

Figure 3 Dial layout.

HUMAN FACTORS ENGINEERING

In using digital readouts, we are also generally unable to take advantage of color to caution or warn us. Early analog dials frequently were coded with green (OK), yellow (caution), and red (danger) zones. This brought into play a vital human factors tool (redundant sensory coding), which will be discussed in this section on sound. Does this mean that digital displays are less useful? Not really, because unlike analog displays, digital displays can BLINK/FLASH, which can be even more noticeable than colored dials!

Auditory Systems

What We Hear

Much of what we do each day is a direct result of auditory inputs. From the ring of the alarm clock in the morning to the late-news report each night, we are immersed in a world of sound. How well we interpret these auditory inputs is a function of both our environment and our own hearing. The following oft-quoted comment is worth pondering as we look at ways in which we can influence our auditory environment: *"I know you believe you understand what you think I said, but I am not sure you realize that what you heard is not what I meant."*

Sound is our perception of rapid changes in the air pressure reaching our inner ear. For practical purposes, this pressure is usually expressed in decibels (a logarithmic ratio). The important point to consider regarding decibels is that a 20-decibel increase in sound level is equivalent to a hundredfold increase in power, while a 3-decibel increase represents a doubling of power. Some representative sound levels are shown in Table 3 using the dbA system where a weighting is applied to the values to more closely track human hearing sensitivity.

As most of us are aware, our ears are sensitive to frequency (hence the tone control on our radios) as well as volume. Frequency of sound is usually expressed in Hertz (abbreviated Hz), which represents the number of cycles the sound pressure wave makes each second. The normal ear responds to sounds in the range from 20 to 20,000 Hz, although hearing has been reported

Table 3 Representative Sound Levels

Sound "power"	dbA	Activity
1,000,000,000,000	120	Rock concert stage
10,000,000,000	100	Pneumatic jackhammer
100,000,000	80	Assembly line
1,000,000	60	Business office
10,000	40	Library
100	20	Broadcasting studio
10	10	Normal breathing
1	0	Threshold of hearing

Source: Adapted from Ref. 3 (Fig. 5.2) and Ref. 4 (Table 10.1).

down to 5 Hz and up as high as 100,000 Hz. High-frequency sensitivity begins to decline for most adults after the age of 50, with few persons past 65 able to detect frequencies over 10,000 Hz. What does this mean to those of us who set up auditory systems (telephone, PA, voice, or warning signals) for others? Very simply, it means that just because you can hear something it doesn't mean that others will and just because you can't hear something it doesn't mean that others can't!

This principle was brought home to me during my student days at Cornell University. I was working part time at a hi-fi store when I suddenly realized that middle-aged male customers would end up buying more expensive (lower-distortion) components when they sought the opinion of a female companion. Later in my career I was discussing this phenomenon with a female manager who had canceled a large order of computer terminals because of the (high-frequency) noise they made. When she tried to explain the problem to the field service engineer sent to correct the situation, they both became frustrated because he was unable to hear any of the noise she was referring to!

HUMAN FACTORS ENGINEERING

The preceding examples demonstrate the importance of taking perception of sound into account. Another important aspect of sound deals with the conversion of sound to information. Consider for a moment the case of the woman who phoned in an order for six wineglasses (model E3401) and received six punchbowls (model V3401). Was this really a case of an inattentive ordertaker or could this problem have been prevented? The similarity of the model numbers could have been avoided by careful reference to Table 4.

In comparing the combinations in Table 4, one is likely to encounter pairings that do not appear at all alike. Pause for a moment, however, and try them again using a strong Southern or British accent—you may well be surprised at the similarity of the sounds. While this points out our regional bias toward phonetic sound-alikes, the lesson has a much broader implication. *We all tend to think that everyone else has the same cultural experience as we have. . .and that thinking. . . is wrong*

Table 4 Sound-Alike Auditory Characters

A-J	B-3	E-G	G-V	N-9	V-Z
A-K	C-E	E-P	G-3	O-0	V-Z
A-L	C-P	E-T	H-S	P-T	V-3
A-N	C-T	E-V	H-X	P-V	Z-3
A-8	C-2	E-Z	H-8	P-3	1-7
B-C	C-3	E-3	I-J	Q-2	1-9
B-D	D-E	F-S	I-Y	Q-U	6-8
B-G	D-V	G-P	I-9	S-X	
B-P	D-3	Q-T	M-N	T-2	

Source: Adapted from Ref. 2 (Table 16.5).

Noise Control

Our sensitivity to noise or undesirable sound depends on its predictability as well as its frequency and loudness. The story is told of a visitor to Niagara Falls asking a resident how he could sleep at night with the constant roar of the falls. The native replied, "What roar?" As we move from one environment to another, most of us have encountered situations where we were unpleasantly aware of the new sounds around us. Yet, like the native, we soon adapted, and in most cases no longer were bothered by the "noise" that had been so apparent. For cases where the general background level is too high for comfortable communication, the use of earplugs can help. In this case, what appears to be an anomaly—blocking one's ears to hear better—actually works! The voice plus the background sound often is too high for auditory functioning. However, the earplugs reduce both sounds so that the ear is no longer overloaded and can pick out the voice above the noise. In other cases, use of acoustic tile in the area can absorb much of the unwanted sound, as can mounting the offending noise generator on a sound-deadening mat.

With noise pollution being an unpopular subject these days, the thought of adding sound to a quiet environment seems another odd distortion of human factors principles. Yet, it is a fact that too quiet an environment can be disturbing to people. The student asleep in the library is a common sight, as is the student with his/her feet propped up studying away in the blare of the student union. What is at work here (although the students are probably unaware of it) is the value of noise as an arousal factor. The second student was taking advantage of the fact that the noise served as a stimulus thereby helping to promote alertness. In the workplace this has been studied, and a background level of about 50 db is generally considered optimum.

One other psychological/human factor issue was also at work here and that is the issue of control. By having control of the noise situation, i.e., the ability to get up and leave, the second student's reaction to the noise was much different than if the same noise

HUMAN FACTORS ENGINEERING

was in the dorm, where the student couldn't feel in control of the situation. This increased tolerance of humans for environmental extremes (noise, heat, humidity, etc.) when they feel in control can help make an undesirable job situation more comfortable. Creating an area where workers can go to escape the disturbance (noise, heat, etc.) whenever they want, with the agreement that they will make up the time, is often enough to relieve the problem.

Warning Systems

Sound has many advantages as a warning system. It can travel over long distances, around and over obstacles, both night and day. Also, for reasons that probably date back to our earliest ancestors, a sudden change in sound has priority over our other senses for getting our attention. Many of us are aware that the sound of fire, police, and ambulance warnings has changed dramatically over the past 20 years. A rescue vehicle speeding through a red light has a need to be recognized, and it was found after many accidents that the siren "wail" was generally not as effective as the "yeow" (descending change in frequency from 800 to 100 Hz every 1.4 sec) or the "squawk" (intermittent horn, 425 Hz, on for 0.7 sec, off for 0.6 sec). What we are observing is that some sounds can mask others, and so the choice of a warning signal should take potential background noise into account.

Another case illustrates the need for a warning that was overlooked. A young driver is hurrying off on an errand. It is a bright, sunny day, the road is dry, and the freeway is moderately busy. Suddenly the car comes to a halt, the cars following the driver barely able to avoid a collision! Flares are set and a wrecker called for. While preparing the car for its trip to the salvage yard, the driver of the wrecker notices that the oil plug had fallen from the car causing the oilless engine to seize up. The small, red oil light (barely visible in the bright sunlight) was still on when he looked inside the car. Later discussion clearly indicated that had an auditory warning been used, the driver would have stopped in time to avoid both risking an accident and losing the engine.

The lesson to be learned from the preceding story is twofold. First, we should use redundant sensory coding (auditory alarms in combination with visual signals) in autos and elsewhere where hazardous situations are involved. Second, just because the equipment is expensive doesn't mean that all the human factors involved in its use have been well considered. The Three Mile Island nuclear reactor, a moderately costly piece of equipment, is a classic example of poor human factors engineering. At the peak of the crisis, over 100 alarms were activated with no way of deactivating the unimportant ones or identifying the important ones. Do we have to wait for disaster to uncover these problems in our own work environments? I, like the other authors of this book, think not. If we encourage individual work groups to examine how their work environments can be made safer, more satisfying, and more productive, then everyone benefits and problems can be avoided rather than corrected after the fact.

Work Station Design

"You're on your own" is a statement that implies a degree of freedom, a chance to be creative. Unfortunately, when it comes to workplace design, few of us are trained in how to optimize those factors which will make our surroundings more comfortable and productive. From secretary, to engineer, to senior manager, all tend to bumble about using what furniture they are given. Yes, we are often allowed to "shuffle" it into an arrangement that we like, but major changes are usually left to an independent group whose major function apparently is to minimize purchase costs. Does this mean you should skip this part as there is nothing that can be done? No, for by studying what can be done, you may be able to (1) make what you have work better and (2) influence how workplace design is approached by your group and your company.

Seating

Aside from when we are sleeping, most of us will spend more time sitting than doing anything else. Whereas we usually get to choose the bed on which we will sleep, we often have no choice over the chair in which we will sit. In restaurants, movies, and at the ballgame, this is probably understandable; at our workplace, this is much less necessary than we think. Fortunately, many work chairs allow the individual users to adjust them to suit their needs and contours. Let's take a look at a few of the principles which should help us in optimizing our seating.

First comes the matter of our back. Proper support of the back is essential for a good seating design. The vertebrae in our spine are much like a stack of books which we can tip forward or backward with our back muscles as shown in Figure 4.

If we tip forward, we increase the pressure on the front part of the bone and cause the back muscles to work more. This forward-leaning, "hunchback" position can promote fatigue and decrease job performance. Adding a back support will reduce the muscle tension and strain on the back. It is worth emphasizing that the back of a chair only helps if it used—and that many highly educated people spend much of their day hunched forward over desk or table with no contact between their body and the back of their chair!

Second come our buttocks and thighs. Like our back, these need proper support for our continued comfort and work effectiveness. Here we are presented with two conflicting needs: stability (favoring a hard seat) and pressure reduction (favoring a softer seat). In general, the more mobility required, the firmer the seating needed. Thus, assembly jobs are usually fitted out with unpadded seating while office chairs have more padding. For people with mobility requirements such as draftsmen, chairs are often provided which allow the user to alternate between standing and sitting. Thigh pressure, however, is a function of our foot placement. The heel should contact the floor while the front of the thigh still receives some support from the seating surface. This can also be accomplished through the use of properly positioned footrests.

Poor Back Support   Good Back Support

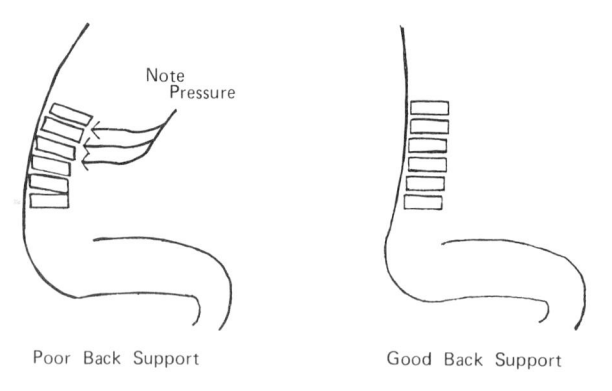

Figure 4 Effect of posture on vertebrae.

Equipment Location and Design

"A place for everything and everything in its place"—a quote from a wise old man that is as valid today as when first uttered. For each of us, the things and places may be different, but the objective remains the same: to have the things we need at hand and easy to use. A casual walk through almost any work area quickly reveals an unlimited variety in workplace layouts. Most, if not all, were generated by fitting the people into the space available rather than creating the space to support the people. Given that that state of affairs will probably persist for some time, let us look at some principles that can help us make the best of our situation.

A good equipment layout considers the reach and clearance envelope of the individual. Articles and controls that require frequent use should be positioned within easy reach. For simple grasping and/or positioning, this means reaching with little or no upper-arm (bicep) movement. The upper arm has considerable weight, and continuous use will contribute to fatigue. By simply repositioning the work surface to 2 in. below the relaxed elbow position, a noticeable improvement in performance can often be achieved. This principle is universal and can be applied in offices as well as on assembly lines.

Once arm motions have been attended to, the head and torso should also be studied. With the head comprising up to 19% of our body mass, any prolonged or frequent viewing should be arranged so as to minimize the strain on the neck and shoulder muscles. This calls for displays to be located in front of the user and slightly below eye level. Obviously, the controls for a display should not interfere with reading that or other displays. One airplane cockpit I reviewed had a flap control so positioned that in use it blocked its signal light. The result was that the pilot had to take his hand off the control to check whether the operation was complete!

Traffic Patterns

"The young fox succeeds by running; the old fox succeeds by cunning." When I first heard this statement, I was reminded of my early days as an engineer at the Sturtevant Division of Westinghouse. Old Russ at the desk next to me was a seasoned manufacturing veteran. I always marveled at how he was able to stay on top of everything and still get all his assignments finished. In later years, as I reflected on his methods, I realized the "old fox" was a lot smarter than he let on!

Each morning and just after lunch each day, old Russ would make a circuit of the shops. On the way, he would drop off any key reports and inquire about the status of jobs for which he was responsible. The rest of the day he spent at his desk doing his job. By contrast, the young engineer would dash off hither and yon at each phone call. Eager to please, full of energy, but spending more time walking than working. If we had analyzed the traffic patterns of the two (Russ and myself), it would have been readily apparent that one of us had found a fine method for minimizing unnecessary traffic!

Work sampling can be applied to traffic pattern analysis to help each of us get more done, with fewer steps. Take the simple problem of how to lay out five desks where the people at them have differing within-group communications needs. Simple counting reveals that there are 10 different possible pairings of the five individuals. By making an analysis of the frequency of communication

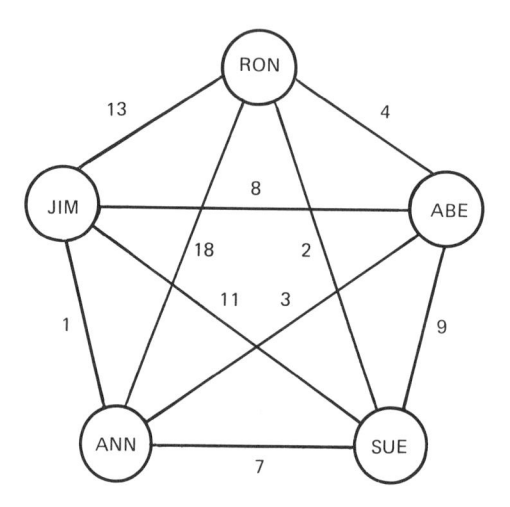

Figure 5 Frequency counts of communications. (Adapted from Ref. 2, Figure 23.5.)

between the people, we get the star diagram shown in Figure 5.

Analysis of the diagram can point to a layout that will be optimal for the group. For example, simply rank-ordering the 10 possible pairs shown in Figure 5 shows that Ron and Ann should be adjacent, as should Ron and Jim. In a similar fashion, people/equipment traffic patterns can be analyzed and an optimum layout developed.

Color

The effect of background color on worker attitudes and productivity is more clouded with opinion than clarified with scientific research. One simple, but useful guideline can be given, however, which is generally agreed upon: light-colored surroundings, such as pastels or beige, used with darker objects (machines, office equipment, etc.) are generally preferred by most workers.

As we move toward more participative styles of management, it is becoming more common to give workers some voice in the selection of environmental colors and decorations. This can provide very positive benefits if properly implemented and is certainly worth some consideration as a factor in the designed experiments discussed at the end of this chapter.

Computers for Human Use

It is late Saturday evening. The young lady places her bank card into the automatic teller machine to withdraw the $40 she will need for a ski trip the following morning. She carefully punches in her account code and so on, and the machine responds by dispensing, side by side, two $20 bills. She pauses to open her purse and locate her wallet. Suddenly, the machine "beeps" and the two bills disappear back into it. She frantically pushes the "Cash Withdrawal" button a number of times until with a second "beep" her card, which she had left in the machine as it was reclaiming her money, also disappears back into the slot. The display goes blank and then flashes back "Welcome to our 24-hr ATM—Please insert card and. . . ."

The preceding incident (which occurred in Bedford, Massachusetts, February 1985) illustrates what can happen when people and computer come together in a poorly planned fashion. Part of making computers "user friendly" involves anticipation of human reactions and the many forms they take. The computer, whether in a digital watch, in an automatic bank teller, or at our place of work, is having a profound impact on many of our lives. Pursuit of the goal that using a computer should always be easier than not using one is filled with human factors considerations. Let us consider, therefore, the most visible features of a computer: its keyboard and its CRT monitor.

Keyboard

One commonly taken-for-granted part of the computer is the keyboard. It is interesting to note that the standard keyboard found on typewriters, referred to as the QWERTY arrangement, is believed to have been designed to SLOW PEOPLE DOWN. The reason was that typists using the early mechanical keyboards were faster than the machines and kept jamming the keys. The answer to this dilemma was to place many of the common letters under the weakest fingers and in a somewhat awkward arrangement. Now that this is no longer necessary, you would think that someone would invent a better layout! Well, While a number of people have tried, so many of us have been trained on the QWERTY keyboard, that it will probably remain the standard for many years to come.

In addition to layout, a great deal of study has gone into keyboard ergonomics in recent years. From these studies the following general guidelines for good keyboard design emerge:

A low profile with an 11-15° slant

Home row keys at 30 mm above work surface

Textured, slightly sculptured keys with a slight, but noticeable change of contour to the f, j, and, in the case of a numeric keypad, the 5 keys

Special function keys such as HELP and STOP which are separated from the alphabetic keys

A large, easy-to-reach RETURN key placed to minimize confusion with other keys

Easy movement of the keyboard relative to the video screen, with coiled cord attachable to left or right side

Ease in forming common non-English characters such as é, ç, and ñ

A more subtle aspect associated with keyboard design is familiarity. Typing is much like driving in that to become proficient, the actions we take must become reflexive rather than conscious. This means that if you have to stop and think about which key to press, your speed will drastically decrease or your error rate will be high. Now all of this should be pretty academic if all of the keyboards used on computers and typewriters were identical—but they aren't! Yes, the alphabets and numbers are all set out in the same locations, but the other characters can vary considerably from keyboard to keyboard. Thus, people who use home computers that differ from their work units invariably find their speed and accuracy diminished on BOTH machines! Some more astute employers, recognizing this, have made arrangements for their employees to obtain professional-quality keyboards and/or computers for home use. This is an area of opportunity for both employers and workers to explore for their mutual benefit.

Video Screens

As with keyboards, good human factors design should be a key consideration in selecting video displays. Among the characteristics of a good display are:

No noticeable flicker. This is accomplished by using a scan rate of at least 60 regenerations per second.

Clear, sharply defined characters which, when viewed from 16 to 28 in., appear solid rather than a string of dots.

Lines and characters that do not "smear" as the display is scrolled upward.

Brightness and contrast controls that are individually adjustable.

A nonglare, scratch-resistant, easy-to-clean surface.

A 30° vertical adjustment to minimize neck strain and allow flexibility in placement.

Freedom from audible sound such as high-pitched transformer buzz.

The choice of color for the display is somewhat controversial. Studies conducted to date show that for single color displays, color is far less important than the quality, sharpness, and stability of the characters. Nonetheless, to assume that one color is "best" for everyone would make no sense at all. A strong case can be made for considering a full-color monitor for most applications involving human input/output. Here color, properly used, can provide significant benefits. The first benefit is more psychological than physical. As discussed elsewhere in this book, workers are more satisfied when they feel they are in control of their work environment. Allowing users to easily change the color of their CRT monitor's display can help enhance their sense of control and increase their job satisfaction.

The second benefit color can provide is to help users differentiate between graphic images on the screen. Just as a multicolor graph on paper can add a new viewer dimension, so color enhances the images on a video screen. Information not readily conveyed in a single color stands out when presented in several colors. Fortunately, this use of color is not limited to the screen: with the low-cost pen plotters and 35-mm film units available today, the multicolor images can easily be transferred to paper and projection media. Thus the vast amount of computer-based data can, through the use of color, be converted into information more readily understood by humans. From a human factors standpoint, the message is clear: failure to take advantage of the benefits of video color is usually a case of being "penny wise and pound foolish."

Software

"We've come a long way...!" While the preceding phrase is often used to describe other things, nowhere is it more apt than in the field of software design. Consider the following lines, which all perform the same operation, namely, adding two numbers together to form a sum.

BINARY: 1001 0110 0000 0000 1001 1011 0000 0001
           1001 0111 0000 0010
HEX: 96 00 9B 01 97 01

HUMAN FACTORS ENGINEERING

```
ASSEMBLY:   LDDA A  ADDA B  STAA C
BASIC:      LET C = A + B
RS/1:       Set Counter = Variable—A + Variable —B
```

Like many of you, I have watched and sometimes participated in the computer revolution. During this time software has progressed from "easy for the machine" code to "easy for the human" code (meaning the programmer). We are now at a stage where "easy for the user" is becoming paramount, and a renewed emphasis is being placed on human factors. This requires, however, that the programmer be simply: (1) electronic engineer, (2) mathematician, (3) psychologist, (4) clairvoyant, (5) teacher, and (6) friendly.

Does this mean that the task can't be done? No, but it does mean that the job is a lot tougher than most of us think it is! In performing this difficult balancing act, there are several guidelines that can help in judging how well a given software program meets the goal of "user friendliness."

- Menus or lists are available for the unfamiliar user to choose from which the more experienced users can bypass with the use of easy-to-remember codes.
- HELP is always available from a clearly labeled (color-coded) key.
- Provision is made for backing up one or more steps (BACKUP key).
- A clearly labeled (STOP) key is provided which will allow the user to gently halt (NOT destroy) the operation being performed.
- Errors should be anticipated and corrected by the system. When the occasional error message is issued, it should clearly indicate to the user what the case was ("Expected a number not a letter" versus "Error 107").

Another aspect of software that is often overlooked is the psychological impact on the user. From data entry to machine control, most software treats the user as if he/she were at best subhuman or a robot. "I can tolerate most people with one exception," a famous actress once pronounced. "And that, my dear, is someone with no sense of humor." With our new awareness concerning quality of work life, we must consider computer software along with other factors having an influence on how we feel about our work. I have long advocated a software approach which would include a "personality setup" in which the user could set the computer responses in one of four modes: (1) friendly, (2) straight, (3) sarcastic, or (4) humorous.

Properly and sensitively implemented, this approach will not only provide variety in a number of otherwise boring tasks, but at the same time give the user a feeling of control which is usually lacking in these situations. Thus, the new question for software quality is not what the software does, but how it makes people feel. This can and should be part of every software specification in the years to come.

DOONESBURY
Copyright, 1985, G. B. Trudeau. Reprinted with permission of Universal Press Syndicate. All rights reserved.

Design of Experiments

Throughout this chapter I have tried to emphasize how different we humans are from one another. In doing this, I pointed out some of the opportunities that exist for modifying the environment to suit the individual. In case after case where the "system" assumed all workers were the same, substantial performance im-

HUMAN FACTORS ENGINEERING

provements have been achieved by slight modification to equipment or environment. Of all the areas for opportunity in American industry, human factors in the workplace probably has the greatest potential.

In one case, output from a tester dropped sharply when a new worker was assigned to the job. After several warnings from the supervisor, the worker was about to be dismissed when someone noted that the "new person" was left-handed. Examination revealed that the testing machine was designed by a right-handed engineer and was so laid out that operation by a left-handed person was almost impossible. A swivel base was proposed and tested to determine the effect of position. After the test results (Figure 6) were reviewed, the machine was permanently modified, and soon the new operator's output was exceeding all previous levels.

In another case, a copy machine was temporarily moved from a remote location to one where it was visible from most offices. This reduced the waiting (lost time) line from two to four people to near zero while improving morale. Needless to say, the move was made permanent.

Both examples show how minor modifications to the man/machine interface can result in significant improvements to perfor-

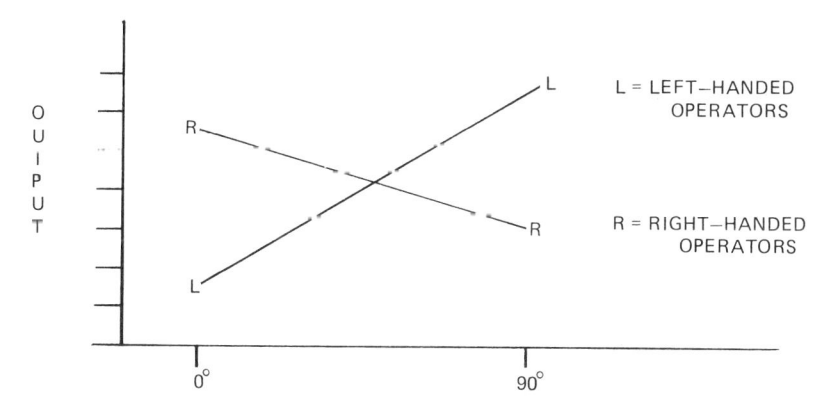

Figure 6 Designed experiment.

mance and worker satisfaction. The opportunities which remain are enormous. All it takes is for a person to be slightly taller, stronger, opposite-handed, or older than the average, and use of an "average-sized" chair, computer, or car can become a painful, demotivating experience. By recognizing these differences and being willing to experiment using human factors principles, true breakthroughs can be achieved.

Conclusion

The field of human factors represents a great opportunity which has been largely untapped by the majority of American workers. The intent of this chapter has been to give a sampling of the subject matter that will motivate readers to attempt meaningful change in their own companies. As a sampling, it shows the richness and potential which the study of human factors can bring to the workplace, yet it has had to leave many fascinating facets uncovered. As we head into the twenty-first century with new tools for the hearts and minds of our work force, it is my hope that we will not forget that the recognition of "human factors" can also have a dramatic impact on performance and quality of work life. While much of the early work in the field was somewhat dry and not workplace-related, newer texts are much more "user friendly." Still, the ultimate test lies in the hands of readers like yourself, for only a "human" can take these words and translate them into action.

Selected Readings

1. *The Human Factor: Designing Computer Systems for People*, Richard Rubinstein and Harry Hersh, Digital Press, 1984.
2. *Human Performance Engineering: A Guide for System Designers*, Robert W. Bailey, Prentice-Hall, Englewood Cliffs, NJ, 1982.

3. *Human Factors in Engineering and Design*, Ernest J. McCormick, McGraw-Hill, New York, 1967.
4. *Ergonomics at Work*, David J. Osborne, John Wiley & Sons Ltd, 1982.
5. RCA.

4

Quality Circles Promote Quality Performance

ROBERT AMSDEN University of Dayton, Dayton, Ohio
DAVIDA AMSDEN Consultant, Dayton, Ohio

Purpose and Outline

Why would a manager want quality circles in his or her organization? That's a good question. There is one answer that many American managers have discovered. As they have become more interested and involved in the drive for better quality and productivity, they are finding that quality circles can help achieve improved quality performance.

Quality circles may appear to be a simple concept, but their incorporation into an organization is not that easy. This chapter will deal with some of the far-reaching effects circles can have. We are going to look at some of the reasons for the push for quality improvements. We shall consider how much circles can really accomplish in furthering this effort. We shall talk about the potential impact of circles on an organization, some practical results circles have had and the relationship of circles to company-wide quality control.

First, we should agree on a definition of quality circles. Circles are small groups of operating-level personnel together with immediate supervision who voluntarily and regularly meet to study problem-solving methods and who identify, solve, and, with management permission, implement solutions to work-related problems. We emphasize that circles, for this chapter anyway, consist of hourly employees together with their immediate supervisors. We are not including management circles, nor do we include "Juran teams."

Major Driving Forces in Business—And Circles

The Drive for Quality and Productivity

There is an increasing realization by North American companies that in order to be competitive in world markets, such companies have to improve quality and productivity as well as reduce costs. This is the reason for growing interest in Juran videotapes, Deming seminars, and Crosby's Quality College. Circles help, at the lowest level of the organization, to improve quality and productivity.

From the spring of 1982, more and more of the large manufacturing corporations, such as Ford and GM, have been pressing their suppliers to prove quality conformance through the use of statistical quality control (SQC) and statistical process control (SPC). It is in this whole area of statistical training that circles can be an effective arm of management. They provide a ready-made vehicle for training and daily practice of SQC/SPC.

Human Resource Development and Circles

Human resource development (HRD) includes many things. We define it simply as attempts to understand human beings better and to involve them in their work more fully.

Quality circles help accomplish HRD. They provide a structure for social acceptance and a sense of belonging. They allow opportunity for recognition and thus develop self-esteem in the circle members. Since they usually select their own projects, circles are a means for self-actualization.

Professionalism/Specialization

Professionalism is a strong factor with circles. First, members of circles find a real sense of professionalism in their circle activity. They themselves identify, choose, solve, and often implement solutions to their work-related problems. Second, because circles address and solve many low-level problems, they free up management and staff to work on more difficult problems. This, in turn, challenges management and staff to grow professionally.

Culture Change Within the Organization

Change, change, change! 3M managers are told that in 5 years 25% of their products will be new (1). Only 2 of the 100 largest firms of the year 1900 are still in existence. Draft beer comes to us in cans, beer that has been filtered, not heated. The list is nearly endless. All these technical and organizational changes result in cultural changes within organizations. By organizational culture we mean the way we work, how we relate to each other, the norms we follow, formal and informal rules of conduct, and management style. Any time technology changes, such as with a new product or process, culture changes. New people interact; new skills are developed; new rules apply. Quality circles can plan for change. Because they plan, the members can control change rather than being controlled by it.

In a Midwestern hospital a circle of technicians in nuclear medicine planned the move from their old quarters into the new wing of the building. They planned arrangement of office space, developed a new system for storing patient files, and controlled many other aspects of their move. Both the hospital administration and the department of nuclear medicine say it is the smoothest departmental move they have experienced.

Acceptance by a circle of change it has helped initiate is very powerful. Here is a mechanism whereby management can introduce change more smoothly and with minimal disruption to the operating personnel.

Development of SQC/SPC and the broader drive for quality and productivity require training, emphasis on data-based decision making, and new ways of thinking and behaving. Circles are a natural to help in this. They begin with training of members and leaders. Data-based decision making is the name of their game. They can be of great assistance in implementing new ways of thinking and behaving at the operating level. Most important, as a group they can wrestle through the implications of change *before* it occurs, and, they can "buy into" or accept the change before it happens.

Perspective—How Much Can Circles Accomplish?

In Seoul, Korea in 1982 we heard Dr. W. Edwards Deming sound a clear, strong warning. We quote him:

> QC Circles is not the way to start quality improvement; it's the *last* thing to adopt, not the first. QC Circles are a raging disease in America and in many other countries, as I see it. A raging disease, supposition that they will solve the bulk of the problems when they can only solve a small portion of them. And they can do nothing unless the management works.... The effect of QC Circles as a raging disease may be to set quality back in America and other places by ten years—a loss of ten years.... Where management is not doing their job, QC Circles will fail and will delay improvement in quality by ten years (2).

There is a basic supposition here, the 20/80 rule. The 20/80 rules, or the Pareto principle, says that 20% of your products account for 80% of your sales dollars; 20% of your projects consume 80% of your time. When applied by Dr. Deming, the rule means that 80% of the problems in a company can be solved by management and only 20% are solvable by the hourly employees.

QUALITY CIRCLES AND PERFORMANCE

Dr. Juran says much the same thing; so does Dr. Kaoru Ishikawa. Top experts clearly state that hourly employees—even when organized and trained in quality circles—can solve *at most* about 20% of the company's problems.

George Sederberg of Cincinnati Milacron stated that quality circles can *identify* 80% of the problems (3). Jerry Schmidt of the Buick Division of GMC has given a clear warning (4). Circles, he said, go through their process of identifying problems, rank them in order of importance, and then look to see which of the most important they themselves can solve. (See Figure 1.) The circle may find that problems A through D are beyond their capability and only management can solve them. The first problem they can work on is E. The warning is this: If the circle sees that management is doing nothing about problems A through D, while they are working on E, the circle will become demoralized and may quit.

Many believe that circles, or some other form of employee involvement, are essential to be fully competitive. We, however, cannot emphasize too strongly that quality circles are not a stand-alone program. They must be part of an overall management-driven strategy for quality/productivity improvements.

Operator-Controllable or Management-Controllable: A Reexamination

Juran's *Quality Control Handbook* (5) gives a simple way to determine responsibility for defects: Is the operator responsible or is management? As a manager, ask yourself the following three questions:

1. Does the operator know what he should do?

2. Does he know whether he is actually doing what he should?

3. Does he have the means to correct his work?

The traditional view says that if the answer to all three questions is "yes," and defects still occur, the operator is responsible for

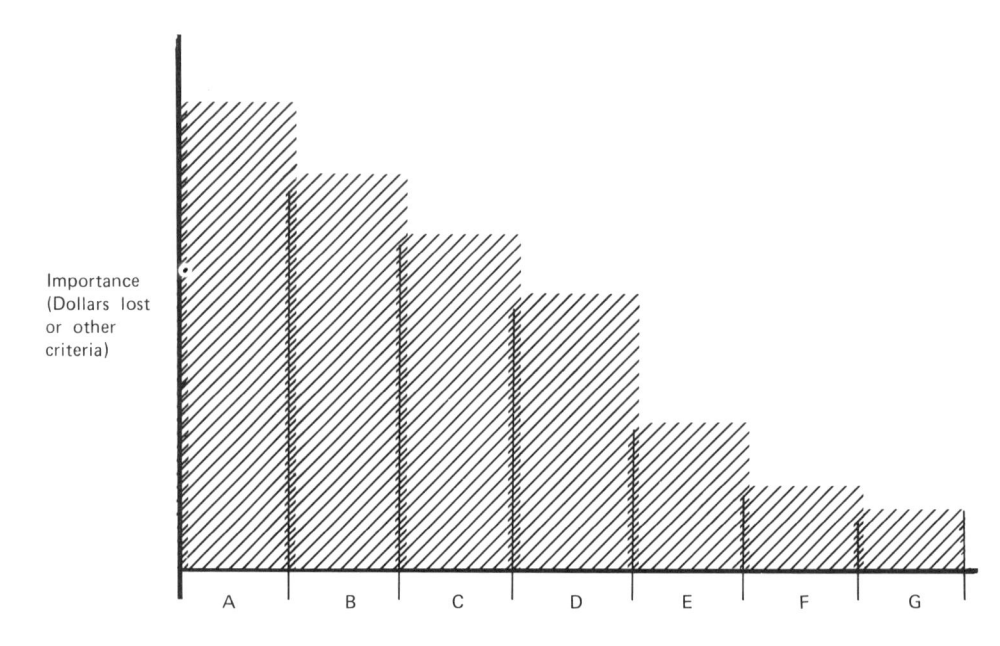

Figure 1

them. However, if the answer to *any* of the questions is "no," then management, *not* the operator, is responsible for any defects that occur. Finally, management is responsible to see to it that the three questions are answered affirmatively.

The traditional view puts all of this responsibility on you, the manager. The operator follows your instructions. If you as a manager are asking these questions, you must assess the need for training and provide it. Determine what gaging or other means are required for feedback to the operator. Provide whatever is required for the operator to correct his process once he discovers it needs correction.

Quality circles give a new twist to *who* is responsible for defects as well as for improvements in quality and productivity. In sitting through presentations by circles and listening to facilitators and others directly involved, we find quality circles, themselves, assuming some of the responsibility for getting "yes" answers to the three questions. Circles identify need for training; they ask for new gages; they request new procedures for correcting a process. But, they do not and cannot assume the right to implement their solutions. That right remains yours, as manager.

In effect there is a twofold change. First, the circle now does a lot of the investigative work, which under the traditional view was done only at the request and direction of management. Second, because the circle is involved in the development work, they buy into its solution. Once you accept their recommendations and implement them, the circle is motivated to make the solutions work.

The quality circle enhances your job as a manager without reducing your power and authority. You now have an investigative arm that looks for continual improvement. Once you implement the circle's solutions, the circle will try to make them work.

Philosophy of Quality Performance

Management's philosophy and understanding of what it takes to achieve good quality and productivity is key to the strategies the organization develops to accomplish these goals. There are many views held by management, but we mention only two.

First, management may truly feel they and their staff have done their job but the work force simply is not motivated enough: "If only the hourly employees would do their jobs as instructed, this would be the best operation in the United States." If a firm holding this view brings in quality circles, circles will tend to go the "touchy-feely" route. They meet, they solve problems; but the problems are concered with communications, interpersonal relationships, the location of the soft-drink machine. Circles will not deal with substantive aspects of the work itself. Such a result is to be expected, because the management philosophy does not encourage anything but this. Should circles ask for new capital investment, this philosophy will not find it necessary. Soon the circles will see which way the wind blows and they will no longer attempt substantive change.

The second view holds (1) that the causes of defective work are primarily system ones: deficient procedures; inadequate equipment, supervision, or training; poor raw materials; or lack or means whereby the most can be achieved with current equipment; etc. These are the things that prevent the worker from doing defect-free work. No matter how well motivated they are, workers cannot, by themselves, overcome such hindrances. (2) Workers welcome the opportunity to assist in solving system problems. Given proper training, environment, and organizational structures, the workers will be effective in helping to solve system problems.

In order for employees to do a good job, management must work to correct system problems. This is a point strongly emphasized by Drs. Deming, Ishikawa, and Juran. If management expects their work force to do a good job and does not provide them with good processes and procedures, good raw materials, good machines, etc., the work force will get mixed signals. They will say, "Why should we care? Management doesn't!"

There is a second element in this point of view: employees can make valuable contributions to the solutions of system problems. Because they have intimate day-to-day knowledge of the job, they see aspects of the work no one else does. Improvements in quality/productivity will be greater if such improvements incorporate the knowledge and suggestions of the work force. The solutions developed have more chance of successful implementation if the work force has already bought into the solutions.

An application of the second view, which also illustrates the preparatory work required before implementing circles, is occurring at the S-10 Truck assembly plant in Dayton, Ohio. From the beginning, management has taken a two-pronged approach. They concentrate on solving system problems *and* they do whatever is necessary to help everyone—hourly employees, support staffs, secretarial personnel—do a good job. There is evidence this approach is paying off. In the spring of 1985, the plant held the number two position in corporate quality for all GM operations (number one was the Pontiac Fiero plant, which has been following Dr. Deming's principles). This plant, along with the other S-10 facilities and Ford, have captured 50% of the small-truck market. This happened in the first year of S-10 production.

Management has planned ways to tap input from the hourly employees. Three of the methods are team meetings, quality lights, and matrix cards. The S-10 plant does not use quality circles as such, but they do use teams. Each Wednesday assembly operations shut down for half an hour for team meetings. The major objective of the meetings is to give the hourly workers an opportunity to talk about the problems they have. The meetings also let management communicate with the teams about all kinds of things that are happening in the plant.

There are quality lights spaced along the assembly line. Should an employee find a quality problem, he or she can signal for help when needed.

Matrix cards accompany the trucks through assembly. If the operator has a problem with some facet of his job, he makes a note of it on the card. This pinpoints where corrections are needed. At a public meeting in October 1984, management reported that they had taken *no* punitive action for such disclosures in the time the matrix cards have been used.

Management at this GM facility is conscientiously trying to fulfill their responsibility for maintaining quality performance and helping employees do their jobs. Management is not willing to muddle along with Band-Aid solutions.

Significance of Quality Circles to Organizations

Quality circles help accomplish several things. They help bring about some of Dr. Deming's Fourteen Points for top management, such as driving out fear and working for continual improvement. Circles are an excellent way to encourage participative management on the shop floor. (A note of caution here: circles may prove to be an enormous jump toward participative management. If done quickly, it may be just too much for your organization to handle [6].)

Quality circles provide a communications net. Such a net will be very valuable for SPC problems. Circles can be a way of pulling operators into the quality function since many of the circle activities in the United States have been quality related. Finally, circles can be a vehicle for quality training.

Results of Quality Circles

Quality circles have had many results. We will look at heightened quality awareness and measurement.

Circles do bring about an increased awareness of quality. This should not be surprising. Working through the steps of the problem-solving process helps the members in several ways. As members study the problem, they look at their own jobs and the quality of their work. They find ways to improve their own work. Furthermore, the members gain a perspective for how their jobs fit into the whole organization. As they discover that improvements can be made, they become more aware of the quality of their own and others' work. Members learn that quality products are important to the long-term survival of their organizations!

We can see several sides to the issue of measurement of circles. It is legitimate to ask why circles should be evaluated according to criteria that are not applied to others. Sometimes it seems that circles are evaluated as though they were nothing more than machines. One reason for such in-depth measurement may come about from the novelty of groups of hourly people solving work problems. This has been outside the traditional way of doing things, and we as managers don't know how to react to it.

Even so, a good manager does need assurance that time and resources invested in circle activities are bringing paybacks to the company. Typical paybacks include scrap reduction, cost-savings improvements, reduction in defects, improvements in morale, and reductions in grievances, absenteeism, and turnover.

Perhaps the simplest measure to use is the problems solved by circles. The literature, conferences, and circle report files are full of successful projects. These are often reported in dollar savings. Circle projects include quality improvements, productivity increases, more efficient handling of robots, etc.

Some companies conduct attitudinal surveys. Some simply watch bottom-line dollars. Some observe culture change in the firm.

Environment for Success

How can you tell whether quality circles will "succeed" in your organization before starting them? What are the essential elements for success? There are no easy answers.

It appears there must be at least one manager who personally backs the concept. Without such a driving force, circles will not have sufficient clout to accomplish anything, and they won't last.

Circles have worked in both Theory X and Theory Y environments. They exist in unionized and nonunionized shops; large organizations and small; manufacturing and service industries; continuous-process plants and batch operations. Where there is a will, there is a way. This seems to be the primary rule: If the organization, especially management, wants circles, they can and will flourish.

This one factor, the will of management, seems to be a prime factor in the success of circles. When management, or enough of the management power structure, decides to back them, circles can succeed. Once management lays the foundation, then the success of the circles is nearly assured. But the *degree* of success will then depend on hundreds of factors. These factors include: types and amount of training; abilities of facilitators; abilities of supervisors, middle management, top management; experience and abilities of the operators; culture of the organization; communication networks; abilities of consultants whether internal or external; and so on.

Companywide Quality Control (CWQC) and Quality Circles

More and more we are hearing about total quality control, total quality process, or some other synonym for complete involvement in quality. As American companies begin to wrestle with their quality philosophy, they are investigating this concept too. Total quality control or TQC is a method for managing quality that grew up in the United States during the 1950s. A. Fiegenbaum published a book with this title in 1960 (7). Like so many other concepts, the Japanese have successfully put to work an American theory, but they broadened it.

In Japan CWQC actually means two things. First, "quality" means the quality of the product or service *and* the quality of how work is done. Second, all employees, from the floor sweeper to president, from the receiving department to marketing, to the secretarial pool, are involved in the effort to maintain and improve quality. Because everyone is involved in the quality function, floor-level people can actively participate by means of QC circles (8).

It is too much to ask quality circles to be the sole means for accomplishing companywide quality control in North American companies, but circles can be of great assistance in the effort. First, circles have training in the problem-solving process, the *how to* of achieving quality/productivity improvements. Second, because of their training in circle tools such as cause-and-effect diagramming, Pareto analysis, and other statistical tools, circles have the means to solve quality/productivity problems effectively. Third, circles are in place. Those companies which have circles and are attempting to do quality control companywide have a head start.

The Japanese started with top management, engineering, and other staff to do CWQC. They soon realized they had to involve the foreman and he, in turn, his workers if they wanted to achieve the kind of advances in quality they wanted. Americans have started the other way round by instituting circles for the hourly employee first. The move for CWQC will involve everyone in the company. By having circles already in place, wise managers will be several steps ahead of the starting point of their Japanese counterparts 25 years ago. Properly guided, circles and companywide quality control can close the quality gap faster.

Footnotes and Selected Readings

1. Videotape, *In Search of Excellence*, 1985
2. ICQCC Seoul 1982. Also published in Amsden, R., and Amsden, D., *Quality Circles Journal*, Vol. 6, No. 3, 1983.
3. Panel discussion on quality circles, Midwest Conference of the Academy of Management, Columbus, Ohio, 1982.
4. Personal communication.
5. Juran, J. M., Editor-in-chief, et al., *Quality Control Handbook*, 2nd ed., McGraw-Hill, New York, 1962, pp. 4-23.
6. Especially see the writings of Rensis Likert.
7. Feigenbaum, A., *Total Quality Control*, 1960.
8. Ishikawa, Kaoru, *What Is Total Quality Control? The Japanese Way*, Prentice-Hall, Englewood Cliffs, NJ, 1985, pp. 23-24.

5

Leadership and Management Training and Development

BARBARA AFFOURTIT
THOMAS D. AFFOURTIT
Interaction Research Institute, Inc., Fairfax, Virginia

Leadership and management have been intriguing topics of interest for both scientists and laymen since the early Greek and Roman periods. The extensive literature published during the first half of this century alone has produced numerous, albeit diverse theories on these subjects. As a result, the concepts of leadership and management have evolved to a complex admixture of descriptive elements and empirical factors that defy simple exposition. Moreover, the collection of data to assess these concepts in a way that permits training and development of skills and abilities has been arbitrary, if not lacking in experimental evidence.

A fundamental problem in writings and research has been the lack of a generally accepted definition of what constitutes leadership and management. In the field of quality management and quality technology, leadership can be described as an outcome such as production yield, scrap rate, etc. However, such distinctions made between individuals or groups can be meaningful for training and development purposes only if all the influencing factors are isolated and a determination is made with regard to the degree of variance for which each influencing variable accounts.

This chapter will attempt to operationally define leadership and management as distinct concepts and describe the process with which each construct can be assessed. In the quality profession, the feedback mechanism that operates within a total quality system will be used to demonstrate how leadership and management skills can be learned under various environmental conditions.

The Nature of Leadership and Management

Leadership and management are the principal concepts that comprise the training and development model proposed in this chapter. Therefore, it is important to understand the nature of each and to describe the elements of each as distinct constructs that can be measured, diagnosed, and improved.

Leadership

Leadership is a learned aptitude, an acquired composite of skills in influencing individuals or groups toward a desired direction. On a very formative level, leadership is the developed ability to inspire "followership." The primary skills of leadership, learned over a long period of time through identification or shaping with role models early in life, and through practice and reinforcement, are directly linked to and often described as personality traits. According to the "trait theory," leadership is an expression of an individual's personality composition (Stogdill, 1948).

Basically, the characteristics or traits of leadership have been identified and measured as a high level of aspiration (Cattell and Stice, 1954), industry and perseverance (Stogdill, 1948), drive for control and power (Krech, Crutchfield and Ballachey,

1962), and need for expression and exhibition (Gibb, 1969).

Since the situation in which a leader must function may dictate which traits predominate, flexibility in trait emphasis has been considered an essential leadership characteristic (Stogdill, 1948). Generally, and especially under conditions of stress, self-assurance (Cowley, 1928), emotional control and adjustment (Holtzman, 1952), ego strength (Cattell, 1956), and an integrated personality (Mann, 1959) have also been established as primary leadership traits.

Moreover, empirical study has revealed that leadership behavior is social or interpersonal to a significant degree: a function of the leader's understanding of and response to the needs and concerns of the group (Affourtit, 1977; Haythorn, Couch, Haefner, Langham, and Carter, 1956; Showell, 1960; Smith, Jaffe, and Livingston, 1955). Empathy (Chowdhry and Newcomb, 1952; Exline, 1960), introception (Smith, Jaffe, and Livingston, 1955), group knowledge (Showell, 1960), and accuracy in interpersonal perception (Gallo and McClintock, 1962) are also socially oriented factors that correlate highly with measures of leadership outcomes.

Finally, the overriding intellectual facility of the individual leader provides insight, sharpens analytical skills, improves judgment, and acts as a catalyst for compounding traits or emphasizing characteristics that are consonant with any given situation (Gibb, 1947; Mann, 1959).

In essence, leadership is the effective expression of an individual's internalized needs or personality makeup. The debate continues as to whether leadership is a constellation of traits common to all situations, or whether leadership is relative to major interaction variables such as the group to be led, the mission to be accomplished, and the particular situation or climate in which the leader must function. Gibb (1969) reports evidence to support both the "trait" and "interaction" theories. Sanford's (1952) early conclusion that focusing on any one theory will yield "positive but unexciting correlations" also suggests that both contentions may be correct.

Management

Management is also defined as a series of skills or techniques that, although learned like leadership, are more formally acquired and are manifested on a more cognitive level, rather than ingrained into one's personality makeup. Leadership is more inductive in that a particularly behavioral style is created from exposure to a series of events over an extended period. Management is deductive in that general knowledge of organizational theory and process is learned and can be applied to particular events. There is overlap. Management capability is complementary to leadership, and vice versa. Some leadership traits facilitate management, and some management skills are instrumental to good leadership. Management, however, is less interpersonal and much less inspirational.

Management skill is akin to administrative ability and is considered more of a method for guiding and directing people toward a desired goal. It is possible for an individual to be a good leader, that is, be able to evoke willing response from subordinates, but at the same time, employ poor management strategies and thereby fail to accomplish an assigned mission. Such an individual would be most successful in a situation where personal dynamics are more important than management capability, a situation in which the "leader" is required to inspire others under a rigidly imposed plan of action devised by an expert manager.

A person with more management than leadership ability, however, would be more successful in an administrative post that requires substantial background in organization processes, but demands little personal contact or charisma.

Management may be also considered the efficiency side of an effective/efficient ratio. A production project may be accomplished effectively—reaching the objective (quota)—but not efficiently—excessive loss of material and wasted effort. Similarly, a project can be well designed and sequenced for ultimate efficiency to avoid loss of material and manpower—but ineffectively executed. In the first case, the leader met production standard at unnecessarily high cost. In the second instance, the manager lost control and failed to inspire subordinates to follow an efficiently designed plan of operation.

Recognizing and taking responsibility for a task, while not knowing which approach or tactic to use, is a leadership strength, but a management weakness. On the other hand, an individual may know how to manage a program well, but have no desire to take responsibility—a leadership deficiency. Management means accomplishing the task at hand in the most proficient way—doing it right. Leadership means inspiring those required to do the task to do it. Doing it right the first time through one's subordinates would be a prime example of efficient management and effective leadership.

Acquiring the Skill

The study of leadership and management seeks not only to understand basic ingredients, but also to control or otherwise transfer knowledge gained to functional behavior. Acquiring the skill, raising the level of potential or incumbent leaders and managers, has always been a primary goal of scholars and behavioral scientists.

Before discussion of how leadership and management skill can be acquired in an organizational setting, a cursory understanding of training and development is necessary. Training connotes a formalized setting in which certain principles and concepts are imparted to trainees through a recognized expert in the field of interest. Moreover, training implies study and the application of planned exercises and activities, more or less controlled in an atmosphere that permits learning through knowledge and experience. Simulation or "hands-on" activity is often used as a method of instruction as well as evaluation of expected behavioral outcomes. Much of training is cognitive; that is, knowledge of what works or does not work when attempting to lead and manage others is gained through rational communication.

Development connotes an informal enhancement of knowledge or skill through experience with or awareness of one's domain of leadership and management. The development of skill can be the result of formal training. But, development normally implies growth or maturation with regard to a broad range of abilities.

Leadership and management development can occur naturally, over a long period through daily experience with a group, through trial-and-error attempts to control or influence a group, or guided by learning techniques that communicate a clear understanding of the group, goal, and situation.

The principal differences between training and development for the purpose of this chapter are more academic than essential. Training requires instruction or guidance from an expert. Development may involve a recognized facilitator or may not. The literature does not make a clear distinction; often training and development terms are interchangeable. Moreover, where a distinction is made, programs frequently utilize both training and development methods in conjunction. The primary purpose of this discourse on leadership and management is to discover what it is and how one goes about learning it.

The basis of all training and development is learning. Learning is the process by which we gain knowledge, skill, and ability to lead and manage others. Both training and development, therefore, can be subsumed under the umbrella of learning. Learning means growth, growth toward an ideal model of leadership and management. Long ago Thorndike (1916) described the progressive nature of learning as a trial-and-error exercise. According to Thorndike's Law of Effect, behavior changes because of its consequences. Humans, animals, all species learn to eliminate inefficient habits and enhance efficient habits through trial-and-error reinforcement.

The principle of feedback, the medium through which trial-and-error information is transmitted, is fundamental to the learning process. Timely and accurate feedback allows adaptation and adjustment and thereby facilitates the learning process. The survival of any organism is based on successful adaptation—that is, learning through proper feedback of trial-and-error behavior. For the contemporary manager and leader functioning in a dynamic environment, behavioral adaptation to a group, goal, and a situation is paramount to his or her success or failure.

The History of Training and Development

In the United States, research on the learning of leadership and management skill through training and development goes back to the turn of the century (Thorndike, 1916). Since then, numerous programs have been offered to anyone seeking to gain more control and influence over others and their environment. Currently available are a variety of seminars, literary materials, videos, laboratory, and longitudinal programs that have emanated from the theories and models presented above, and purport to train, teach, develop, or otherwise instill leadership and management capability. Assessment of the effectiveness of these programs is often accomplished through attitude surveys or rating scales conducted by proponents of the approach that reveal positive claims by participants of improved awareness, more confidence, and increased abiility to lead and manage others. Criterion-based validity studies concerning the sustained effectiveness of these programs, however, have been disappointingly sparse, inconclusive, or scientifically unsound.

Laboratory methods such as role playing and some form of sensitivity/awareness training comprise the most popular approaches used to improve leadership and management. These methods are designed to modify participant behavior toward the use of "effective" leadership/management practices, or to increase effectiveness by gaining insight into the motives of self and others.

Of the 102 references studied, Corsini, Shaw, and Blake (1961) list only five that made any attempt to evaluate the behavioral-impact role-playing methods. Mann and Mann (1959a, 1959b) concluded that role-playing experience increases role-playing ability and social adjustment, but not necessarily leadership and management. Stogdill (1974), summarizing the results of 10 studies, reports that sensitivity training tends to change attitudes regarding warmth, acceptance of self and others, and openness. However, he found little conclusive evidence that lasting change occurs in overt behavior.

Studies conducted by Blake, Mouton, Barnes, and Greiner

(1964), Miles, Milansky, Lake, and Beckhard (1965), Beckhard (1966), and Kuriloff and Atkins (1966) claim that managerial training accounted for improved operating efficiency and productivity. However, none of these studies used control groups, leaving the findings open to alternate plausible hypotheses.

Some studies using control groups reported that individuals experiencing laboratory training were actually less productive than the control groups. Deitzer (1967), for example, found that a control group of district sales managers outperformed a management training group on several key criterion variables, such as number of new agents recruited, volume of new policies sold, etc. Deep, Bass, and Vaughn (1967) studied 93 participants of a stimulated management exercise. Those receiving management training prior to the exercise reported more cooperation and openness between members, but performed significantly more poorly. Similar findings were reported by Stinson (1970). "Intact" groups, those trained in management sensitivity, were high in cohesiveness, but low in productivity compared to control groups. Underwood (1965), in a study of 15 training and 15 control groups, found that laboratory training changed participants' attitudes, but had an adverse effect on productivity.

Many reviews of the literature on various types of training and development methods, however, are generally mixed. Stock (1964) summarized reports of training benefits indicating 60-75% experience improved self-insight, sensitivity to others, role flexibility, diagnostic ability, and self-confidence. However, Stock also reported that personality predisposition affects response to training. For example, task-oriented and anxious persons, according to Stock, respond negatively to standard leadership and management training efforts. Odiorne (1963) analyzed 51 books and 68 journal articles and found no study demonstrating that any type of laboratory training changes behavior back on the job. And, from a review of the literature, Campbell and Dunnette (1968) concluded that training and development programs can change behavior in the setting where they are administered, but there is little conclusive evidence for transfer of such training to the job situation.

Stogdill (1974) suggests that the reason for disappointing outcomes is perhaps due to a concentration on (1) group participation and (2) transition of leadership and management. This emphasis prepares individuals to surrender control to the follower group. Popularity rather than productivity then becomes the measure of leadership/management effectiveness. Emphasis on learning behavior patterns, functional techniques, and practices that characterize successful (i.e., productive) leaders and managers may prove more fruitful in terms of task accomplishments via acceptance by subordinates.

More discouraging evidence of management program effectiveness comes from Argyris (1964, 1976). Working with senior executives over many sessions using various training and development techniques, he discovered that, while executives did recognize their own dysfunctional patterns and were able to learn effective behaviors in the laboratory, they were not able to change their performance on the job. This phenomenon occurred after repeated sessions in which the executives admitted returning to ineffective ways and pledged to respond with more appropriate behavior once they returned to their jobs. Argyris paints a dismal picture for those expecting to reap great benefits from short courses or popular books on how to lead and manage.

Summarizing these studies suggests that, content validity notwithstanding, transferring cognitive awareness training and practice exercises from the classroom to effect actual performance change on the job is an arduous and time-consuming process, requiring perhaps total concentration and diligence to avoid slipping back to old habits. Relevancy of activities during training and development sessions may also be a factor contributing to program effectiveness. The climate of the organization, the assigned group, and the demands of the particular situation to which the individual returns may do more to condition behavior than any outside training or development session.

After more than 50 years of research, the question of how to best train or develop leadership and management is still not easy to answer. Many aspects of changing or improving behavior remain unexplained, and there are many ways of characterizing and organizing what is known. Without denying the value of traditional leadership and management programs, what is needed is a mechanism that allows an individual the opportunity to systematically develop his or her skill on the job, a technique designed to assess and evaluate the relationship between the leader/manager and a group that is oriented toward a particular mission and functioning within the context of an organizational culture. A training and development program is needed that allows leaders and managers to shape their behavior to their actual group, goal, and situation and, through reinforcement, evoke the most optimal response for quality and productivity objectives.

Leadership and Management Improvement Through Process Control and Breakthrough Methods

To develop expertise in the quality profession, the practitioner learns the specifications required for the product and conducts measurements of the process in order to make proper adjustments for optimal quality. The control and influence over the process by the quality practitioner is mediated by the signals received: from the customer, through gauges and other devices, and from statistical process control techniques. Moreover, timely response to correct or improve the process after analyzing the signals is crucial to producing and maintaining optimal quality.

Measuring production outcome alone does not provide enough information about the process to know how to change it. Without a basic understanding of variation and complete assessment of the process, the quality practitioner is reduced to screening out bad product and approving good product for shipment to the customer. Under such a quality system, judgments about the production process usually regress to arbitrary assignment of causes, the correction of which can only be randomly correct. According to Deming (1975), measuring outcomes and treating quality conditions as "special" causes dooms an organization to high production waste, poor morale, and loss of competitive position.

Similarly, the leader/manager, operating within parameters of expectations for the people under his or her charge, becomes a skilled professional by applying appropriate and accurate techniques of assessment, and by responding to feedback in a manner that achieves the best possible results. The process to control and influence in this case is motivational.

Measuring only the quality and quantity of motivational output (i.e., personnel performance) results in the same arbitrary decisions, the same emphasis on special causes, and the same randomly effective corrections that may lead to learning dysfunctional leadership/management habits. Like the ideal quality-improvement program that utilizes appropriate process data to control and influence outcomes, the ideal leadership/management improvement program involves collection and analysis of the appropriate motivational process data.

The Motivational System: The Domain of Leaders and Managers

The concept of motivation evokes a certain mystique, but the motivational system is not unlike any other system or organization, following the same basic rules and principles. It is a system with a structure, comprised of a series of integrated, dynamic processes and subprocesses in which a consistent quality or direction can be discerned. The processes represent orderly and persisting interrelations between parts of the whole, and all of the processes work together to perform a given function.

People are motivated by a series of internalized biological, emotional, and cognitive conditions that direct them toward certain actions. The motivational system is comprised of instincts—inborn mechanisms that function in the interest of organism survival; needs—life-sustaining physiological elements and acquired characteristics that are culturally reinforced; values—potent psychological drives such as religion, social mores, and politics; attitudes—learned states that represent more specific predispositions to act in a particular way; and finally, opinions—relatively inconsistent cognitions that are easily modified and that defy long-range predictions (Affourtit, 1976). While there are relationships and patterns of connection among them, each element represents a level of strength and stability. Some of the elements of

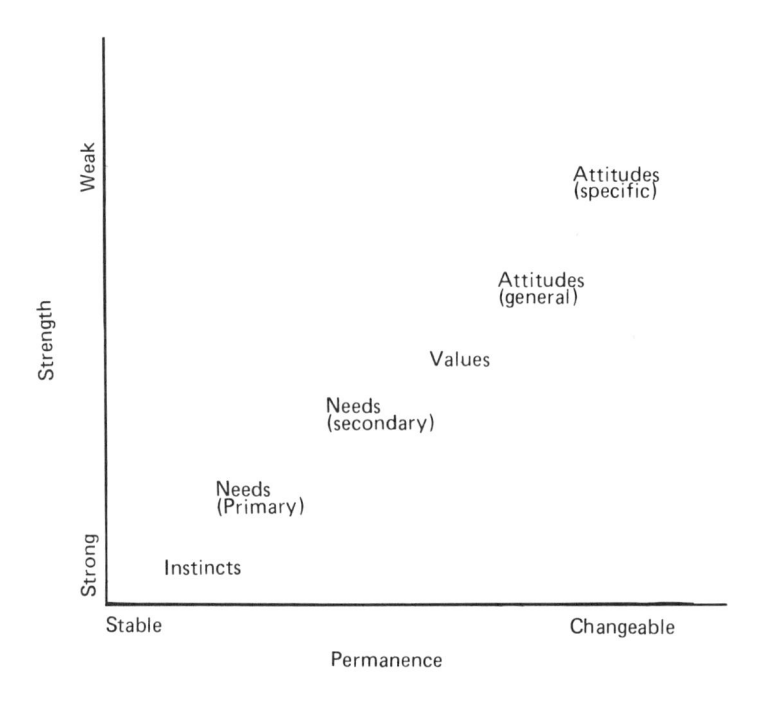

Figure 1 The strength and stability of the motivational system.

motivation are strong, definitive, and pervasive, while others are relatively weak, vague, and capricious. Figure 1 illustrates this concept of the motivational system.

The motivational system of each individual or collectively of the group is the domain or component for which the leader/ manager is responsible. In consideration of the purpose or mission for which this component is designed and the environment in which it must function, the content of a relevant leadership/ management program is contained in the motivational system of the group under charge. Anyone desiring to enhance skill in leading and managing this system, must learn about the system, how it operates, what its idiosyncrasies are, and which inputs, manipulations, or interventions will control and influence its behavioral outcomes.

Motivational Climate Factors

What is labeled work motivation or motivational climate is a process within the motivational system that functions to produce work behavior. People bring to the job certain motivational predispositions, that is, attitudes and values about work in general or expectations about the job in particular. Some have a strongly ingrained "work ethic" that emanates from religious or philosophical values. Others, with a more egocentric value set, may impose a "what's in it for me?" predisposition while on the job. With certain restrictions imposed to protect the constitutional rights of the individual, groups of workers are selected by personnel departments to fit the organization in terms of job skills and personal characteristics. Organization leaders and managers take this collection of individuals and, notwithstanding background or motivational diversity, must mold them into a cohesive unit capable of optimal behavioral output.

Once assigned to a job, employees begin to form opinions and develop new attitudes or reinforce and revise existing ones. Judgments are made about such organizational concerns as opportunity for advancement, policy, supervisors, co-workers, etc. These judgments, colored by preexisting motivational sets, collectively represent the motivational climate of the organization. Concepts such as job satisfaction, communication flow, supervisor support, solidarity, training readiness, recognition, and equality have been operationally defined as internal motivating conditions that inhibit or promote optimal performance and commitment to corporate goals (Affourtit, 1977; Likert, 1967). Motivational climate, a by-product of its members, encompasses the entire milieu of the company.

The individual who intends to develop skill in leadership and management must take cues and other signals from the organization's motivational climate. Motivational climate signals enable an individual to learn, develop, train, grow, or otherwise enhance skill in leadership and management. Through trial-and-error feedback, the law of effect will promote the precise type of leadership and management behavior required for constantly improving performance.

The Perceptual Process

Motivational climate factors that comprise a group's work orientation can be read directly from perception of experience in the work environment. Perception, an integral part of the motivational system, supplies information about the environment to the brain. To assess the motivational climate process, it is necessary to measure experience on the job as perceived by the employee. When attempting to understand any aspect about human motivation, perception is reality. Moreover, perception is a transactional process; that is, what is experienced is translated into meaningful concepts by the motivational system. Meaning does not always come from experience; meaning is brought to experience. A work situation cannot adequately be assessed without measuring the individual or group involved. Figure 2 depicts the transactional view of the perceptual process.

Stated perceptions are judgments about experience and, if stated truthfully, perceptions represent predispositions for action. For example, if a worker states, "From my experience, there is no opportunity to advance in this company," it can be assumed that the individual is predisposed toward leaving the company or at least will not produce as much for the company as an employee who perceives the company as having some opportunity for advancement. Moreover, the probability is high and can, in fact, be established statistically, that one or both those actions will result. The individual charged with changing such negative perceptions and its behavioral ramification must take action. If the action is effective, say by providing more opportunity for advancement, or by correcting an erroneous perception (revealing opportunities unknown to the employee), then the person in charge learns an important leadership/management lesson. This lesson will, in turn, transfer to similar situations in the organization. Through the law of effect, experience on the job will have a greater impact on leadership/management improvement than external training/development programs in laboratories, through films and lectures, or from literature. The key to success with this model (i.e., decreasing the probability of leader/manager error in judgment)

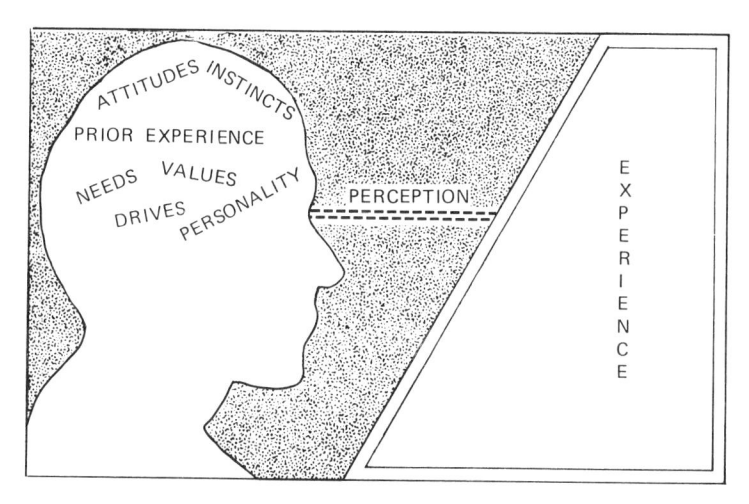

Figure 2 Transactional view of the perceptual process. (From the U.S. Marine Corps Leadership Evaluation and Analysis Program [LEAP]. Reprinted by permission of the publisher.)

is systematic feedback through accurate measurement and analysis of motivational climate factors.

Motivational Climate Assessment

The individual interested in enhancing leadership/management skills must accurately assess the needs and concerns of the group with regard to the work situation. If the information is valid, the leader/manager has the content for the most relevant personal training/development opportunity. The object of measurement is a complex human component. The primary assumption is that motivational climate factors, expressed as perceptions of needs and concerns with regard to the work situation, will predict performance on the job and, therefore, represent the conditions that the leader/manager must learn to control and influence.

The first step toward motivational climate assessment is to either select or develop the proper instrument of measurement. The leadership/management improvement model proposed here requires just as much precision of instrumentation, technique, and procedure as a well-designed quality improvement program. Motivational climate assessment begins with a plan that includes the purpose for which assessment is made, a theoretical framework to guide assessment, delineation of the forms of investigation, and a technique that is designed to satisfy the requirements of assessment.

Of the various techniques used to assess motivational climate, the survey questionnaire overcomes most of the problems and biases that can occur. Table 1 lists the benefits and shortcomings of direct observation, personal interview, and the mail-out or group-administered survey questionnaire. While the observation and interview techniques allow more flexibility to probe, expand, and discovery additional concerns previously not considered, the survey questionnaire can eliminate distortions due to interviewer bias and fear of recrimination that usually destroy the validity of survey methods (McBer, 1970). Moreover, interviews require much more professional training than survey administration. Generally, interviews are used prior to and after a questionnaire is administered to generate ideas and items for questionnaire design and to probe and clarify group responses, respectively. The observation method of assessment is least desirable due to personal distortions of the observer and/or violations of the Privacy Act. To measure motivational climate through the perceptual process, the questionnaire survey is superior to other available techniques. Confidentiality, anonymity, and representativeness can be assured, interviewer bias is eliminated, and cost and administration skill required are minimal.

Selection of a readymade or a custom-designed survey questionnaire depends on individual preference and the theoretical base considered most appropriate for the situation.

A formal theoretical foundation is based on an identifiable theory of motivation such as Fiedler's Contingency Theory (Fiedler, 1968), Maslow's Hierarchy of Needs (Maslow, 1943), or Blake and Mouton's Two Factor Theory (Blake and Mouton, 1964). Supporting literature, creditability, and validation along with available survey techniques are benefits of this approach.

Table 1 Comparison of Motivational Climate Assessment Techniques

	Technique			
			Questionnaire	
Criteria	Observation	Interview	Mail	Group
Confidentiality	?	—	+	+
Anonymity	?	—	+	+
Assessor bias	?	—	+	+
Flexibility	—	+	+	+
Representativeness	+	+	—	+
Comprehensiveness	—	+	—	—
Skill Required	—	—	+	+
Cost	+	—	+	+

However, each theory is strongly biased toward a management approach that may be too broad, inappropriate, or not relevant to a particular organization.

The shotgun theory fosters unbiased data collection of a wide range of motivational climate factors that can correlate with actual performance. But, results may not be relevant or coherent and may be difficult to interpret. Collecting data from a variety of sources, based on a plethora of ideas and assumptions, is an example of the shotgun approach.

The grounded-theory approach that produces a customized survey design is probably the most ideal method for most training and development programs. The database is relevant to the organization, and results focus on the particular concerns of the group under charge. Grounded theories emanate from interviews, group sensing, and observation within a department or throughout an entire organization. The expressed interest and critical concerns of the group guide the survey design and the data collection procedure.

Selecting or designing the right technique for motivational climate assessment is the most critical aspect of the leadership/management improvement plan. Just like a "high-tech" testing device, the motivational climate survey instrument must be appropriate for the target population, precisely calibrated, and reliable. The guidelines and standards for motivational assessment techniques published by the American Psychological Association (1966) require evidence of validity and reliability for instruments that purport to measure any mental state. Through factor analysis, content validity is established revealing the degree to which the content of the items logically defines the concept being measured. To avoid response set, defensive inhibition, acquiescence, and other biases, items must cover the full range of feeling and tonality about an issue being measured. In order to produce a meaningful score from a scale of measurement, items must be unidimensional; i.e., item statements that comprise the score must measure the same concept. If evidence of scale unidimensionality and nonambiguity is not provided, scores between individuals, groups, or periods may not be comparable. Internal and temporal consistency is also established by statistical methods that measure item correlation within the instrument and over time. Finally, concurrent and predictive validity must be demonstrated. If a questionnaire measures a motivational construct that is associated with certain types of behavior, then a score on the scale should correlate with and predict the expected behavior or performance. Specific performance, then, becomes the final criterion for validation of the motivational scale. This type of validity is essential for applied programs.

Unless validity and reliability estimates are substantially demonstrated for a questionnaire technique, there can be no guarantee that the results of a survey are any better than random speculation. The current limited acceptance of survey data-gathering methods is not due to the state of the art, but can be accounted for by widespread failure to adhere to the requirements established by the science for instrument precision.

Empirical validation of the motivational climate assessment technique is accomplished through a pilot study for a prototype

LEADERSHIP AND MANAGEMENT TRAINING

instrument to weed out ambiguous, redundant, and nonrelevant items, or by administration to the target population for a standardized survey questionnaire. Correlation coefficients calculated between motivational climate scales and both criterion items and performance measures will establish critical (i.e., statistically significant) cause-and-effect relationships. Table 2 displays results of validation studies for three separate motivational climate assessment techniques designed specifically for the type of organization and particular environmental situation.

The Self-Improvement Method

The planning and development phase complete, the emergent and incumbent leader/manager need only administer the motivational climate assessment technique, review the results, and then respond to the signals given to maintain control or to improve the performance of the group. In this way, leaders and managers elevate their own capability to deal with the motivational conditions for which they are responsible.

Group Motivational Issues and Performance Outcomes

The motivational climate scales listed in Table 2 can be analyzed by individual item statements that represent more specific group judgments, as shown in Tables 3 and 4. These items offer diagnostic clues and causes for the performance outcomes that the leader/manager is obliged to change.

Table 3 lists the seven items that correlate highest with lateness on the job. The motivational climate score for each item is also given. The scores represent one-directional percentiles; i.e., converted scales range from 0 to 100 with 50 being the midpoint. Regardless of the tone of the item (positive or negative), scores below the midpoint indicate that the majority of personnnel perceive the issue in the negative, and vice versa. Some of the issues that influence lateness most require a management solution such as assuring accurate information and clarification policy and procedures. Other personnel concerns call for the responsible party to exercise more leadership skill regarding recognition and participa-

Table 2 Correlation Coefficients Between Motivational Climate Scale and Subscale Scores and Various Criterion Variables

	Criteria		
Interaction inventory Scale 1	Production errors	Punctuality	Turnover
Organization	***	*	*
Corporate policy	*	*	**
Work group proficiency	**	—	—
Solidarity	**	**	*
Communication flow	***	*	***
Workload	*	—	—
Job quality	**	**	***
Task satisfaction	**	*	***
Task significance	*	**	**
Personal development	*	*	***
Reward and advancement	**	*	***
Equality	**	*	***
Recognition	***	*	**
Wages	—	—	**
Supervision	*	—	—
Motivational climate	***	*	***

Scale 2	Reenlist	Drug	Alcohol	Theft
Senior proficiency	***	**	**	**
Senior support	***	**	***	**
Communication flow	***	**	**	**
Organization and planning	***	**	**	***
Recognition	***	—	—	—
Discipline	**	—	—	—

Scale 3				
Job quality	***	—	—	—
Task satisfaction	***	—	—	—
Task significance	***	—	—	—
Functional readiness	—	—	—	—
Training readiness	—	—	—	—
Individual training readiness	—	—	—	—
Solidarity	**	***	***	**
Individual development	***	—	—	—

*$p < 0.05$; **$p < 0.01$; ***$p < 0.001$.

Table 3 Motivational Climate Scores for Items Most Significantly Associated with Lateness

Item	Score
Employees participate in decisions affecting their job.	47.8
All employees have an equal opportunity for advancement in this company.	32.0
Employees have little influence on what goes on in the company.	46.0
There is not enough recognition for doing a good job in this company.	38.8
Some employees are required to do more in order to get ahead.	31.7
The information employees receive is accurate.	49.6
Company policy and procedures are not clearly understood.	46.7

Table 4 Motivational Climate Scores for Items Most Significantly Associated with Production Errors

Item	Score
The management is unaware of the problems employees face.	32.9
Personnel in my department are not sufficiently trained for their jobs.	57.2
More formal training is needed in my department.	27.4
Company policy and procedures are not equally enforced.	35.2

tive decision making. And finally, the equality issues require research into federal compliance and promotion statistics first, before a rational response can be made.

Reviewing Table 4, the leader/manager, seeking a reduction in production error, will have to address the issues of training, equal enforcement of company policy, and awareness of personnel problems. The latter condition, although more ambiguous than the others, may be satisfied simply by communicating awareness as well as interest in actual personnel problems by virtue of response to the motivational climate survey.

Personal Assessment Scales

From a review of Table 2, the leader/manager becomes aware that the manner of supervision, as judged by the group, is somewhat correlated with both production errors and punctuality. Using a control chart to assess these personal leadership/management characteristics, Figure 3 reveals that "providing the essential training" and "technical proficiency" are judged to be significant shortcomings.

At this point, it is unknown whether the rated individual is not providing the training that the group feels essential because he/she lacks technical competence or is merely perceived as not being technically qualified because training is not provided. What is known is that these characteristics must be improved in the eyes of the group for production and punctuality to be improved.

Perceptual Disparity

Analyzing motivational climate data from the perspective of various groups within an organization provides yet another dimension of leader/manager responsibility. Perceptual disparity (i.e., differences in perceptual judgment between selected groups) has proven to be an excellent measure of basic causes for and predictors of organizational behavior (Affourtit, 1979a). The disparity index (DI) calculated between seniors and subordinates of military units predicted significant differences in unauthorized absences, career

LEADERSHIP AND MANAGEMENT TRAINING

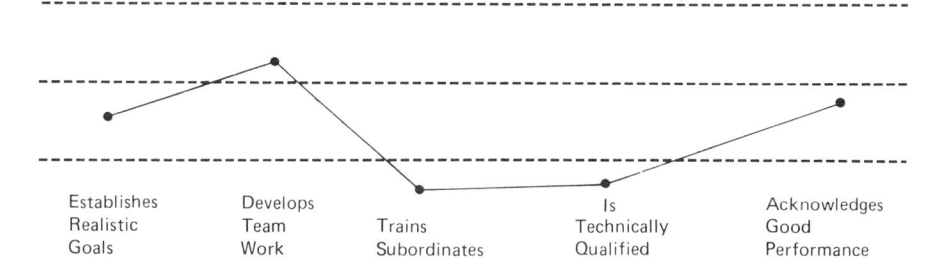

Figure 3 Control chart of supervision scale categories for Department E.

intention, and reenlistment rates (Table 5). Notwithstanding the overall motivational climate level of a unit, if both leaders and followers agreed with regard to areas requiring improvement, unit performance was higher than in units where leaders and followers disagreed over existing conditions. It was concluded that, if conditions within the organization are low, but both senior and subordinate judgments are in concert, then the organization is collectively oriented toward improvement. The forecast is positive. However, if seniors and subordinates disagree over the conditions assessed, the total situation is not conducive to improvement. The future seems bleak for unit members, compounding current concerns and producing a more severe impact on performance.

Disparity, then, represents the gap between those in charge and those who function to produce a service or material output. This gap and the concerns that produce the disagreement are the content of leadership/management training and development. As the individual learns to close the gap, insight is gained, expertise is enhanced, and performance is improved. Table 6 shows the disparity indices for several subscale categories. This information directs the leader/manager's attention to the area of disparity that produces the greatest impediment to performance.

Further analysis is conducted for disagreements over particular concerns. Table 7 lists individual items and disparity indices for leadership staff and subordinate members of a military unit.

Table 5 Significant Correlation Coefficients Between Motivational Climate Scores and Subscale Scores and Criterion Variables

Interaction Inventory Scale 4	Disparity		
	Unauthorized absences	Career intention	Reenlistment rates
Command preparedness	***	—	***
Command efficiency	**	—	**
Command cohesion	**	—	***
Command equality	—	***	***
Minority discrimination	—	—	***
Majority discrimination	—	**	—
Intergroup climate	—	—	***
Justice	—	***	***
Motivational climate	***	—	***

**$p < 0.01$; ***$p < 0.001$.

Table 6 Disparity Indices: The Organization Scale

Subscale	Disparity index
Policy	20.5
Solidarity	18.6
Communication flow	6.8
Group proficiency	5.4
Workload	4.9

Table 7 Individual Concerns and Disparity Indices

Interaction inventory item	Disparity index
Most of the troops in this command are dissatisfied with their job.	18
The troops in this command are well informed.	13.2
Most of the troops would rather serve in another command.	13
The troops of this command are confused much of the time.	12.5
Morale and spirit are high in this command.	12
This command is well organized.	10

The leadership (i.e., officers and staff) of this unit can easily recognize some areas where their development is essential if the unit is to improve performance. The job satisfaction issue may require more probing for clarification. However, the level of disparity over being well informed and confused reveals a fundamental communication problem between leaders and followers. When confronted with these results as related to a unit dysfunction, one junior officer exclaimed, "I read them [the troops] the order last week!" In an impromptu training session conducted by his senior, the officer quickly "learned" the difference between reading an order to unit members and assuring understanding and retention of the order through proper communication.

Case Histories

As can be seen from the data given above, the information supplied by the motivational climate survey is a considerable aid to the leader/manager's quest for improved talent and proficiency. The content for self-training and development clear, the course of action toward improvement is primarily a matter of individual preference and personal style. For the leader/manager to derive benefit from analysis, the information must be used in a manner that upgrades his/her ability to deal effectively with the group under charge. The case histories described below offer several approaches available to the leader/manager.

Open Forum

A recently arrived infantry company commander announced to his unit that he would post the motivational climate survey results in the living quarters for all members to review. Unit members were initially skeptical, although platoon leaders were in favor of any method of improving the poor performance record of the command. The approach conveyed a sense of openness and communicated immediately to unit members that the new commanding officer was interested in doing something about their concerns.

Bimonthly training sessions were held with officers and staff noncommissioned officers during which they would address selected problem areas, determine the accuracy of command perceptions, brainstorm arbitrary and complex issues, gather facts to support or refute perceptual judgments, and develop potential solutions for improving conditions. This exercise also allowed the senior members to acknowledge the points of view of the junior members of the unit.

As pertinent issues were clarified and recommended courses of action were outlined, the commanding officer and senior members addressed the entire command on a particular issue or series of issues. Input from other members of the unit was solicited, hard evidence of conditions was displayed by the leadership, and recommended courses of action were presented by the company commander.

The initial effect of the process was a diminished disparity between seniors and subordinates in the command; that is, the process itself increased group solidarity. Troop involvement in correcting deficiencies was encouraged, but the seniors maintained control of the situation by selecting the issues and preparing to meet disagreements or differences in perception logically and factually. In instances where troops had misjudged a condition or

LEADERSHIP AND MANAGEMENT TRAINING

misperceived a company policy, the leaders were prepared to present the "facts" concerning, for example, disciplinary procedures, duty assignments, or promotion policies. The command gatherings were brief, relevant, positive, and to the point.

Knowledge of the critical issues and preparation for meetings made the leaders more confident when addressing the troops, and the process avoided the potential loss of control that can occur when groups try to communicate from different points of view. When an issue that was not prepared for surfaced, the leaders clarified and recorded it for response at the next meeting.

Delegation of Authority

An aviation maintenance manager reviewed the results of a motivational climate survey and found the scale scores to be a thoroughly accurate reflection of his own estimate of the situation. He then circled those areas and issues he felt required priority attention and discussed each at a meeting with his directors and supervisors.

He then directed each supervisor to deal with the issues identified by delegating responsibility down to the shop heads to exercise them in reviewing, investigating, and correcting any discrepancies uncovered. He requested informal periodic feedback concerning the outcome of any intervention, as well as recommendations and suggestions from members participating in organization improvement projects. In this manner, the manager satisfied the leadership/management training requirement from the parent organization and at the same time addressed relevant needs and concerns of his organization.

Several months later another survey was administered. This time personnel were very enthusiastic about the process and about the potential progress the approach could bring. Improvements were noted in most motivational areas, particularly in closing the perceptual gap between senior and subordinate members of the organization. The supervisors met and were informed by management that they were on the right track and to continue as directed. The positive feedback had a catalytic effect on the junior management and supervisors, as they realized their efforts were paying off and were being recognized by top management.

Six months later, a third survey was administered. The results were particularly revealing. Scores increased significantly in all but one of the motivational areas measured. Performance measure also improved since the first survey; repair rates, turnaround time, and no-defect rates improved significantly compared to sister organizations.

In consideration of the mission and organization of his company, the general manager in this case functioned primarily as a director, training and exercising his subordinates in leadership and management activities that had a direct impact on group performance. He utilized modern organizational techniques, investigated problems, gathered facts, developed policies as needed, and then delegated authority to address critical issues. He provided support and position power to supervisors and thereby exercised developing leaders/managers and promoted positive transition of authority when the time for promotion occurs.

Classic Approach

After administering the motivational climate survey to the organization, a plant manager had a formal report prepared of the results. The data were grouped according to mission-oriented categories for the total organization and for the two exempt/nonexempt groups. In this manner, the most critical areas of concern (lowest scores) and specific issues were identified within the categories of organization, communications, and morale.

The plant manager published a list of problem areas and established a study group composed of selected managers, supervisors, and operators to further investigate each condition and to design a solution/action program for review. With the survey results as a guide, the study group uncovered numerous instances where appropriate action would improve the motivational level of the organization. Check-in and administrative procedures created a poor first impression for newcomers; sick leave procedures were annoying and inefficient; intrasection planning activity was practically nonexistent; interdepartment functioning was considered fragmentary, diffuse, and in some cases isolated; many members did

LEADERSHIP AND MANAGEMENT TRAINING 119

not understand company requirements, pay policies, or how to deal with personal problems.

Two chains of command were apparently operating, one for managers and staff and one for supervisors and operators. As a result, communication was not consistent or timely, and complaints came from both sectors. Moreover, operators in all sections generally felt their accomplishments were not recognized, punishment for generally misunderstood policy was considered unfair, and members did not seem to understand the difference between rights, responsibilities, and privileges. Generally, the personnel saw a large gap between themselves and management. Management was seen to abuse the privileges afforded them, and they did not seem to understand or be concerned about subordinate issues.

Corrective actions and solutions were rapidly established and published formally with a full description of the action to be taken, the decisions made, and the target data or goal to be reached. Some modifications were structural, some represented changes in process, others involved establishing educational programs. For example, the administration office was moved to a more central location to facilitate the check-in process and to avoid loss of important paperwork; the "buddy system" was established for newcomers; and a thorough indoctrination program was implemented for new employees.

To improve communication flow, lower-level staff meetings were established; supervisors and shop heads were included once a month at the plant manager's weekly conference; the company newsletter was used to further inform members about personal, local, and organizational matters; periodic intersection "field trips" were promoted to broaden the appreciation of employees in other departments and to generate group pride. To improve general morale and corporate identification, field days and family days were planned by operator committees, and individual/section achievement awards were initiated and publicly presented.

Finally, a training program was organized to address pertinent motivational concerns. Training was conducted for separate management and staff groups that covered relevant concrete subject areas, such as rights, privileges, and responsibilities of employees, principles of counseling, and briefing techniques. In addition, critical company issues identified by the survey were broached by separate groups and then addressed during a second stage of training that included all levels of employees. A primary goal established for this approach was to prepare senior and junior managers to effectively answer questions concerning organization and structure, promotion systems and policies, record book entries and annual rating reports, and even matters of courtesy.

The entire process was recorded and produced in a formal report along with presentation aids and charts that monitored progress. Resurveys were planned periodically to obtain feedback on decision-making effectiveness. The report was voluntarily submitted to the parent organization for the purpose of sharing the experience and the findings, and to recommend potential solutions for other divisions in the organization.

Reorganization

Shortly after taking control of a somewhat hybrid engineering support company, the new CEO realized that conditions in the organization were not as good as they appeared on the surface. According to the records, however, maintenance levels were maintained, equipment was functional, spare parts were available, repair rates were steady and efficient, etc. On the employee morale side, the record showed that absenteeism was down, as were employee reprimands. The employee complaint report did not reveal any major problem areas. On paper, the command looked well organized and proficient.

Yet, the CEO quickly detected that the records were not quite accurate. Vehicles would not start; equipment failed to function properly; key staff and other managers were not readily available to respond to mishaps. Beyond that, responsibility seemed to be diffused; grumbling and excuses among employees were rampant; even the employee break area was unkempt and disorganized.

A thorough investigation of the organization revealed a Pandora's box of problem areas. The CEO discovered that complaints from clients the company was supporting were usually rejected

LEADERSHIP AND MANAGEMENT TRAINING 121

as unsound or excused as negligence on the client's part. Communication lines between client organization and maintenance sections were unstructured and disorganized. Section heads frequently had to use informal channels or other means to obtain support and/or equipment. Often one manager would handle requests from several sources insufficiently, while those supposedly responsible for action were not available.

The records concerning equipment readiness did not accurately reflect the situation. The company was a long way from efficient; many of the problems that were not included in official reports were forgotten or disregarded and remain unattended. Accordingly, repair rates and equipment viability were not exactly falsified on the records; they were "estimated."

Results of the motivational climate survey revealed that operators had little respect for or confidence in the management. They felt they could not communicate up the chain of command; managers were uncaring about their personal and job situations, and they were sufficiently dissatisfied with their assignments. The supervisors and shop heads were particularly dismayed about not being supported and not given responsibility. No one cared about his job. Since absenteeism and tardiness were easily excused (and often not officially reported), the offense was committed frequently without fear of disciplinary action, a condition no one really complained about. Legitimate complaints, formally submitted, were generally left unresolved or rejected, a condition that made employees reluctant or cynical about getting involved or conveying other problems to management.

The most revealing analysis was provided by a time-with-company breakdown of the survey results. New arrivals to the company were generally highly motivated; in fact, the group with less than 3 months on the job had higher motivational scores than those with 3-4 years. After 3 months with the company, however, the motivational level plummeted and remained low until employees left the company. At the 3-month point, the novelty of the experience seemed to wear off. Employees realized that the company was not representative of the job or profession they sought, and they became aware that responsibility on the job meant little support from above or personal guidance when needed.

The management and staff, on the other hand, saw those below them as unmotivated, although they felt that communication, support, and response to subordinates were much more adequate than the other employees estimated. In short, the company was not functioning well, and the true situation was reflected through accurate assessment of unit performance and motivational climate.

The CEO's mission was clear. He had to train and develop his managers expeditiously on the spot. Although the efficiency and morale problems that now "surfaced" were mostly their doing, replacing the entire staff was unfeasible. And sending them off to "management school" would not solve immediate problems.

The CEO went to work establishing visual charts indicating actual work accomplished, repair rates, etc. The work setting had to be the manager's classroom. Objectives or goals were also established, and progress was measured on a daily/weekly basis for all unit members to see. The lines of communication were corrected by creating a maintenance control center through which all message traffic was received, recorded, and tracked. Motivational and morale problems were systematically addressed. Section heads were briefed together and individually as warranted by the initial survey results. Policy changes considered necessary to modify perceptions and to improve conditions were implemented.

The process and structural change eventually had a positive impact on the company. Equipment was functionally upgraded; deadline items were tracked efficiently; spare parts were ready or on order. The CEO also displayed, for the benefit of both employees and clients who visited the company, before-and-after charts indicating the degree and rate of improvement over time.

After 8 months, a motivational climate resurvey revealed that employees developed more pride in their company. A renewed sense of professional competence and achievement was not apparent. Corporate cohesion also increased as management developed a better appreciation for employee problems and realized that leniency and unchallenging work neither improved morale nor afforded them respect.

Self-Awareness

The director of operations of a large manufacturing organization suspected that one of his department heads was promoting racial bias and thereby causing dissension between the minority and majority employees in his department. There was no evidence to put his finger on exactly: an attitude expressed by the manager, his demeanor toward certain individuals, and some casual comments made by personnel in the department.

Realizing a potential racial confrontation was brewing, the director summoned the department head and outlined the situation and his assessment of it. The man (a good engineer with much more time on the job than the director) became defensive and denied any preferential or discriminatory treatment of members of his section. The manager questioned the director's judgment by explaining he knew how to handle employees; many years of successful service and rise in leadership position were proof of his capability. He further explained that there were a few vocal malcontents in his department who were responsible for the director's impression.

The motivational climate survey was administered to the entire company but processed by directorates. This procedure gave the general manager an opportunity to review his corporation as a whole as well as to analyze differences in conditions between the various functions.

The results were revealing insofar as perceptions of discrimination and efficiency within each department were concerned. The department in question displayed a generally negative condition for minority discrimination as judged by both minority and majority employees. Most of the employees in the department were aware of the manager's bias but could not effectively communicate the situation to him. Furthermore, other department results revealed no such negative judgments in the area of perceived discrimination.

With this evidence in hand, the director summoned the department head for counseling, showed him the data, and directed him to explain how a couple of malcontents could produce such results. After the counseling, some of the staff supervisors were gathered, and along with the director and department heads they reviewed the situation, analyzed assignments, and individual impressions, etc., and planned several courses of action toward modifying the conditions that produced the negative perceptions. The department head did a lot of soul searching and finally realized that he was treating people differently merely on the basis of color. He modified his actions accordingly.

Investigation Process

An incident occurred between two groups of Marines in one command that resulted in one Marine's requiring medical attention for a knife wound. A formal investigation of the incident produced contradictory explanations and judgments about the probable cause and the events that led to the altercation. The outcome of the investigation did not conclusively reveal which group instigated the incident, whether the action was ethnically motivated, or who was actually involved. Several alternate theories were pieced together for the final report.

Realizing that witnesses, being liable for their testimony, were intimidated by the investigators and were pressured by peers to communicate accepted versions of the incident publicly, the commanding officer administered motivational climate surveys to the entire command and also requested verbatim comments about the incident, as well as suggestions for improving relations between Marines in the command.

Unit members were able to communicate anonymously without fear of reprisal, and they were not reticent about expressing their opinions and suggestions. Furthermore, the items in the questionnaire were structured to cover the full range of factors that represent standard concerns of Marines in a number of areas, including intergroup climate. The items helped respondents organize their thoughts and stimulated a number of verbatim comments in an effort to qualify the response categories of the survey. The activity also gave members a sense of involvement and unity in solving command problems.

The commander was able to elicit additional information about the incident to support or refute the theories generated by the formal hearing. Moreover, he could judge the degree of tension remaining between groups, systematically determine probable underlying causes, and establish a course of action designed to improve relevant conditions. The suggestions made by troops toward diffusing the situation were quite beneficial, according to the commander.

A leadership lesson on how to avert future confrontations also emerged from the data. It seems that an NCO had the adversary groups under control before any actual contact was made. However, the NCO left the scene to get additional help in resolving the conflict and in dispersing the groups. In the absence of a responsible intermediary, emotions of the groups increased and the altercation occurred. Had the NCO remained to maintain order and sent another Marine for additional support, the incident probably would not have escalated. A critical lesson in leadership was learned by all.

Establish Priorities

Upon assuming command of a military unit just prior to a demanding tactical training exercise, a new commanding officer administered the motivational climate survey to his unit during the initial staging period. In preparation for taking command, the officer had previously reviewed the survey results of a division cross-section and identified some general conditions and concerns that served as management and leadership guides. He also took note of those conditions that appeared most disparate between senior and junior enlisted men, i.e., the issues that showed the largest gaps between the two rank groups, such as information dissemination and command organization.

By administering the motivational questionnaire himself, he informed the unit that he wanted to begin his tour as commanding officer by getting a fix on the primary concerns and issues that were important to unit members. Administration of the questionnaire immediately after his statement of intent made it clear to the unit that he was sincere in wanting to upgrade the morale and efficiency of the unit.

The data provided by the survey gave the commanding officer substance to train subordinates and to organize his priorities and establish goals for the unit. The information also helped confirm some initial impressions he had formed and aided in the interpretation of judgments he received informally from junior officers and key staff, most of which had slightly different priorities and perceptions about the command. He now had a balanced view of the command, and by knowing which judgments were most accurate, he was able to determine some measure of credibility among his subordinate leaders. He felt more confident about making decisions in preparation for the difficult exercise that the unit faced.

During the days of the tactical exercise, the commander, pressed with numerous demands and details that required immediate attention, forced himself to deal alternately with at least some of the concerns that the survey printout revealed as prominent among unit personnel—issues that were considered to have been insufficiently addressed in the past. Even though the immediate tactical demands seemed more critical at the time, he realigned his priorities to allot some effort toward personnel issues— issues that conventional wisdom dictated should be placed on the "back burner."

In addition, as he interacted with the troops during field exercises, rather than engaging primarily in small talk, he was able to take the initiative and communicate more directly with the troops on relevant issues, probe for further information, and solicit suggestions about upgrading unit climate.

This approach, according to the commander, had a very positive effect on his own leadership development. Admittedly, he normally would not have considered many of the conditions he eventually delat with during such a hectic schedule. But, the fact that he did utilize some of the time on issues that troops felt were personally important had a motivating effect on unit members. The unit performed exceptionally well and achieved an outstanding score during the exercise—100% training attendance during the entire period, no absenteeism, no one missing muster, good coordination between seniors and subordinates, and all duty watches responsibly carried out. The spirit of group solidarity expressed was officially noted by the senior training officer in an after-action report.

Although the totality of leadership displayed by the commander deserves full credit for the outcome, the commanding officer felt that adapting his priorities to include some key management issues and the manner with which he was able to approach his troops were primarily responsible for gaining the confidence, respect, and response of the Marines in this new command.

Poor Communication

In an effort to identify some definitive causes for an inordinate number of absences in his food service organization, the manager administered the motivational climate survey to his group immediately following a very hectic weekend. After reviewing the results, the manager focused on the single most negatively perceived issue shown on the motivational profile. The manager reasoned that this issue was not only the most critical but the one about which employees were most certain. He reasoned that this issue would be used by employees as a premise to deduce a number of other negative conditions for which little evidence might be available.

According to the survey, most of the employees considered the promotion system to be unfair and discriminatory. Moroover, when the data were processed for ethnic groups, all groups saw racial bias as a factor for their advancement in the organization. In this case, at least, one group had to be wrong.

Since the manager considered the promotion policy to be fair and conducted in accordance with corporate policy, he was surprised by the results of the survey. Further inquiry into the allegation revealed that most of the employees considered time-in-grade as the ultimate criterion for promotion. They did not fully understand how the promotion system worked, they could not calculate their individual composite scores that considered other criteria, and many claimed they were unaware of a composite scoring system or standard promotion policy.

As a result of this misconception, whenever a black or white employee received a promotion with less time-in-grade than another employee of a different race, the group associated with the nonpromoted employee surmised that discrimination was the reason. Moreover, the manager's initial assumption was correct. The certainty of the "evidence" of racial bias in promotion was the basis for a number of other misperceptions concerning discrimination in the company. The employees rationalized, excused, or filtered out any evidence contradicting their "theory" as an exception to the rule.

Supervisors and key staff members were generally unaware of the intensity of the situation and shrugged off comments overheard as meaningless. But, if resentment was not vocal, it was intense, as indicated by the anonymous comments on survey forms.

The solution was simple. The manager quickly modified the training schedule to include a concentrated educational project The morning after the next hectic weekend, he summoned his supervisors and key staff and directed them to gather the employees in small groups and, with company policy in hand, explained precisely how the promotion system actually functioned, and exactly what each individual had to accomplish before a promotion could be awarded.

This case is a good example of poor communication between management and employees. Management was certain that the employees had previously been informed about the promotion system and assumed that all employees understood why they were or were not promoted. However, whether they received a lecture on promotion when hired by the company, were initially briefed during company training, or were informally told during work hours, the fact remained that they did not understand the system, and their performance reflected a critical misjudgment of company policy.

The manager took the stand that he and other lead personnel were not only responsible for communicating such information, but they were also responsible for assuring comprehension.

Developing Leadership

An amphibious assault vehicle commander directed his platoon leaders to administer the survey to their respective sections. Each officer was required to develop motivational profiles for several different groups (by education, rank, ethnic group, EAS, etc.) as an exercise in learning about the members that comprise the unit.

At an informal officers call, the leaders discussed their results from the standpoints of the different groups within the command. They identified common command weaknesses and attempted to deduce reasons for certain trends that were peculiar to groups with different backgrounds or at different periods in their tour in the military. The exercise was an attempt to analyze group motivation, understand expectations, and promote more flexibility in dealing with diverse groups. The company commander theorized that, although unit members were a generally homogeneous group, there were important individual differences among them that, properly considered by leaders, could be instrumental in controlling and influencing their behavior. Considering individual differences will promote command solidarity and individual identification with unit goals.

The company commander felt that this exercise was not only beneficial in gaining knowledge about unit concerns and priorities, but was also a valuable lesson in understanding the rationale behind various perceptions of members. Accordingly, the insight acquired from this exercise became a catalyst for positive and productive interaction between the leaders and the troops. Young officers became less reluctant to approach junior members in the unit. The leaders were able to address relevant matters with a group and on a one-to-one basis, generate rapport, and communicate more intelligently and rationally with unit members. The young officers expressed the feeling that they had learned something that enhanced their value as leaders.

As these case histories illustrate, the information obtained from a motivational climate survey can be addressed in any number of ways depending on the individual's approach to problem solving. The primary purpose of an intelligence-gathering technique like the survey is to gain control and influence over the group the leader/manager was assigned to. In this respect, the manager's philosophy or style of leadership is not a real consideration. Whether the one in charge is more disposed toward Machiavellian principles or espouses Jeffersonian concepts, he or she is more able to manipulate incentives or be guided by group desires, as the case may be, by having a firm understanding of the motivational orientation of the unit and by learning those behaviors that elicit the best performance results.

Summary

The motivational climate survey is an ideal training and development technique for anyone in a leadership and management role. First to improve are insight and adaptability, two essential ingredients for further growth. The only requirement is openness or willingness to adapt to the environment.

Since the motivational climate assessment technique allows equal participation and equal expression by all group members, it overcomes defensive listening on the part of the leader/manager. As the ultimate participative management technique, the survey, properly validated against performance criteria, communicates the "truth" about the leader/manager's domain. It highlights which motivational factors are vital, which are significant, and which concerns have impact on performance outcomes. Most important it reveals evidence of the leader/manager's shortcomings and assets, as well as his responsibilities for improvement.

The truth, however, is not for the fainthearted. While "the truth shall make you free," it may first make you miserable. The leader/manager will most likely suffer growing pains with this model of training and development. As an alternative, the leader/manager may elect to participate in a laboratory training session, watch a management film, or read about leadership and management in a book. But, as the literature shows, nothing much will change.

In the rush to compete with the Japanese and regain preeminence in the world marketplace, U.S. managers are, more than ever, obliged to devour reams of new ideas, facts, techniques, theories, and procedures concerning management and leadership. Some of the modern philosophies of management, like Deming's "14 Principles" are insightful and profound, if unproven, but many are vague, abstract, and contradictory. Some of the new offerings are so well packaged and marketed, strike the right cords, and use the right "buzz" words that they have become monumental financial successes for authors and publishers. For the most part, the popularist writings, propaganda pitches and grand pronouncements notwithstanding, offer overly simplistic approaches to those seeking a quick-fix solution. "Theory S," for simplistic, sensationalistic, and superficial, is an apt label for such entertainment without substance.

The quick-fix approach is like working in the dark, hoping something will turn out right, but not willing to be identified if it fails. In 84 pages, the *One Minute Manager* (Blanchard and Johnson, 1983) advises managers to spend their time doling out 1-min rewards and 1-min reprimands. Good advice. However, as a rule of thumb, the more simplistic the method, the more assumptions one is obliged to bring to the situation. For example, disciples of the *One Minute Manager* must assume that: the manager's perception of the situation is accurate; the manager's on-the-spot judgment of right or wrong is correct; the problem represents a "special" case; the system is blameless; impulse is superior to an analytical approach; there is only one side to an argument; those in positions of management are superior to those beneath them; people are best when treated like Pavlov's dog; a 1-min mistake won't beget months of disintegration; leaders cannot learn from subordinates; people who are treated like Pavlov's dog will increase productivity; all situations are either black or white; discussion and investigation are ineffective and unnecessary; democracy is outdated; authoritarianism is sound practice; all managers possess the insight of a philosopher king. The *One Minute Manager* is testimony to the fact that in a complex and demanding world, most of us are inclined toward expediency, and if packaged properly, the majority will acclaim pap.

In the popular publications *In Search of Excellence* (Peters and Waterman, 1982) and *A Passion for Excellence* (Peters and Austin, 1985), the authors present a collage of anecdotes that define "excellent" leaders. Readers aspiring to excellence are encouraged to emulate the personages whose achievements are described as legends. But beyond reiterating that the selected successes were "people oriented," Peters et al. merely recount outcomes. Without full analysis of the processes that lead to these outcomes, inspired readers can only hope for random success.

The anecdotes, presented as scientific "fact," are what may well be only scientific fiction. For any method to be scientifically meaningful, that is, capable of being transferred to other situations, it must somehow be capable of being studied, measured, or tested in a scientific fashion. If it cannot be measured—as in the case of most of what is termed "leadership and management," then the label is at best a metaphor and at worst a myth. And, learning the skills of what is described, is an equally amorphous and unscientific enterprise.

Consider one example offered by Peters of an Air Force Commander who assumed leadership of a unit during a 4.1-hr average part-replacement rate. After 2 years the part-replacement rate changed to 7.6 min. Notwithstanding the fact that personal charisma accounted for much of the variance, the readership is left to surmise all the intervening variables that occurred over the period of change that produced the outcome. What is offered is merely specious argument for an emphasis on the people under one's charge.

Leadership and management are both an art and a science. The art comes from current capability; characteristics acquired over a long period of time; a "feel" for the situation; our character expressed as appropriate to an assignment. The science of leadership and management transpires from systematic assessment and analysis of the motivational climate for which we are responsible, and appropriate response to improve group performance toward a desired goal. Successful leaders and managers utilize the data they receive from application of motivational climate assessment techniques to reinforce functional and extinguish dysfunctional behavior patterns. In this way, they can hone their leadership and management character, emphasize certain traits and skills, and learn new behaviors in response to the group, goal, and situation. Whatever the skill or natural ability one possesses, it can be improved. Like quality, the leadership/management goal is continuous improvement. Humans are a complex and dynamic species. Successful leaders and managers must constantly evolve to different and unique levels of control and influence. The most certain route to improvement is through the scientific method, application of appropriate techniques for data analysis, and corrective response to diagnosed causes.

Selected Readings

Affourtit, T. D. *The Marine Corps Leadership Evaluation and Analysis Program (LEAP) Volume 1; Manual for the Leadership Analysis Form and LEAP Interaction Inventory* (2nd ed.) (Technical Manual 77-1). Fairfax, VA: Interaction Research Institute, Inc., March 1977.

Affourtit, T. D. *Contemporary Marine Corps Leadership Issues: Final Report* (Technical Report 79-10). Fairfax, VA: Interaction Research Institute, Inc., August 1979a.

Affourtit, T. D. *The Leadership Evaluation and Analysis Program (LEAP): Manual for the Interaction Inventory Adjunct Questionnaires* (Technical Manual 79-C). Fairfax, VA: Interaction Research Institute, Inc., June 1979b.

Affourtit, T. D. *The Leadership Evaluation and Analysis Program (LEAP) Economic Feasibility Report* (Technical Report 79-8). Fairfax, VA: Interaction Research Institute, Inc., July 1979c.

Affourtit, T. D. *The Leadership Evaluation and Analysis Program (LEAP) Corporate Intervention Report I*. Fairfax, VA: Interaction Research Institute, Inc., July 1980.

Affourtit, T. D. *Quality and Productivity*. A seminar/workshop on statistical quality control and organizational development. Fairfax, VA: Interaction Research Institute, Inc., 1918.

Affourtit, T. D. and Affourtit, B. B. *The Japanese Connection: Statistical Methods for Process Management.* Fairfax, VA: Interaction Research Institute, Inc., 1982.

Argyris, C. T. Groups for organizational effectiveness. *Harvard Business Review*, 1964, *42(2)*, 60-74.

Argyris, C. T. *Increasing Leadership Effectiveness*, New York: Wiley, 1976.

Beckhard, R. An organization improvement program in a decentralized organization. *Journal of Applied Behavioral Science*, 1966, *2(1)*, 3-25.

Besterfield, D. G. *Quality Control.* Englewood Cliffs, NJ: Prentice-Hall, 1979.

Blake, R. R. and Mouton, J. S. *The Managerial Grid.* Houston: Gulf, 1964.

Blake, R. R., Mouton, J. S., Barnes, J. S., and Greiner, L. E. Breakthrough in organizational development. *Harvard Business Review*, 1964, *42*, 133-155.

Bowers, D. *Perspectives in Organizational Development.* Ann Arbor: University of Michigan, Institute for Social Research, Technical Report Contract #170-719/7-29-68, September 1970.

Buckley, W. (ed.). *Modern Systems Research for the Behavioral Scientist.* Chicago: Aldine, 1968.

Campbell, J. P. and Dunnette, M. D. Effectiveness of T-Group experience in managerial training and development. *Psychological Bulletin*, 1968, *70*, 73-104.

Campbell, J. P., Dunnette, M. D., Lawler, E. E., and Weick, K. E. *Managerial Behavior, Performance, and Effectiveness.* New York: McGraw-Hill, 1970.

Cattell, R. B., Second-order personality factors in the questionnaire realm. *Journal of Consulting Psychology*, 1956, *20*, 411-418.

Cattell, R. B. and Stice, G. F. Four formulae for selecting leaders on the basis of personality. *Human Relations*, 1954, *7*, 493-507.

Chowdhry, K. and Newcomb, T. M. The relative ability of leaders and non-leaders to estimate opinions of their own groups. *Journal of Abnormal and Social Psychology*, 1952, *47*, 51-47.

Comte, A. *The Positive Philosophy*, Vol. II, Book VI. Trans Harriet Martinson. London: George Bell Sons, 1896.

Corsini, R. J., Shaw, M. E. and Blake, R. R. *Roleplaying in Business and Industry*. Glencoe, IL: Free Press, 1961.

Dowley, W. H. Three distinctions in the study of leaders. *Journal of Abnormal and Social Psychology*, 1928, *23*, 144-157.

Deep, S. D., Bass, B. M., and Vaughn, J. A. Some effects on business gaming of previous quasi-T-group affiliations. *Journal of Applied Psychology*, 1967, *51*, 426-431.

Deitzer, B. A. Measuring the effectiveness of a selected management development program. Columbus: Ohio State University, *Dissertation Abstracts*, 1967.

Deming, W. E. On some statistical aids to economic production. *Interfaces*, August 1975, *5*, pp. 1-15.

Exline, R. V. Interrelations among two dimensions of sociometric status, group congeniality and accuracy of social perception. *Sociometry*, 1960, *23*, 85-101.

Fiedler, F. F. Personality and situational determinants of leadership effectiveness. In D. Cartwright and A. Zandler (eds.), *Group Dynamics*, 3rd ed. New York: Row-Peterson, 1968, Chap. 28.

Fleishman, E. A., Harris, E. F., and Burtt, H. E. *Leadership and Supervision in Industry*. Columbus: Ohio State University, Bureau of Educational Research, 1955.

Gallo, P. S. and McClintock, C. G. Behavioral, attitudinal and perceptual differences between leaders and non-leaders in situations of group support and non-support. *Journal of Social Psychology*, 1962, *56*, 121-133.

Gibb, C. A. The principles and traits of leadership. *Journal of Abnormal and Social Psychology*, 1947, *42*, 267-284.

Gibb, C. A. Leadership. In G. Lindzey and E. Aronson (eds.), *The Handbook of Social Psychology*, Vol. 4, 2nd ed. Reading, MA: Addison-Wesley, 1969, 205-282.

Haythorn, W., Couch, A. Haefner, D., Langham, P., and Carter, L. The effects of varying combinations of authoritarian and equalitarian leaders and followers. *Journal of Abnormal and Social Psychology*, 1956, *53*, 210-219.

Hobbes, T. *Leviathan*. Oxford: James Thornton, 1881: original publications, 1651.

Holtzman, W. H. Adjustment and leadership. *Journal of Social Psychology*, 1952, *36* 179-189.

Juran, J. M. *Quality Planning and Analysis*. New York: McGraw-Hill, 1970.

Krech, D., Crutchfield, R. S., and Ballachey, E. L. *Individual in Society*. New York: McGraw-Hill, 1962.

Kuriloff, A. H. and Atkins, S. T-group for a work team. *Journal of Applied Behavioral Science*, 1966, *2(1)*, 63-93.

Litwin, G. H. and Stringer, R. A. *Motivation and Organizational Climate*. Boston: Graduate School of Business Administration, Harvard University, 1976.

Mann, J. H. and Mann, C. H. The importance of group task in producing group member personality and behavior changes. *Human Relations*. 1959a, *12*, 75-80.

Mann, J. H. and Mann, C. H. Role playing and inter-personal adjustment. *Journal of Counseling Psychology*. 1959b, *22*, 64-74.

Mann, R. D. A review of the relationships between personality and performance in small groups. *Psychological Bulletin*, 1959, *56*, 241-270.

March, J. G. and Simon, H. A. *Organizations*. New York: Wiley, 1958.

Maslow, A. H. A theory of human motivation. *Psychological Review*. 1943, *50*, 370-396.

Miles, M. B., Milansky, J. R., Lake, D. G., and Beckhard, R. Organizational improvement: effects of management team training in Bankers Trust. New York: Bankers Trust Company. Unpublished monograph. 1965.

Miller, J. G. Toward a general theory for the behavioral sciences. *American Psychologist*, 1955, *10*, 513-553.

Odiorne, G. S. The trouble with sensitivity training. *Training Directors' Journal*. 1963, *17(10)*, 9-20.

Peters, T. J. and Austin, N. *A Passion for Excellence. The Leadership Difference*. New York: Random House, 1985.

Peters, T. J. and Waterman, R. H., Jr., *In Search of Excellence. Lessons from America's Best-Run Companies*. New York: Harper Row, 1982.

Rapoport, A. The diffusion problem in mass behavior. Ann Arbor: University of Michigan, *General Systems Yearbook*, 1956, *1*, 6.

Sanford, F. H. *Research on Military Leadership*. In J. C. Flanagan

(Ed.), Psychology in the World Emergency. Pittsburgh: University of Pittsburgh Press, 1952.

Showell, M. Interpersonal knowledge and rated leader potential. *Journal of Abnormal and Social Psychology*, 1960, *61*, 87-92.

Smith, A. J., Jaffe, J., and Livingston, D. G. Consonance of interpersonal perception and individual effectiveness. *Human Relations*, 1955, *8*, 385-397.

Spencer, H. *The Principles of Sociology*, Vol. II, Book II. New York: Appleton, 1898.

Speneer, L. M., Klemp, G. O., and Cullen, B. C. *Work Environment Questionnaire and Army Unit Effectiveness and Satisfaction Measures* (Technical Report). Boston, MA: McBer Co., September 1977.

Stinson, J. E. The differential impact of participation in laboratory training in collaborative task effort in intact and fragmented groups. Columbus: Ohio State University. *Dissertation Abstracts*, 1970.

Stock, D. A survey of research on T-groups. In L. P. Bradford, J. R. Gibb, and K. D. Benne (Eds.). *T-Group Theory and Laboratory Method*. New York: Wiley, 1964.

Stogdill, R. M. Personal factors associated with leadership. *Journal of Psychology*, 1948, *25*, 35-71.

Stogdill, R. M. *Handbook of Leadership*. New York: The Free Press. 1974, Chap. 16.

Stogdill, R. M. and Coons, A. E. (Eds.). *Leader Behavior: Its Description and Measurement*. Columbus: Bureau of Business Research, Ohio State University, 1957.

Thorndike, E. L. Education for initiative and originality. *Teachers College Record*, 1916, *17*, 405-416.

Underwood, W. J. Evaluation of laboratory training. *Training Directors Journal*, 1965, *19(5)*, 30-34.

Vroom, V. H. and Deci, E. L. (Eds.). *Management and Motivation*, New York: Penguin, 1982.

6

Participative Management

JILL P. KERN   Digital Equipment Corporation, Stow, Massachusetts

The Los Nietos plant of the National Supply Company, a Division of Armco:

- Reduced finished goods inventory 12%.
- Reduced raw materials inventory 40%.
- Increased inventory accuracy to 96% from 64% (1).

A unit of Lincoln National Corporation:

- Saved $425,000 annually.
- Increased employee responsibilities and satisfaction through radical reorganization (2).

The Winnipeg plant of Memorex:

- Reduced scrap 62%.
- Saved $168,000 annually (3).

A Texas Instruments warehousing operation:

- Reduced dock-to-stock time from 3 weeks to 3 days.
- Cut the value of material tied up in the warehousing flow 50% and increased productivity 25% (4).

All of these breakthroughs were achieved through the actions of employee teams, volunteering to work together to solve problems within their job areas. Management's primary role was not in the creation of temporary task forces, in the identification of trouble spots, or in the dictating of policy. Rather, management at each of these companies recognized that an important and valuable resource, available at no extra charge, was being neglected: the brainpower of *every* employee.

Participative managment means that employees have the opportunity to participate or become involved in making decisions that affect their job or work. This may occur on an individual or a team basis, at any level of the organization, and even cross-functionally. Often the focus is on problem solving. The concept is known as *employee involvement*.

Background

During the Industrial Revolution, machines and automation took on ever-increasing importance in the work environment; the role of the human worker diminished correspondingly. Labor unions, founded on the basis that management was naturally opposed to the interests of workers, were an early reaction to reduced reliance on human inputs to industry.

Individuals such as Federick W. Taylor and Frank B. Gilbreth pursued scientific management and motivation methods based on wage incentives and efficiency improvements through standardization of tasks. Unfortunately, these methods continued to treat humans as extensions of machines rather than recognizing their strengths and needs as people. The importance of employee attitude, and hence of human relations, was finally revealed by Elton Mayo through work at Western Electric (the "Hawthorne Effect"). Mayo and others found that group cohesion and involvement in control and management of the work situation can have powerful consequences for productivity.

The behavioral sciences grew from the emerging need to understand human motivation. Pioneering efforts of Douglas McGregor, Abraham Maslow, Frederick Herzberg, Rensis Likert, and others led to the application of certain motivational concepts in the industrial environment. These concepts form the philosophical basis for an infinite variety of participative management, or employee involvement, processes.

Concepts

As Maslow and others discovered, all individuals' needs extend beyond basic survival to social and ego needs. Today, adequate wages and benefits generally satisfy survival needs. Motivation efforts must therefore address higher-level issues: the need to be an accepted part of the group, the need for individual recognition and esteem, and the need to achieve one's own particular brand of self-actualization.

Participative management is based on two fundamental concepts. First, every individual in every organization is capable of contributing to improvements in the way work is done. It makes sense that the person doing a particular task is the one most knowledgeable about it and therefore most suited to enhance it. Moreover, individuals are motivated to perform better and with greater satisfaction through having the opportunity to influence the work situation. People also tend to be more committed to the accomplishment of goals and changes that they have helped to structure.

The second concept is that the output of a group working together can be far greater than the sum of the individuals' separate efforts. This is known as *synergy*. Not only are more effective decisions made when all those affected are part of the decision-making process, people also like to be part of a successful, productive team.

Participative management gives individuals new opportunities to contribute, and builds dynamic teams from individuals. The forces of individual contributions and synergy are harnessed through the process of identifying, analyzing, and solving work-related problems. The way in which the problem solving is structured and carried out depends on the particular involvement technique that has been implemented.* However, regardless of the methodology, several principles are critical to long-term success in this area.

Principles for Implementation

Perhaps the most overriding requirement for the success of the participative approach is *management commitment*, with particular emphasis on the word "commitment." Many programs begin at the grass-roots or worker level, where the desire for involvement is often most keen, and many such programs survive and prosper. But even the strongest of these must eventually win over all the management ranks, including the most senior executives, or they will ultimately fail. It is far better to begin with high-level commitment—lip service does not count! Management must have a strong and visible presence in the participative process.

In order to achieve management commitment, it is frequently necessary to begin with *management motivation*. Efforts along these lines can begin with education of management as to the benefits—stated in terms of bottom-line dollars—that have been experienced by others in your industry through participative management. Motivation continues through measurement and tracking of the accomplishments of pilot efforts within the organi-

---

*For more in-depth discussion of two well-known versions of the participative management process, see Chapters 4 and 2, on quality circles and on quality of work life (QWL), respectively.

zation—again: talk dollars. Measurement must also become an integral part of the participative process, in order to maintain management motivation in the face of the other strong pressures operating in the business.

Evaluating the organizational culture is an important step in developing a successful involvement process. Companies vary greatly in their management styles, and not all of these are suited to the smooth integration of employee involvement. Thought must be given to the receptiveness of key individuals to participative concepts. The current economic health of the organization, the success or failure of other recent motivational programs, and similar intangibles must also be considered. (See the preceding chapter.)

Because every company has its own character and its own level of readiness, *tailoring the process* to the company is vital. Intermediate programs, designed to move the corporate culture toward acceptance of participative management, may be necessary. And, regardless of the organization, it is seldom appropriate to implement a process taken directly from an outside source without careful consideration of how well it will fit the circumstances involved. The most striking examples of problems arising in this style of motivation resulted when American companies embraced Japanese techniques without accommodating the very different culture and expectations of workers in the United States.

Communication is at the heart of employee involvement processes. Open communication must begin during the earliest planning stages of the program, to make clear the goals as well as the benefits anticipated for both individuals and the organization as a whole. One of the most important points to stress is the people-building nature of employee involvement: the individual learns new skills, and achieves more responsibility and greater control of his/her work life. As progress is made, communication must be maintained and enhanced, to spread the word to other parts of the organization, and to keep interest and motivation high.

Teams should be made up of *volunteers* at the member level as a minimum, and at all levels if possible. Teamwork requries the full and willing participation of every individual involved.

This is difficult to obtain when membership is required or forced, although some companies have taken this route successfully.

Team members may come from *all levels and all areas* of the organization, as long as they have common problems or situations to discuss. Although employee involvement tends to focus first on those who have had the least opportunity to participate in the past—hourly workers—involvement efforts that encompass professional, clerical and managerial employees have been highly successful. Indeed, involving all levels may be the best strategy for eliminating one of the biggest roadblocks such processes have faced: middle-management reluctance to relinquish control over subordinates.

Training is essential. Employees are asked to identify, attack, and resolve problems, as well as to understand and work within the framework of a team effort. For most, this is alien territory; they must be given tools and skills to help deal with the challenge. This is most important at the start of a new involvement program, but training should be ongoing as well, to refresh employees on skills learned earlier, and to upgrade those skills as the teams' efforts become more sophisticated.

Providing *recognition* for employees who participate in the involvement process is highly recommended. Recognition need not be monetary—posters and bulletin boards congratulating individuals and teams for their contributions; team hats, pins, or jackets; award dinners; contests for the best management presentation; articles in company newsletters—there are a multitude of ways to reward people effectively and sustain motivation. However, monetary rewards can play a major role—see section on productivity gainsharing later in this chapter. (Employee involvement also has the advantage of giving people continuing satisfaction and pride in overcoming problems as a team without management's intervention. In addition, an individual who has learned from and contributed to a successful involvement effort is frequently seen as a more valuable, and hence promotable, employee!)

Planning for the long-term integration of employee involvement into the culture of the organization should begin immediately. If

PARTICIPATIVE MANAGEMENT

an involvement process is implemented with the intention of curing short-term problems only, its full potential will never be realized. Instead, plans should be made to permit participative management techniques to permeate the organization, until teamwork at all levels becomes a way of life. A number of companies whose programs are very mature no longer have designated "quality circles"—the skills and methods that were initially focused under such an umbrella are now second nature. Such should be the ultimate objective of an employee involvement effort.

Individual Involvement Processes—Examples

Opinion Survey

Via a series of questions regarding the organization, the management, the job, the strategy, and so forth, management solicits employees' opinions, identifies areas where improvement is needed, and takes action. Preserving confidentiality is critical if honest and worthwhile answers are to be obtained. An opinion survey is often the first step taken by a management team that recognizes the need for change.

Suggestion Programs

Employees are asked for any ideas they may have to make improvements in the job they or others do. Ideas are evaluated and implemented by management. Cash rewards based on anticipated dollar savings are generally provided to encourage participation; public announcements of awards often supplement the monetary incentives.

Open Door/One-On-One

Management encourages employees to communicate ideas and concerns by eliminating traditional barriers. Though some managers operate this way by nature, many organizations specifically prescribe these practices.

Performance Management

Employees develop a set of performance goals for themselves and communicate them to peers and superiors by publicly displaying progress charts. Each individual is thus encouraged to achieve goals through peer support. In addition, knowledge of all others' goals enables people to assist their fellow employees as well as to accomplish their own objectives.

Self-Assurance/Self-Control

Employees are trained to be fully responsible for their own work output. This requires knowledge of the desired results, knowledge of what the present level of performance or conformance is, and the means to make whatever adjustments are needed to achieve the desired outcome (including rejection of inadequate inputs from others).

Team Involvement Processes—Examples

Work Simplification

An organizational unit creates a flow chart of part or all of the process for which it is responsible, be it production or service oriented. Each step is examined in detail, and then the process is simplified by removing redundant steps, combining others, streamlining, preventing recurring errors, etc.

Task Forces

Management often creates temporary task forces or teams of employees to solve one-time-only problems. Although this provides those involved with unusual opportunities, the temporary nature of the task force makes it difficult to sustain motivation among the entire work force over long periods of time.

Quality Circles

These are small groups of people performing similar work, who meet regularly to identify, analyze, and solve work-related problems in their area. In contrast to task forces, quality circles (and other processes of a similar nature but with varying names) are ongoing. As one problem is solved, another is taken up, and the team continues although membership may change over time. For more information, see Chapter 4.

Quality of Work Life

QWL utilizes many of the same concepts and tools of employee involvement as quality circles do. However, QWL is felt to be broader in scope, integrating a larger set of organizational goals through participative methods. It is closer to *autonomous work groups*, which solve the wide range of problems and usually do not need management's permission to implement solutions (5).

Productivity Gainsharing (6)

Various methods existing (including suggestion systems and Scanlon plans) for sharing the monetary gains achieved through the efforts of workers with those workers. Generally a formula is agreed upon for sharing a portion of the dollar savings achieved, based on value added, bonus pools, labor hours, etc. Such systems tend to be more effective when linked with a team-based method for generating ideas and improvements, such as quality circles. Further improvement might be achieved by keeping the size of the group for which the formula is calculated small, to promote a team approach, and by providing (for example) a 50%-30%-10% split of savings achieved over 3 years, to foster long-term thinking and to keep the flow of benefits smooth.

Job Enrichment

This refers to redesign of jobs or tasks to provide employees with more meaningful and hence more rewarding and enjoyable work. Job enrichment can be accomplished through management intervention or, preferably, through participative approaches. Such approaches may include employee suggestion programs, direct solicitation of enrichment ideas from individuals or groups (e.g., the

Scanlon Plan), and creation of teams, such as quality circles, to address and manage such issues on their own.

Labor/Management Advisory Board

Labor agreements in recent years have sometimes included provisions for labor representation on an organization's executive or advisory board. This provides an opportunity for the interests of workers to be considered and addressed at a high level. Other efforts along these lines include joint worker/management safety councils and the like.

Just as there are a multitude of ways in which to increase employee involvement and participation as a means for worker motivation, there are a multitude of publications on the subject. Several sources of information on the broad issue of participative management are described briefly below; more are presented in the specific chapters on quality circles, on quality of work life, and in the Selected Readings.

Additional Information

Working Together, William Mares and John Simmons, A. A. Knopf, New York, 1983. *Working Together* is a comprehensive, easy-to-read history of the development of participatory management in American industry. The stage is set with a description of the productivity problem and a flash back to the foundation of classic scientific management in Taylor's theories. Five fascinating case studies in participation are followed by a frank discussion of the barriers that arise in trying to accomplish this radical shift in management style. Two appendices list data on productivity improvements achieved through participation and examples of the wide range of firms that have broad employee ownership.

Systematic Participative Management, Quality Control Circles, Inc., Saratoga, CA, 1983. This work is in three volumes: *Principles*, *Problem-Solving Guide*, and *Data-Gathering Guide*. The three constitute an excellent introduction to participative management as well as providing a set of tools, training materials, and implementation guidelines appropriate to any effort in the employee involvement area. Of particular interest is the material on group management and group dynamics.

Every Employee a Manager, M. Scott Myers, McGraw-Hill, New York, 1970. Myers addresses the subject of job enrichment, including a historical perspective on the relationships making jobs more meaningful. The reader is led to the conclusion that participation of the individual in the enrichment of his/her own job is most effective. The bulk of the book deals in detail with the achievement of job enrichment.

Work and Motivation, Victor H. Vroom, John Wiley & Sons, New York, 1967. Vroom examines the motivational bases of work, and determinants of job satisfaction. He concludes that a work role most conducive to satisfaction provides, among other characteristics, considerate and participative management, the opportunity to interact with one's peers, and a high degree of control over work methods. It is noted that participation leads to productivity as well as to satisfaction, and the book covers several ways to taking advantage of such effects.

The following books also address motivation via participative management to some extent, generally tying it in to larger campaigns to motivate workers toward quality and productivity improvements.

Quality Control Handbook, J. M. Juran, McGraw-Hill, New York, 1979. See Chapter 18.

Management of Quality, J. M. Juran. See Section L.

Total Quality Control, A. V. Feigenbaum, McGraw-Hill, New York, 1983. See Chapter 9.

Quality Planning and Analysis, J. M. Juran and F. M. Gryna Jr., McGraw-Hill, New York, 1960.

Summary

Employee involvement/participative management provides the opportunity for individual workers to be a part of a group, to contribute (and be recognized as contributing) more than the basic job requirements, to learn and develop new knowledge and skills, and to have a voice in the management of the work environment. The results of such involvement go far beyond the achievement of worker motivation, though people building must be at the heart of the process for it to succeed. Not only do motivated employees perform better, but the problem-solving nature of many of these processes pays off in bottom-line profitability improvements that are tangible and satisfying to management.

Selected Readings

1. American Productivity Center, *Case Study 33: National Production Systems—Los Nietos*, 1984.
2. Rolland, Ian, The human equation in the new corporation, *Vital Speeches of the Day*, October 15, 1982.
3. Burroughs internal publication, authorized for inclusion.
4. Ways, Max, The American kind of worker participation, *Fortune*, October 1976.
5. Mares, William and Simmons, John, *Working Together*, A. A. Knopf, NY, 1983.
6. Graham-Moore, Brian E. and Ross, Timothy L., *Productivity Gainsharing*, Prentice Hall, Englewood Cliffs, NJ, 1983.

7
The Art of Statistics

WILLIAM G. BARNARD   Vita-Mix Corporation, Cleveland, Ohio

> We will see, for instance, that understanding entails making inferences and results in the ability to make further inferences.
>
> —Dehn and Schank (1982, p. 365)

Introduction

This chapter discusses some stimulating things that I have become aware of over the past several years from contact with thinking in various fields. I will try to tie these thoughts together and point to where more information can be found. The chapter title comes from a desire to point to the vital role and potential of human and humanlike abilities in statistics. "Art" seemed to say that without limiting the subject. The chapter is short to serve as an introduction. Every attempt to say more led to an explosion of words and ideas. Better that the details be left to another time so that the flavor can be sampled here.

Although we think of formulas and formal procedures, statistics is very dependent on the user. This chapter is concerned with this "softer," less formal side of statistics characterized by human insight and rules-of-thumb (heuristics). Because it strives to model study human thinking, and even to surpass human thought at its own informal game, artifical (computer) intelligence (AI) will also be discussed. This is not a chapter about which statistical methods to use where. There are many excellent sources for that. Generally the key to this chapter is how the human (or human-mimicking computer) might approach statistics and statisical problem solving.

Another way to look at our topic is by studying the "nonalgorithmic" aspects of statistics. An algorithm is essentially a procedure that can be carried out without creative intervention and that can obtain an error-free answer (if there is one) in a finite number of steps. The contrast of algorithms and heuristics is a recurring theme, both in human thought and in artificial intelligence. Dehn and Schank (1982) give an excellent in-depth discussion of this area, as do various other sources on AI.

The study of nonalgorithmic statistics can pay dividends. Dehn and Schank (1982) compare the relative advantages of heuristics and algorithms in thinking. Tukey (1977) discusses the benefits of exploratory data analysis versus confirmatory data analysis. Some of these ideas will be discussed in this chapter. Campbell (1976, p 147) mentions how rigid outlook can sometimes put us in a bind.

> ...a sobering reminder that an exclusive concern with methodological models and rigorous technique can blind us to larger issues and concerns. . . industrial and organizational psychology should not get so engrossed in research methodology that it loses sight of the questions it is trying to answer.

We will develop briefly some of the ways that intuitive and heuristic methods can enhance the use of statistics. Ideas are drawn from recent statistical literature, quality control, literature on teaching statistics, psychology, and artificial (computer) intelligence.

First, it is important to understand what data sets try to tell us. Mention will be made of Ehrenberg's teaching methods, Tukey's exploratory data analysis (EDA), Cleveland's work in graphical techniques, Shewhart's control charts, and Ott's analysis of means (ANOM).

Second, it is important to understand how to apply statistical methods and what the methods can be expected to do for us. It is not enough to follow a cookbook approach if we intend to get the most out of our efforts.

Third, it is important to understand the problem enough to know what to do when assumptions are not met. Fisher and others have engineered many problems out of experimentation with superb formalized designs. However, when assumptions for these formal methods are not met, problems are clearly thrown back on the user to solve by applying methods according to insight, ingenuity, and a number of patched-together heuristics. Quasi-experimentation, as discussed by Cook and Campbell (1976, 1979), pulls together a number of heuristic approaches to handle this type of situation.

Artificial intelligence will be discussed, including the possibility of the user developing statistical applications through use of expert systems, essentially augmenting his ability to use rules-of-thumb (heuristics). Packages might be developed to permit the quality-control person or other substantive user to utilize statistics in a more proficient way, cataloging and evaluating research results, or even developing tailor-made quality control programs. Expert systems encourage developing an effective working knowledge base incrementally, a little at a time, as new information becomes available, similar to the way a human adds knowledge (Davis, 1982). Like human learning, expert systems evolve and are never logically completed.

AI is also used to model or simulate human mental activity. AI has been a driving force in cognitive psychology, providing better insight into ourselves and how we learn and understand (Simon, 1983; Dehn and Schank, 1982).

Usually when we use statistics our mind is on the problem to be solved and/or the statistical methods. Here our focus is on that which guides the process toward solving the problem.

The "Psychostatistical" Wellsprings of Quality

Quality and statistics both depend on psychological factors, such as performance, ability, training, motivation, attention, and understanding. Good research and communication methods using statistics can play an important role in the study and improvement of behavior and lead to an improvement in quality.

Quality fundamentally relates to people, not statistics. It stems from our mutual interdependence. Quality can be viewed on the most intimate level—the quality of mothering or the quality of a child's contribution to the family's chores. The relationship need not be economic in a money exchange sense. The perception of quality (or nonquality) can be viewed as a feedback process valuable for learning and improvement of performance. Statistics, or at least the heuristics and mind-set developed from the use of statistics, can augment this process so necessary for performance improvement.

Quality is most often recognized when one produces an object or service for another. In an organizational sense, good quality requires inspired and trained performance of management and employees to consistently produce safe, workable, long-lasting, cosmetically pleasing, and inexpensive products and services. On a mass scale, these concepts of quality can best be defined and understood statistically (Deming, 1982).

Quality requires excellent communication between organizations and their customers and suppliers. There must be quality objectives with a "community" understanding of quality and how to achieve it. Schilling (1984b) espouses statistics as a fundamental language of communication in achieving quality.

Statistics as Learning Strategy

Statistical heuristics includes inductive strategy for learning about the empirical world. Statistical algorithms are tools in the implementation of this strategy. Statistics, as heuristics and algorithms, helps us to collect and digest the broad, detailed information often needed to determine the nature and scope of quality problems, or to demonstrate that good quality exists (Shewhart, 1931; Deming, 1982). Schilling (1984b) says:

> The need for statistical methods in quality is based on the empirical nature of the solution to quality problems. Quality problems generally require an empirical not a theoretical solution. . . . Poor quality is not deliberately designed into a product and so, when quality problems occur, the most efficient approach to a solution is usually a statistical one. Statistical methods . . . are often the only recourse, not only in solving problems in the face of variation, but also in designing the product, determining capability, assessing conformance, and attaining and retaining control in all aspects of the quality system.

Statistical thinking can also make one more aware of his own performance and how to improve it. This is one thing that makes it so effective for statistically trained production workers to monitor and be responsible for the quality of their own work. Not only are defects reduced, but there is also a tendency for the nature of the production process to evolve and improve.

Campione, Brown, and Ferrara (1982) discuss learning strategy at some length from a psychological viewpoint, particularly in its relationship to mental retardation research. Their discussion of blind training, informed training, and self-control training are particularly interesting for the analogies that one can draw to various approaches in industrial management and training.

Artificial Intelligence and Human Intelligence

Researchers who use AI methods to study intelligent activity have not been able to completely simulate human thinking. Consequently, computer simulation has been more effective in shedding considerable light on what human thinking is not (Dehn and Schank, 1982). The human brings a vast background to bear against a problem. It has been suggested that a human toddler has a deeper and more varied background than the most powerful computer. Computers gain power by specializing and processing accurately and very fast. Humans make mistakes, but they can cut through a mass of irrelevant information to get to the heart of a matter. The computer is more powerful when all of the details can be tied up in an algorithm; the human when not all details are available.

Algorithms, which are calculatorlike procedures that have only "right answers," are effective only in situations well defined by heuristic thinking. Plugged in as formal "chunks," algorithms make thinking more precise and efficient. Heuristics have multiple "good answers," not right answers. Computerization started with algorithms, which are easy for machines, though hard for humans. Now AI tries to handle information heuristically, making machines think in the imprecise way that we do to gain more power! Algorithms are more powerful when all parameters can be defined; heuristics when thinking is imprecise and probing. For other comparisons see Dehn and Schank (1982).

Learning by Toying with Data

What do statisticians do to take advantage of intuition and heuristics in applying statistics? Search through recent statistical literature turns up some interesting illustrations.

Some authors emphasize developing good preliminary understanding of data sets.

> We have thus learned a very important lesson in statistical analysis—look at the data. A few minutes with pencil and paper will answer most of the questions that one could ask of the data.
>
> —Deming (1982, p. 115)

THE ART OF STATISTICS

Always graph your data in some simple way—*always*.

—Ott (1975, p. 2)

Tukey (1977) starts his book by saying, "It is important to understand what you CAN DO before you learn to measure how WELL you seem to have DONE it." He compares formal "confirmatory data analysis" to his flexible "exploratory data analysis" (EDA), which is more graphical, intuitive, and rule-of-thumb. He advocates aggressive exploration of data (p. vi).

> Consistent with this view, we believe, is a clear demand that pictures based on exploration of data should *force* their messages upon us. Pictures that emphasize what we already know—"security blankets" to reassure us—are frequently not worth the space they take. Pictures that have to be gone over with a reading glass to see the main point are wasteful of time and inadequate of effect. The greatest value of a picture is when it forces us to notice what we never expected to see.

Tukey discussed many devices to discover the unusual and unexpected. He says some exploratory methods are so new that we really don't know why they work.

Exploring and understanding data is also an effective introduction to statistics. Reznick (Marx, 1984) urges teachers to recognize the need for students to develop early qualitative understanding and not be forced prematurely into quantitative methods. Otherwise, there is a tendency for students to revert to an earlier, nontechnical, nonscientific approach.

Likewise, Ehrenberg (1982) is concerned that taking a theoretical rather than a user-centered approach to teaching introductory statistics can make statistics forbidding and incomprehensible. In *Data Reduction* (1975), he carefully discusses data and their significance as a vehicle to understanding theoretical distributions, probability models, and computation. I relate to this approach from personal experience. Years after I originally studied statistics, the simplicity and careful development of Ehrenberg's *Data Reduction* helped to make statistics a fascinating pastime and tool. Joiner (1982) also expresses excitement and intellectual stimulation in reviewing the book.

> Data Reduction is a very innovative, different kind of basic statistics book. . . .
> The freshness and importance of this book are all the more remarkable in that the material covered is not new in any mathematical sense. Rather, Ehrenberg is working at the core of statistics—teaching us to look at simple things . . . with fresh insight.

Graphs are an area of considerable recent publication (Tuft, 1983; Cleveland and McGill, 1984). Graphs have many uses and in some ways outperform computational methods. When they can be applied effectively, they provide excellent communication capability, facilitating quick absorption of vast quantities of information with good mental retention. They combine the ingenuity of the artist and the analytical ability of the statistician in a picture form—essentially a different kind of picture than the original data or the computational analysis. One can see relationships more quickly, and outliers and irregularities are more noticeable.

Cleveland and McGill (1984) discuss experimental research to understand and design new graphical methods making use of theory and methods from psychophysics as opposed to a strictly intuitive artistic approach. This is a case of using the scientific method to develop methods to improve human perception and intuition through better data displays.

Statistical Teaching and Organization

The journal *Teaching Statistics* and portions of *The American Statistician* discuss teaching philosophy and methods. Posten (1981), in the "Accent on Teaching Materials" section of the *The American Statistician*, mentions educational growing pains.

> Many of us who are teaching general introductory statistics at the college level are not doing it as well as we would like.

Two important reasons for this condition are the newness of our field and the lack of conceptual background previously afforded our students. Statistical inference has, unfortunately, not been around long enough to produce the methodology, curriculum sequencing, and broad development of superior teaching materials, all of which require many decades of curriculum work.

Teaching of statistics must proceed at many levels for many applications. The study of probability and statistics can proceed through the highest doctoral levels, and it can start very early. There are teaching materials for the primary- and secondary-school grades starting as low as the first grade (see Hoffer, 1984). The following source materials, used judiciously, can be used to develop or supplement introductory training materials for the workplace.

Statistics in Your World	ages 11-16 (Schools Council, Series)
Teaching Statistics 11-16	ages 11-16 (Schools Council, 1980)
Statistics and Information Organization	grades 5-9 (Hoffer, 1978)
What Are My Chances? Book A	grades 4-6 (Shulte and Choate, 1977)
What Are My Chances? Book B	grades 7-9 (Shulte and Choate, 1977)

There are sources (Ishikawa, 1982) for teaching statistics in the context of quality circles in industry. However, the organization must look beyond quality circles and in plant training to organize for applying statistics. Deming (1982, p. 353-362) discusses organization for statistical work, including ways of recruiting and developing statistical talent from within and outside the corporate body. Deming advocates that statistical work within an organization be guided by a competent statistician.

There are a number of sources of information on statistics in the context of quality control. The American Statistical Association (ASA) has a new Committee on Quality and Productivity (Hahn and Boardman, 1985). ASQC (Eaton, 1985) supplies program help to the American Association of Junior Colleges. ASQC's Educational Training Institute (ETI) has correspondence and special seminar training in quality methods. ASQC's certification programs are excellent, as are the courses that its various sections (chapters) offer. Vardeman and David (1984) discuss what a graduate-level course in quality and productivity should cover and present a model lecture schedule and an 83-item source list covering key topics. All of these sources make important contributions to the application of statistics.

Acceptance Sampling—The Cost of Misunderstanding

Acceptance sampling is a good place to begin discussing the importance of understanding in applying methods, for it is an example where statistical methods, used blindly, solve few problems and may create many (Deming, 1982). However, if properly used, acceptance sampling is a valuable decision tool (Schilling, 1982, 1984a). It requires consumer/producer agreement on the limits of acceptable and unacceptable quality and applies pressure for improvement.

Fundamentally, acceptance sampling merely "decides" whether incoming product is good enough to be used. It uses standards of acceptable, not desirable, quality. Using the analogy of school grades, acceptance is the equivalent of a grade of D or better, rejection of the equivalent of an F grade. Clearly, in this sense "acceptable" is not "good."

However, one key thing makes acceptance sampling absolutely indispensable to the consumer—preventing an unmanageable flood of bad quality. It's like building a garden fence to keep the rabbits out. The fence does not make a good garden, but it assures the garden has a chance. Likewise, acceptance sampling assures that attention can be devoted to real quality improvement, but in no direct sense does it produce good quality.

Schilling (1982, 1984a) discusses how a comprehensive acceptance quality-control system by the consumer can apply pressure for quality improvement on the producer. However, this approach can work only if it induces the producer to remedy causes of poor quality. Failure to remedy causes coupled with blind lot after lot use of acceptance sampling leads to misuse by essentially creating an ongoing chance lottery. Such a situation produces minimal improvement, even by sorting out bad parts after lot rejection (Schilling, 1982). The cost of the ritual can be immense in time, money, and lost opportunity for real quality improvement.

Just as causes of poor grades are usually not found by looking at a youngster's school record, causes of poor quality will probably not be found by looking at a producer's acceptance—rejection record. However, either can scream loudly for attention. Getting at causes of poor quality generally requires other statistical methods such as control charts, trouble-shooting methods or experimental design.

In Search of Causes

Areas of statistics with excellent formal research designs and algorithms still require intuition and heuristic thinking. Discussion of causal research is an excellent way to illustrate this.

Cook and Campbell (1979, p. 36) discuss a number of theoretical definitions of cause before settling on working common-sense ideas, some of which follow.

> ... the manipulation of a cause will result in the manipulation of an effect. ... Causation implies that by varying one factor I can usually make another vary. For many valid causal laws we may not in practice be able to manipulate the ... cause at will, if at all. This has grave consequences for our ability to test the law, but it does not negate its truthfulness. However, it does decrease the immediate practical importance of the law, for it suggests that the causal powers implicit in the law cannot be easily used to make desirable changes

in persons or environments. . . . If we define the meaningfulness of causes in terms of their ability to create testable, dependable, and planned changes, then the most meaningful causes are those which can be deliberately manipulated.

Fisher and others have engineered many problems out of experimentation with superb formal designs. Fisher pioneered methods to virtually eliminate many problems of experimental interpretability right in the planning stage. These powerful methods can be used as tools in conjunction with not-so-formal thinking about research problems. There are interesting vignettes of Fisher's activity (Box, 1984; Kempthorne, 1983; Steinberg and Hunter, 1984).

To illustrate, Fisher's randomized experimental design was a major advance. With random assignment of subjects to experimental conditions he was able to take experimental research into field settings where not all environmental conditions can be known or directly controlled. Randomization makes the experimental and control groups equivalent in statistical analysis, even though not all extraneous conditions are known or directly controlled. Randomized experimental design has become a highly acceptable way to structure research to relate causes to their effects.

In contrast, quasiexperimentation (Cook and Campbell, 1976, 1979) deals with many of the same problems, but under conditions of research and design handicap that are very common in the social sciences. It improvises strategy and heuristics to overcome design handicaps and helps to further focus on the art, ingenuity, and understanding of research issues.

Quasiexperimentation addresses situations where randomized assignment of subjects to conditions, directly comparable control groups, experimental manipulation, or other niceties of experimental design are either not feasible or even desirable. Cook and Campbell (1979) discuss the interpretability of many nonexperimental designs that can be grouped as (1) nonequivalent control group designs, (2) interrupted time-series designs, and (3) inferring cause from passive observation. The interpretability of the various quasi designs is situation dependent and varies with the nature of the design, nature of the research problem, peculiarities of the data, and other considerations.

Active Methods—"Make It Happen"

Experimental design studies are classic active research studies designed to forcefully demonstrate causal relationships. Some quasiexperimental methods also take an active approach. Suspected causes are directly manipulated to see whether they produce expected effects. In terms of the working ideas of causation above, the results of active research are easy to interpret and apply. As long as the suspected cause can be manipulated at will, it is usually relatively easy to track its effect.

Passive Methods—"Watch It Happen"

In passive studies the researcher is an observer, not a manipulator. Passive studies are generally weak at identifying causal relationships, for if you do not manipulate a suspected cause to see whether it produces a suspected effect, then you have to wait for the two to happen together. If you wait for the two to happen together, you still may not know which is the cause and which is the effect—or whether there is another cause of the two. Passive observational research also has trouble isolating causes from background irrelevancies. In spite of this, Cook and Campbell (1979) do discuss the use of passive methods for identifying causes.

Passive research lends itself to prediction and forecasting without knowing or controlling causes (Argyris, 1976). Prediction merely has to say that within a certain defined context something will happen again, not why it happened. Note the limitations of the following useful reactions to prediction. We use weather forecasting by staying in if the weather is to be bad, not knowing or altering the causes of bad weather. We use employment tests by not hiring the least promising, not trying to alter human capability. We use economic forecasting by making or not making economic ventures, not trying to alter the economic situation. Prediction generally foretells a situation one must adapt to, not how to change the fundamental causes of the situation.

Four Kinds of Validity

To know what to manipulate to improve the fundamental situation we generally have to understand the relationships between the causes and effects acting in the situation.

Cook and Campbell (1979) discuss four types of conclusion validity to establish in causal research. Differences between the kinds of validity are arbitrary, but are useful for discussing questions to be addressed. These four types of validity form a hierarchy where one type is a foundation for the next level of validity. Establishing validity demands heuristic thinking and detective abilities of the researcher. An important key to establishing validity is ruling out threats to validity. The reader is referred to Cook and Campbell references for detailed discussion.

Statistical conclusion validity is concerned with whether a statistical (not necessarily causal) relationship has been established between two or more variables. At this level we are concerned with tests of significance and the logic, adequacy, and appropriateness of the statistical algorithms or methods used. This is where we are concerned with the sensitivity of the methods, whether there is reasonable evidence that the variables covary, how strong the degree of covariation actually is, etc. Statistical conclusion validity can be demonstrated in either active or passive research designs. In short, statistical conclusion validity applies to the heuristics of applying formal statistical methods and consequent demonstration of relationships in the data, regardless of the nature of the relationships.

Internal validity is concerned with the behavior and direction of the causal relationship, or whether there is any causal relationship at all. Active designs have a marked superiority over passive designs in demonstrating internal validity, because they show more easily that one thing leads to another. Without direct manipulation of variables, it is hard to prove causality. Internal validity is concerned with the heuristics of research design.

Construct validity goes beyond statistical methods and demonstrated relationships to attach abstract meaning and labeling to the cause, the effect, and their relationship. Development of constructs is part of developing theories. What is the nature of the cause, the effect, and their interaction? Do we have the right notions or can the mechanism be explained some other way? We proceed from statistical covariation (statistical conclusion validity) and direction of cause (internal validity) to notions of actors in the relationship. This can be an area of considerable creativity, perhaps even artistic input.

External validity is concerned with whether the relationship demonstrated between two or more causal constructs can be generalized to different persons, settings, and times. Establishing constancies is basic to developing broad scientific generalizations or theories (Ehrenberg, 1982). The basic question of external validity is whether we can take this information and use it elsewhere.

Control Chart Methods

Some basic methods can be used in a variety of ways depending on the situation and the heuristics involved. Five applications of Shewhart control charts illustrate this.

Shewhart control charts are a group of convenient paper-and-pencil semigraphical methods with variations for attributes (discrete data) and variables (measurement or continuous) data. Producing process stability is the main use of Shewhart control charts (Shewhart, 1931). A process in control is essentially a random, but predictable "white-noise" process. Deming (1982) says that only if a process is "in control" are we able to generalize or predict from process data. In standard control chart usage, a process is generally not disturbed (passive role) unless the chart indicates it needs adjustment. Then, variables are actively manipulated to identify what it takes to bring the process back on target or reduce its variability. Control charts work better for monitoring and identifying visible causes that have a clear-cut effect ("assignable causes") than those whose effect is consistent or blends into white noise and is only suspected ("constant systems of chance causes").

The second use of control charts is called analysis of means (ANOM), a refinement of Shewhart charts for trouble shooting and experimental design. ANOM evaluates the statistical significance of all data values at once. In contrast, control charts for process control evaluate only the most recent data value in a series. Those intending to use Shewhart control charts should read Ott (1967, 1975) to better understand the differences, some of which may be important to a particular application.

Other approaches to using control charts use the standard format with differences mainly in how active or passive the research is. In the third approach, we study processes passively in a totally natural state without artificial or corrective input and consequently have to wait and watch for natural causal disturbances. Control charts can be used to detect process irregularities as evidence of causal relationships with outside disturbances. Time series analysis (Box and Jenkins, 1976) is an alternative approach with other analytical options.

In the fourth approach, control charts are used for active quasi-experimentation similar to Cook and Campbell's (1979) "interrupted time-series design." This approach looks for causal relationships in "blips" or effects in an ongoing process in response to deliberate "tweaking" of suspected causes.

In the fifth approach control charts are used to rule out threats to validity in preparation for experimental design or quasiexperimentation. That is, they are first used to establish a stable baseline of process behavior by removal of assignable causes. Reponses to "tweaking" in the process or in experimental design then stand out from the background with a minimum of interference. In reality, this is an application of the first method, but in support of other research methods.

Shewhart's classic development of control chart theory (1931) has been republished by ASQC (1980). Deming (1982, pp. 111-192) gives important control chart philosophy. AT&T (1958) discusses use and interpretation. Standard texts are by Grant and Leavenworth (1980), Duncan (1974), and Burr (1976, 1979). These sources treat control charts primarily for process control.

Information Handling

Researching and compiling information on the many causes that can affect a single process or variable can create a research and information-handling crisis. Fisher developed up-front planning innovations such as factorial designs to draw broad and meaningful generalizations directly from data.

A simple graphical method of summarizing causal relationships comes from quality control and is called the "Ishikawa diagram" (Ishikawa, 1982). The Ishikawa diagram is used to brainstorm causal relationships and to catalog their substantiation. This simple information system speeds search for causal constructs to help discover causes for particular quality problems.

Future contributions to research organizations may come from AI. Expert systems could be designed to catalog and access data from studies, and even to draw conclusions and make suggestions for further study including statistical methods to use.

The Computer as Heuristic Tool

How can we apply AI to statistics? The term "artificial intelligence" causes a problem, because its meaning is constantly in flux. As AI applications become better understood, there is a tendency to no longer consider them to be "intelligent." AI remains a domain of the mysterious and not well understood. So perhaps it is better to think in terms of heuristic use of the computer and how it might be applied to statistics.

Through heuristic processing the computer may become an onhanced aid to statistical application. An attractive package, semi-automatically driven by heuristics, might conduct an exploratory data analysis, help us to interactively phrase the problems, make recommendations as to the proper confirmatory statistical design and research needed, and then drive the selected statistical algorithms. Finally, it could help us draw conclusions from the data. Statistical algorithms would be reduced to plug-in modules or "chunks" in heuristics for problem solving much as they are in human thinking.

Early work in AI dealt largely with contrived problems. Recent research work has tended toward real life problems. TEIRESIAS is a system that by analogy hints at the possibilities of an expert system for applying statistics. It forms an interface between an expert system and a human expert to facilitate the loading of expertise by a human expert. Davis (1982) describes applying TEIRESIAS to MYCIN, an expert system designed to help physicians in the diagnosis of bacterial diseases. TEIRESIAS is called a "metaknowledge" system and essentially "knows" what knowledge is in MYCIN and how to manipulate and develop it while interacting with the human expert.

> TEIRESIAS does not attempt to derive new knowledge on its own, but instead tries to "listen" as attentively as possible and comment appropriately, to help the expert augment the knowledge base. It thus requires the strongest degree of cooperation from the expert. . . .
>
> TEIRESIAS is designed to work with performance programs that accommodate inexact knowledge. Such programs find their greatest utility in domains where knowledge has not been extensively formalized. In such domains there are typically no unifying laws on which to base algorithmic methods; instead there is a collection of informal knowledge based on accumulated experience. As a result, an expert specifying a new rule in this domain may be codifying a piece of knowledge that has never previously been isolated and expressed as such. This process of explicating previously informal knowledge is difficult, and anything which can be done to ease the task will prove very useful.
>
> —Davis (1982, pp. 288-289)

Someday computers may even develop new statistical algorithms (see Lenat, 1982). The two approaches might work together to create algorithms for hitherto underdefined areas of inquiry. Will that relieve man of the need for understanding and heuristics? Probably not. It will give him higher-level "chunks" to use in his intuitive and heuristic thinking, hopefully on a higher and more productive level. Man has been building on knowledge passed on to him from time immemorial. The pace should only pick up.

Summary

We discussed briefly ways that insight and heuristic methods enhance the use of statistics. Ideas are drawn from recent statistical literature, quality control, literature on teaching statistics, psychology, and artificial (computer) intelligence. Attention was given to Ehrenberg's teaching methods, Tukey's exploratory data analysis (EDA), Cleveland's work in graphical techniques. Shewhart's control charts, and Ott's analysis of means (ANOM). Quasi-experimentation was used to discuss the art of research to find causes, to rule out threats to research validity, and to discuss active and passive research methods. Artificial intelligence (AI) was discussed, including the possibility of the user approaching the statistical application through expert systems, essentially augmenting the user's heuristic capabilities. The use of AI to model human mental activity was also discussed.

Selected Readings

Argyris, C. (1976). Problems and new directions for industrial psychology. In *Handbook of Industrial and Organizational Psychology*, Dunnette, M. D. (Ed.) Rand McNally College Publishing Company, Chicago.

AT&T (1958). *Statistical Quality Control Handbook*, 2nd ed., AT&T Technologies, Indianapolis, IN.

Box, G. E. P. (1984). The importance of practice in the development of statistics, *Technometrics*, Vol. 26, No. 1. pp. 1-8.

Box, G. E. P. and Jenkins, G. M. (1976). *Time Series Analysis: Forecasting and Control*, Holden-Day, Oakland, CA.

Burr, I. W. (1976). *Statistical Quality Control Methods*, Marcel Dekker, New York.

Burr, I. W. (19790. *Elementary Statistical Quality Control*, Marcel Dekker, New York.

Campbell, J. P. (1976). Methodological foundations of industrial and organizational psychology. In *Handbook of Industrial and Organizational Psychology*, Dunnette, M. D, (Ed.) Rand McNally College Publishing Company, Chicago.

Campione, J. C., Brown, A. L., and Ferrara, R. A. (1982). Mental retardation and intelligence. In *Handbook of Human Intelligence*, Sternberg, Robert J. (Ed.). Cambridge University Press, Cambridge, England.

Cleveland, W. S. and McGill, R. (1984). Graphical perception: Theory, experimentation, and application to the development of graphical methods, *Journal of the American Statistical Association*, Vol. 79, No. 387, pp. 531-554.

Cook, T. D. and Campbell, D. T. (1976). The design and conduct of quasi-experiments in field settings. In *Handbook of Industrial and Organizational Psychology*, Dunnette, M. D. (Ed.) Rand McNally College Publishing Company, Chicago.

Cook, T. D. and Campbell, D. T. (1979). *Quasi-Experimentation: Design and Analysis Issues for Field Settings*, Houghton Mifflin Company, Boston.

Davis, R. (1982). Teiresias: Applications of meta-level knowledge. In *Knowledge-Based Systems in Artificial Intelligence*, Davis, R. and Lenat, D. B. (Eds.) McGraw-Hill, New York

Dehn, N. and Schank, R. (1982). Artificial and human intelligence. In *Handbook of Human Intelligence*, Sternberg, Robert J. (Ed.). Cambridge University Press, Cambridge, England.

Deming, W. E. (1982). *Quality, Productivity, and Competitive Position*, MIT, Cambridge, MA.

Duncan, A. J. (1974). *Quality Control and Industrial Statistics*, 4th ed., Irwin, Homewood, IL.

Eaton, J. (1985). Community colleges and ASQC join forces for SPC training, *Quality Progress*, March, pp. 14-16.

Ehrenberg, A. S. C. (1975). *Data Reduction: Analysing and Interpreting Statistical Data*, Wiley, New York.

Ehrenberg, A. S. C. (1982). *A Primer in Data Reduction: An Introductory Statistics Textbook*, Wiley, New York.

Grant, E. L. and Leavenworth, R. S. (1980). *Statistical Quality Control*, 5th ed., McGraw-Hill, New York.

Hahn, G. J. and Boardman, T. J. (1985). The statistician's role in quality improvement, *Amstat News*, March, No. 113, pp. 5-8.

Hoffer, A. (Project Director) (1978). *Statistics and Information Organization*, Creative Publications, Palo Alto, CA.

Hoffer, A. (1984). Review of a collection of papers on the teaching of probability and statistics in an elementary school curriculum, *The American Statistician*, Vol. 38, No. 3, p. 213.

Ishikawa, K. (1982). *Guide to Quality Control*, Asian Productivity Organization, Tokyo.

Joiner, B. L. (1982). [Review of] data reduction: Analysing and interpreting statistical data [revised reprint], *Journal of the American Statistical Association*, p. 692.

Kempthorne, O. (1983). A review of R. A. Fisher: An appreciation, *Journal of the American Statistical Association*, Vol. 78, No. 382, pp. 482-490.

Lenat, D. B. (1982). AM: Discovery in mathematics as heuristic search. In *Knowledge-Based Systems in Artificial Intelligence*, Davis, R. and Lenat, D. B. (Eds.) McGraw-Hill, New York.

Marx, H. M. (1984). Psychology. In *1985 Handbook of Science and the Future*, Encyclopaedia Britannica, Inc., Chicago, IL.

Ott, E. R. (1967). Analysis of means—A graphical procedure, *Industrial Quality Control*, August, 1967. Reprinted in *Journal of Quality Technology*, Vol. 15, No. 1, January 1983, pp. 10-18.

Ott, E. R. (1975). *Process Quality Control: Troubleshooting and Interpretation of Data*, McGraw-Hill, New York.

Posten, H. O. (1981). Review of statistical teaching materials for 11-16 year-olds, *The American Statistician*, Vol. 35, No. 4, pp. 258-259.

Schilling, E. G. (1982). *Acceptance Sampling in Quality Control*. Marcel Dekker, New York.

Schilling, E. G. (1984a). An overview of acceptance control, *Quality Progress*, April, pp. 22-25.

Schilling, E. G. (1984b). The role of statistics in the management of quality, *Quality Progress*, August, pp. 32-35.

Schools Council (1980). *Teaching Statistics 11-16*, W. Foulsham & Co. Ltd., Berks, England.

Schools Council (series) *Statistics in Your World*, W. Foursham & Co. Ltd., Berks, England.

Shewhart, W. A. (1931). *Economic Control of Quality of Manufactured Product*, Van Nostrand, New York. Commemorative

Reissue by American Society for Quality Control, Milwaukee, WI, 1980.

Shulte, A. P. and Choate, S. A. (1977). *What Are My Chances?* Books A and B, Creative Publications, Palo Alto, CA.

Simon, H. A. (1983). Why should machines learn? In *Machine Learning: An Artificial Intelligence Approach*, Michalski, R. S., Carbonell, J. G., and Mitchell, T. M. (Eds.). Tioga Publishing Co., Palo Alto, CA.

Steinberg, D. M. and Hunter, W. G. (1984). Experimental design: Review and comment, *Technometrics*, Vol. 26, No. 2, pp. 71-97.

Tuft, E. R. (1983). *The Visual Display of Quantitative Information*, Graphics Press, Cheshire, CT.

Tukey, J. W. (1977). *Exploratory Data Analysis*, Addison-Wesley, Reading, MA.

Vardeman, S. and David H. T. (1984). Statistics for quality and productivity: A new graduate-level statistics course, *The American Statistician*, Vol. 38, No. 4, pp. 235-243.

8

Developing a Quality Selection System

JOHN A. BERGER   RIMS, Oak Brook, Illinois

Prevention Not Detection

One of the basic tenets of effective quality management is to *prevent* problems from occurring rather than *detect* the defect or problem once the production or service process has been completed. It is too late at that point, and a waste of valuable resources has occurred.

Most executives and managers responsible for the quality function would agree with this point. We would like to extend this philosophy not only to the management of physical resources but to the management of human resources as well. The trend towards total, company-wide quality control has to include sound management of a company's greatest and most expensive resource, its people.

Payroll and labor costs vary by industry and company, but usually range from 40 to 60% of every sales dollar. The most profitable companies realize the value of paying close attention to every detail of human resource management.

Voluntary turnover of highly trained personnel, underutilizing the talents of high potential employees, having people work at 40% capacity because of demotivating working conditions are but a few of the ways human resources are mismanaged.

If the United States is to regain its competitive advantage in world markets, it will have to invest as much in its people as in its technology. Training and development is not an expense, it is an investment.

Statistical Process Control for Human Resources

Deming, Juran, Golomski, and other quality experts have continued to assist companies to get their production and service processes in a state of statistical control. That is, to control the variability of the process by understanding all the factors that cause the process to function so that when something goes wrong the cause of the problem can be easily diagnosed and corrected.

We would like to see quality and other management personnel work toward having each individual's performance, each work group, each department, and each division within the company reduce the variability of performance, but maintain the performance at a very high level. This requires a thorough understanding of the interplay between culture, values, technology, and individual differences.

The process of selecting quality personnel can be conceptualized as a number of very distinguishable activities that must occur for maximum performance to occur. A look at each step will provide insight into how each activity can be improved using the latest in human resource management technology. The social sciences are still more art than science, but recent research can provide valuable clues on being more effective.

DEVELOPING A QUALITY SELECTION SYSTEM

This chapter will not make you experts in selection, but hopefully will give you a better understanding of some of the tools available to make more effective hiring decisions. To become proficient in their use will require further study and experimentation on your part. We feel the effort will be well worthwhile for you and your organization.

The Cost of Guessing Wrong

The first step in achieving excellence in human resource management is to hire the right person for the right job, that is, matching the person's abilities, motivations, interests, and skills with the demands of the job and the "personality" or climate of the work group and company.

This "matching process" is not as easy as it sounds, and in fact, much of the waste and mismanagement of human resources is because of making a mistake in this phase of the human resource management process. Selecting the wrong person causes valuable training time and money to be spent on the wrong employees, makes supervisors waste time on subordinates who cannot or will not perform no matter how skillfully managed, and demotivates other co-workers who do not get their needs met.

Schmidt and Hunter (1983) determined that a productivity increase of 40% can be achieved if the incumbents on a job are selected such that their average level of output is one standard deviation above the average for employees who otherwise would have been hired for the job. This estimate is in general agreement with findings reported from industrial engineering studies that the best worker on a job often produces 2.25 times as much as the poorest producer (Niebel, 1982).

Using human resource cost-accounting principles, Berger (1978) figured the cost of turnover for one computer programmer who stayed with the company for one year and was making $25,000 per year.

An Example—Turnover Cost Analysis for One Computer Programmer

I. Recruiting costs	
A. Want ads	$ 600-1200
B. Executive search/placement fees	$ 3750-7500
II. Selection costs	
A. Application processing	$ 10-25
B. Interviewing and screening	150-300
C. Testing	250-400
D. Medical/physical exam	50-100
III. Training cost	
A. On the job	
1. Week 1 (100% salary, 0% productive)	$ 500
2. Weeks 2-6 (70% salary, 30% productive)	1750
3. Weeks 7-26 (40% salary, 60% productive)	3800
4. Weeks 27-52 (20% salary, 80% productive)	2600
B. Formal training	
1 week technical seminar (travel, seminar costs)	$ 750
IV. Fringe benefits (30%-40% of base salary)	$ 7500-10,000
V. Administrative costs	
A. Orientation time and material	$ 150-300
B. Insurance, pension, health claims (clerical time)	75-150
Total estimated costs	$21,935-29,375

These figures are direct estimated costs and do not include lost opportunity costs such as supervisor's time, trainer's time, or the impact the departed programmer had on other programmers' morale or productivity. In addition, it is impossible to calculate the damage to customer good will because of bugs in the software or terse customer interactions.

Schmidt and co-workers (1979) developed a methodology to estimate the impact of valid selection procedures for hiring computer programmers for the federal government and extrapolated those findings to the U.S. private sector. Using valid selection procedures, they demonstrated productivity gains from *$5.6 million to $97.2 million* for the government alone. Projecting this to the national economy, the estimated productivity gains would range from $93,000,000 to $1,600,000,000.

These are almost unbelievable statistics, but are *conservative* in the authors' eyes. Nevertheless, the fact that one programmer can cost a company over $29,000 for 1 year's service makes a selection error very costly indeed.

What, then, are the basic steps in selecting the right person for the right job?

Accurate and Valid Job Descriptions and Job Specifications

First, accurate job descriptions and job specifications must be developed that give the recruiter a clear picture of the types of abilities, skills, experience, qualifications, and personality you, as the hiring authority, are looking for. This beginning task, in itself, can present problems since many managers do not know the type of person who will be successful in the job.

Before you can ask a recruiter to search for suitable candidates, you must give him valid and reliable data to work with. Therefore, you must analyze the differences between the most and least successful people who are currently working in the job or have worked in the job in the past. You must make sure the job has not significantly changed so that the success profile you develop for the recruiter is current and valid.

Many times there will be more than one pattern of success, and this can be confusing. Trying to develop the "one" pattern of success so that a one-mold or "cookie cutter" selection decision process can be developed is one of the major reasons validation studies have shown lower than expected validities and utilities. The insightful manager will recognize individual differences and see how combinations of characteristics have led to success in the job. Strengths and weaknesses that balance and complement each other are usually the most fruitful way to determine what exactly goes into making someone successful in this job.

By analyzing these relationships, the manager can better understand what the necessary and sufficient behaviors are for success on the job. Once the manager understands this, he or she will be more effective in selection, training, coaching, counseling performance feedback, and team building—the major components of a manager's job.

Developing a Candidate Specification Sheet

A *candidate* specification sheet should be developed that lists the most important abilities, skills, personal characteristics, qualifications, and past job experiences. Once this is completed, the recruiter can begin the search process in a rifle shot and not a shotgun fashion. The candidate specification sheet is also useful internally since each person who interviews the candidate can fill out the sheet and compare notes. Using the same selection criteria increases the likelihood that the best selection decision will be made.

Red Flags on the Employment Application

The applicant should fill out the company's application even if he has brought a résumé. Résumés might have been prepared by someone else, and the applicant is telling you what he or she wants you to know, not necessarily what you need to know.

The following are a few danger signals or "red flags" to look for on the application:

Has the applicant had a sketchy and erratic job history, with many brief periods of employment?

Are there time gaps in his/her employment record during which he or she did not work?

DEVELOPING A QUALITY SELECTION SYSTEM

Are there indications that because of past compensation the applicant's salary requirements will be higher than the amount the company can offer? If the applicant has to take a pay cut, then he may be using this as a "stopgap" job until something "better" comes along.

Has the applicant moved frequently from one part of the country to another, or from one type of work to another, suggesting a lack of personal stability or maturity?

Is the applicant's past job experience and education directly related to the job specification and job description?

Do the applicant's reasons for having left previous jobs suggest that he or she might be troublesome or difficult to work with? Ninety percent of job failures are due to interpersonal difficulties, not lack of ability to do the job.

Does the applicant have any physical or mental disability that would prevent him from carrying out the job effectively?

If the applicant answers "yes" to any of these questions or a number of the answers are obviously bad, then you have to decide whether to screen out the applicant at this step or continue to step two—the employment interview.

Conducting an Effective Employment Interview

Five Steps to Prepare for the Interview

1. Review the job description to clarify and focus on the exact duties, tasks, and responsibilities.
2. Review the job specifications to visualize the critical and essential qualifications the applicant must have.
3. Review the application and résumé.
4. Determine the most important areas to talk about. What questions or doubts do you have from reading the application or résumé?

5. Allocate enough time to get the data needed to make a valid and informed judgment. Don't shortcut the interview to get it over with so you can get back to your "real job."

Remember, time invested before hiring will more than pay for itself down the road.

Six Steps in Conducting the Interview

1. Introduce yourself and welcome the applicant.
2. Build rapport and trust by discussing people or work situations you have in common. This allows you to "get on the same wavelength" quicker.
3. In the interview explore the following areas: job knowledge and skills, education, experience and work background, intelligence and mental alertness, communication skills, energy level, interpersonal skills, maturity, positive mental attitude and self-confidence, independence, self-initiative, drive, resourcefulness, motivation, and flexibility.
4. Provide the applicant with information about the company. You must "sell" the applicant as much as he or she "sells" you.
5. Answer any questions the applicant may have.
6. Conclude the interview and tell the applicant what the next step is in the selection process.

Interviewing Effectively

Interviewing is an art, not a science. Getting past the "social mask" into the real person is the objective of the interviewing process and is the most difficult task an interviewer has. Every applicant will tell you what he or she thinks you want to hear in order to get the job; therefore, you must become very skilled at hearing not *what* an applicant says but *how* he says it.

Nonverbal behavior is 60-65% of the communication message; the actual words are only 35-40%. Voice intonation, body posture, eye gaze, and general body movement are the keys to telling whether a person is being truthful and in what areas he is most sensitive. The skilled interviewer will want to probe those areas that are most unnerving to the applicant, for this gives clues to weaknesses and exaggerations of strengths, skills, and past accomplishments.

The interview is the situation where two people see whether "the chemistry" is right between them. This is very important in determining whether the person will fit in with the group and be successful in the environment. If the new person is not liked, then he or she will not get the support and help needed to successfully learn the new job and will most likely than not start doing the less important parts of the job. The information work group is a very powerful force in shaping a new employee's attitudes and expectations. If the new employee is accepted, then the chances of success are increased dramatically; if he or she is not accepted, then failure is almost certain. The job of the interviewer is to determine whether the applicant can work with him or herself and the work group at large. Ninety-five percent of job failures are not due to lack of ability but due to personality differences and difficulty "learning the ropes" from co-workers.

The interview has been empirically shown to be *unreliable and invalid* as a predictor of future success on the job, but continues to be used in almost every job-hiring situation. Interviews are necessary but not sufficient as data-gathering sources and should be one of the steps in the selection process. The interview is much more than a "talking session" and all hiring authorities should undergo extensive training in learning the skills involved in effective interviewing. These skills include: asking open-ended questions, not yes-no types; listening for variations in voice intonations; deep probes into sensitive areas; and techniques to get the applicant to trust and open up to reveal his "true self."

Effective interviewing skills are critical to many aspects of the management process: selection, performance appraisal, counseling, coaching, goal setting, and career development. Therefore, each manager should take an audit of his interviewing strengths and weaknesses to determine where he needs to improve.

Testing and Evaluation

Since the interviewing process is so "subjective," many companies have started using tests as an objective way to assess the probability a candidate will be successful in their environment.

The 1964 Duke Power v Griggs landmark legal decision gave testing a "black eye," and many companies stopped using tests because they did not want to go through the expensive "test validation process." Test validation is a procedure that measures the relationship between the test (predictor) and some criteria of success (percent of sales quota, paying health claims, making microchips). Usually, correlations and multiple regression are used to determine how well the test predicts success of current employees (concurrent validation). Once the profiles of success are developed for currently successful employees, a new applicant is compared against this success profile and the probability of "likeness" is calculated, the assumption being if the new person has many of the characteristics of your most successful employees, chances are he will be successful too. Generally, this validation strategy has worked and proved cost-effective in terms of upgrading the work force and reducing turnover of the best performers.

A new type of validity research, called *validity generalization*, is being conducted. This research has shown that certain types of skill tests—clerical, computer programming, and mechanical—are transportable. That is, a successful programmer who is good at coding and testing in one company is likely to be good at a second company. These types of findings allow companies to use professionally developed tests without having to validate each test in their own environment. Validation is still recommended in most circumstances since validity generalization is still being debated in the professional community and no legal precedents have been established one way or the other. However, because of business necessity, many companies have started testing again since they cannot afford the expensive process of hiring and training employees who do not work out. Affirmative action quotas have become less threatening since the Reagan administration has become more sympathetic to the employer.

Testing has been attacked by "protected groups" since it is objective and easy to demonstrate numerical differences between group scores. The interview, on the other hand, is much less valid and reliable and harder to quantify to determine whether discrimination is occurring. This is the major reason testing and interviews have been the target of attacks by "protected groups."

The 20-year decline in testing has reversed itself, and testing is on the climb again. Computerized test administration and interpretation at affordable prices seems to be the wave of the future for testing and one of the major reasons for its increased use. The use of computerized testing allows companies to internally develop testing programs and not rely on outside experts to interpret the results. Usually outside consultants are needed to help design, develop, and implement the computerized testing programs, but their role and importance decrease over time.

The Role of Testing in Selection

Much of the criticism of testing stems from mangers who are disappointed or disillusioned by the fact that tests themselves cannot be used to do the entire selection job. They would like to give tests to a group of applicants, hire the person who scores the best, and then have a productive, loyal, honest, stable, and self-starting work force. This cannot be done. Human nature is too complex. All we can do is establish a pattern of characteristics based on what successful people in specific jobs are like and try to select and hire individuals who are like them. This improves the odds that our choice will be right. Essentially, in selection we are playing the percentages, and a selection program using tests will increase the odds of selecting the right person for the right job.

Testing should be one of the data sources in making the final hiring decision. Interviews, applications, reference checks, and tests are the four major sources of information most recommended by selection experts. Judgments made through the analysis of personal history (applications), interviews, and reference checks are *subjective* judgments. Each depends on the likes, dislikes, and prejudices of the person doing the selection. Tests are less subject to error and less misleading than the judgments made by other methods. The test is the only *objective* hiring tool we have to work with, yet it should never be used as a substitute for the application form, interview, or reference check.

Most people are swayed by the assured, glib candidate. Test measurements go beyond surface impressions to the heart of the person. Tests measure such qualities as level of intelligence, personality traits and behavioral styles, values and motivations, and vocational interests that make up the internal structure of the person and are formed over the life-span of that individual.

Testing is a way to determine the individual strengths and weaknesses of the candidate so that training dollars are not misspent, and the supervisor has a head start in determining how best to manage a new employee. Experience has shown it takes roughly 6 months to really learn what makes a new employee "tick." Testing can accelerate that process and time schedule by breaking through the social mask and emotional shell.

Testing and selection is much more important to improving quality and productivity than training and management development. Many companies are finding this out too late after spending hundreds of thousands of dollars on low-potential employees who should never have been hired in the first place.

Performing Effective Telephone Reference Checks

Reference checks are becoming more and more difficult to perform sucessfully because companies are afraid of legal action from terminated or departed employees. The best way to get reliable and valid job performance information is to bypass the personnel or human resources department and talk to the immediate supervisor, who is probably less sophisticated and legal wise.

Reference checks are very important in establishing the track record and past performance of the applicant. One must be very sure that the supervisor has no emotional grudge or "hidden agenda" in detailing both overly positive or negative information. The best way to guard against this is to get at least three references and compare the degree of agreement. If all three references are

DEVELOPING A QUALITY SELECTION SYSTEM

fairly consistent in their perceptions about performance and personal characteristics, then you can be more assured about the validity of the applicant's track record.

Areas to Probe with Supervisor

Identify yourself, your position, and your company. Start out by saying, "I would like to verify some of the information given to us by Mr./Mrs./Ms. —." This signifies to the ex-supervisor that you have certain facts and you merely want to verify or confirm the information you have.

The major areas to find out about include: dates of employment, nature of the job performed, thoughts concerning his or her work performance, job progress made, earnings history at company, reasons for leaving, eligibility for rehire, strengths and weaknesses, ability to get along with others, attendance, dependability, ability to take responsibility, potential for advancement, degree of supervision needed, and overall attitude and performance.

Making the Final Selection Decision

The most effective selection decisions occur when the company and hiring authority have a number of quality candidates to choose from. Potential employees are attracted to a company for a variety of reasons: company image, physical proximity, a friend works there, the industry is perceived as a growth industry, likable and persuasive college and personnel recruiters, employment agencies, and alluring want ads.

Whatever source or method an applicant chooses to begin the selection process, it is critical that the company obtain as much data upfront as possible to determine the degree of fit and probability of success of the applicant.

The final selection decision should be made by the hiring authority based on the four selection steps:

1. The company application.
2. The employment interview.

3. The appropriate test battery.
4. The telephone reference check.

The mistake most often made is to "short-circuit" the selection process, which normally takes 3-5 weeks once the applicant has been contacted, and to hire the first "warm body" that makes a good impression and seems to have "industry experience." This short-circuiting is a short-term gain because 6 months down the road, when the employee is terminated or leaves, all the training and supervisory time will have been wasted.

Hiring the right person for the right job is difficult at best. Our knowledge of human nature is not precise enough for us to predict with absolute certainty how an individual will behave in the future. With all the countless variations in human behavior, and the changing environment, it will probably never be possible. However, one of the most valid psychological theorems is: *a person's past behavior is the best predictor of future behavior.* That is why it is so critical to complete the four-step selection process outlined above.

The quality and performance of your company is only as strong as your weakest employee.

Selected Readings

Brodgen, H. E. and Taylor, E. K. The dollar criterion: Applying the cost-accounting concept to criterion construction. *Personnel Psychology*, 1950, 3, 133-154.

Carlson, R. E. Selection interview decisions: the effect of interviewer experience, relative quota situation, and applicant sample on interviewer decisions. *Personnel Psychology*, 1967, 20, 259-280.

Cascio, W. F. *Costing Human Resources: The Financial Impact of Behavior in Organizations.* Boston, MA: Kent, 1982.

Fear, R. A. *The Evaluation Interview.* New York: McGraw-Hill, 1978.

Flamholtz, E. *Human Resource Accounting.* Encino, CA: Dickenson, 1974.

Ghiselli, E. E. The validity of a personnel interview. *Personnel Psychology*, 1966, 19, 389-394.

Goldstein, I. L. The application blank: How honest are the responses? *Journal of Applied Psychology*, 1971, 55, 491-492.

Guion, R. M. Recruiting, selection and job placement. In *Handbook of Industrial and Organization Psychology*, edited by M. Dunnette, Chicago: Rand-McNally, 1976.

Hunter, J. E. and Schmidt, F. L. Fitting people to jobs: The impact of personnel selection on national productivity. In *Human Performance and Productivity*, Vol. 1, M. D. Dunnette and E. A. Fleishman (Eds.), Hillsdale, NJ: Erlbaum, 1982.

Janz, J. T. and Dunnette, M. An approach to selection decision: Dollars and sense. In *Perspectives on Behavior in Organizations*, J. R. Hackman, E. Lawler, and L. W. Porter (Eds.), New York: McGraw-Hill, 1977.

Mobley. W. H. *Employee Turnover: Causes, Consequences and Control*. Reading, MA: Addison-Wesley, 1982.

Schmidt, F. L., Gast-Rosenberg, I., and Hunter, J. E. Validity generalization results for computer programmers. *Journal of Applied Psychology*, 1980, 65, 643-661.

Schmidt, F. L., Hunter, J. E., McKenzie, R., and Muldrow, T. The impact of valid selection procedures on workforce productivity. *Journal of Applied Psychology*, 1979, 64, 609-626.

Tucker, D. H. and Rowe, P. M. Consulting the application form prior to the interview: An essential step in the selection process. *Journal of Applied Psychology*, 1977, 62, 283-287.

9
Strategic Quality Planning

WILLIAM A. GOLOMSKI
W. A. Golomski & Associates, Chicago, Illinois

Planning

There are many types of planning in any organization. They vary by

1. Time span
2. Functional departments
3. Subsidiary or business unit

Material in this paper has been taken from materials copyrighted by W. A. Golomski & Associates. Permission is granted to ASQC to publish this chapter in the first edition of this book.

4. Cross-functional activity

5. Purpose, e.g., strategy, operations, tactics

All employees are affected by more than one of the above plans. Some types of planning are inwardly directed, such as the

1. Safety plan
2. Personnel development plan

Others are primarily externally oriented, such as

1. Stockholder relations plan
2. Community relations plan
3. Vendor relations plan
4. Security analysts relations plan

The best known plans in any organization are the

1. Annual operating plan
2. Strategic or long-range plan
3. Personnel plan
4. Marketing plan
5. Operations or production plan

Why Plan?

Everyone famous has come up with a reason. I'll paraphrase some of them.

> People seldom hit that which they do not aim at.
> —Thoreau

STRATEGIC QUALITY PLANNING

> We are very good at planning, but not very good at implementing.
>
> —Nehru
>
> Plan and act so that error is not inevitable.
>
> —Chief Thundering Horns
>
> I don't believe in planning; just be ready for the future.
>
> —Yogi Berra
>
> It is not enough to be busy. . . . The question is: What are we busy about?
>
> —Thoreau

There are some critics who feel that long-range plans are of little value, because conditions change rapidly and make them useless. Many in the steel, air transportation, and electronic components industries have felt that way recently. Others truly feel that you can invent a future for yourself. Still others feel that strategic plans should be constructed to enable you to seize opportunities. Much like a boxer or wrestler, you have to get your corporate self in shape to take advantage of any opportunities that may occur.

Planning can be viewed as a top-down, authoritarian process. If the planning process works right, there is also a bottom-up stage.

Strategic Quality Planning

The purpose of strategic quality planning is to assure the viability of the organization using concepts of quality and quality measure improvement. This assures a flexibility in meeting the future successfully. Of the options available to use the resources of the firm, which set, considering the role of quality, is the best? Far too often, quality is ignored as the usual marketing and finance centered plans are developed.

The role of quality is often under attack by those who look at the short run, or do not have a sufficient customer focus. In the late 1960s, the Joseph Schlitz Brewing Company started to become more marketing oriented. Growth was great as the Old Milwaukee brand expanded. Promotional costs were high. Strong financial people were brought in to offset the power of those in marketing. Products were reformulated and processes were changed. Cost advantages occurred. But two things were wrong. First, taste-testing research was done by those with simple survey skills and not by those who understood the physiological aspects of sensory perception. The signals received were wrong! Second, the processes were not validated to assure that the controls were in place for making it the same time after time. In the mid-1970s, the heritage of quality was lost as a series of executives with strong financial and traditional sophisticated planning skills departed. Finally, the officers and board stopped working together as a team. Eventually, the assets of the proud company were sold. The major brand, Schlitz, is hardly known today.

It is hard to gain a reputation for quality, but easy to lose it.

Some customers are not sufficiently knowledgeable on how to evaluate products. For initial purchases they rely on the recommendations of famous people, those around them whom they respect, or consumer evaluation magazines, newspaper columnists, and similar services. Some industrial goods buyers rely on the choice of industry leaders. "If Oscar Mayer bought it, it must be good." Large appliances and vehicles pose an especially difficult problem for customers. Often these are purchased based on *perceived quality*, and *not actual quality*. This poses a severe problem for executives who conduct engineering tests on durability and reliability of their products versus those of competitors. They might find that their product is the best, but the marketplace thinks otherwise. This is happening today with U.S. autos. Some have better quality, but the marketplace wrongly perceives otherwise.

There is no good substitute for careful objective marketing research. Just as in any other field, some are more expert at doing it than others. Far too often executives hold group meetings to discuss the future of a potential product. People in the meeting learn how to read subtle body language signals from the key decision

STRATEGIC QUALITY PLANNING

makers and are influenced by them. I've seen far too many of these sessions drift in the wrong direction.

We have conducted tests in which we have had three groups do the following.

1. List the product quality attributes of the product.
2. Rearrange the list from the most important to the least important.
3. Give importance ratings for each item on a scale of 1-10, where 10 is the highest rating.
4. Do the same for one to three competitive products that come to mind, using the column developed in item 2 above.

We have done this study with consumers and industrial buyers of goods and services. The results were seldom the same. In fact, they were usually significantly different. The groups used were: senior executives or plant managers, marketing executives, product developers, quality managers, and buyers. This is ample reason to consider plans. First, we try to determine why the differences exist and, then, which results we should use for strategic quality planning.

Quality measures such as these govern purchasing behavior. To be of operational value, however, some additional information is needed.

1. What is the likely trend of each of the product quality attributes over the next 3-5 years?
2. What is the value in revenue to move up one point in ranking for each product quality attribute, separately?
3. Do interactions occur that will give synergy?
4. What are the risk and penalty for not improving, or not improving fast enough?

Strategic quality plans affect both the revenue curve and the cost curve of a break-even chart. The above factors mainly affect the revenue curve. Improvements prevent price erosion and enable the firm to be a price leader within its price/quality segment.

When we approach the cost curve, there are a variety of quality measures. The best known is that of Josef V. Talacko, Privat Docent of Charles University in Prague. His work from 1946-1947 in Prague dealt with cost of poor quality in government and industry.

A current adaptation of Talacko's work has led to viewing military products or costly durables as having not only

1. External failure costs
2. Internal failure costs
3. Appraisal costs
4. Prevention costs

In addition, they are sometimes subdivided to emphasize life-cycle cost concepts. As an example, in autos,

1. What does it cost you to have your vehicle serviced?
2. What is the cost of a standby or rental vehicle?
3. What did you lose as a salesperson because your vehicle was not working? Or as a heart surgeon because you couldn't get to the hospital in time?

Quality costs as used today are somewhat different from the earlier formulations. Those early concerns were with

1. Sales likely to be lost or to drift downward because of poor quality
2. Sales you could get if quality improved
3. The advantages of being a quality leader

Following are some costs based on recent work with some 150 companies:

| | Quality costs as % of sales | |
Technology	Marketing company	Production organization
1. Simple, low-tolerance, agribusiness, basic textiles	0.0-0.5	0.2-1.5
2. Normal mechanical industries fabricated foods, medical devices, packaging, metal stamping, plastics	1.0-5.0	1.5-6.0
3. Precision industries, drugs, fine furniture, ceramics, steel	1.0-5.5	3.0-15
4. Complex products such as electronics, space drugs, artificial organs, fine chemicals, powdered metals	3.0-8	8.3-60+

These costs are from the four quality cost categories listed previously.

Generally speaking, there is no real value in knowing what the costs are. That doesn't solve any problems. The primary advantage is in getting the attention of upper management on the problems the firm faces and the opportunities to lower costs, and thereby increase profits.

A quality cost matrix helps to identify opportunities for cost reduction project work. The cause of the problems can often be determined with an Ishikawa diagram. The solution may involve simple brainstorming, statistical methods, or engineering work.

Approaches such as these have proved to be successful at the Eastman Kodak Company in Rochester, New York, and in the high-tech Precision Castparts Company in Portland, Oregon.

More Definitions

Many people get confused about quality because sometimes they are talking about the *design aspects of quality*. This has to do with the choice of the components and materials that go into a product.

At other times, they are talking about the *conformance aspects of quality*. This has to do with the consistency or uniformity of the product or service.

The PIMS studies are concerned primarily with quality of conformance. In these,

Superior quality is associated with a higher price and helps profits.

The higher the relative quality, the higher the cash flow and ROI in good times and bad.

Poor quality cannot be overcome by advertising.

The Productivity Problem

For years the common wisdom in manufacturing plants was that increased quality meant decreased productivity. Part of the confusion came from the reliance on detection systems as the major quality thrust. In companies where the causes of error have been removed, and where processes are in a state of statistical control, productivity goes up as does quality.

I usually conduct a survey in workshops to determine which of the following best represents the thinking of each participant, whether in manufacturing or in a staff, service, or support group.

People view concern for quality and concern for productivity in different ways.

1. Improvements in quality do not affect productivity.

2. Improvements in quality have a small impact on productivity improvement.

3. Improvements in quality have a major impact on productivity improvement.

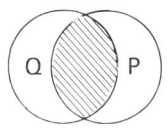

Good improvement requires

1. Good product design for products and services
2. Reliable and capable vendors
3. Processes that are capable of meeting the requirements of customers at a profit
4. Concentrating on prevention of imperfections rather than detection
5. A timely and accurate feedback system
6. Unified strategic and annual quality plans
7. Aiming for perfection as a state of mind

Certainly, there are cases where productivity changes with no effect on quality. This happens in multiple operations or higher-speed equipment.

The Strategic Quality Planning Process

Many corporations have a corporate strategic plan. In examining a few hundred of these, I found little or nothing on quality. Likewise, in examining corporate mission and policy statements, quality was ignored or discussed in a limited or inappropriate way. Mission statements indicate what we stand for; policy statements indicate what we must do; and procedure statements indicate how to do it.

The strategic quality planning process has the following parts:

1. Quality mission statement.
2. Key result areas (KRAs). What upper management believes we should emphasize in the years ahead. Not quantified. Customer focus.
3. Objectives. What we are committed to achieve in each responsibility unit. These are usually stated in quantifiable terms relative to the benefits to internal or external customers.
4. Programs. How to get it done, by whom, at what cost/benefit, and when. The better programs are based on multidepartmental and multilevel teams.
5. Review. Periodic coaching and counseling to assist in being successful.

Who Should Do It?

The quality strategy of a firm is developed by upper management. Quality professionals might participate to the extent that they can generate a variety of options to be used as inputs to the discussion sessions. The initial sessions will often be difficult because it is a new experience. Furthermore, there will be a shortage of customer-based measurements.

Some elements to consider are:

1. Product quality level
   To be the same for all products?
   To be the same for all countries?
   Current product quality image.
   Competitive product quality image.
   Role of marketing research in quality and production decisions.
   Management process to improve quality.
2. Employees
   Ideal selection and affirmative action.
   Restrictive work practices.
   Training for craftsmanship.

STRATEGIC QUALITY PLANNING

3. Production
    New equipment versus better understanding on how to control variation.
    Seriousness of running plants to make nonconforming product.
    Degree of flexibility in using standard operating procedures.
    Pioneer new processes or be a follower.
4. R&D
    When are products really ready for release to production?
    Use of statistically valid test procedures.
    Processes that are user friendly and validated.
    Do we want to satisfy customers immediately or 6 months after production starts?
5. Vendors
    What is the advantage of many vendors? A sole superior vendor?
    Do we wish to assist vendors in improving their processes?
    Does our evaluation of purchasing agents get in the way of good quality?

Morality

Private morality has to do with free, responsible human actions that affect another person. The conscience must be instructed and informed for a person to be acceptably moral.

Public morality has to do with actions we wish to criminalize. Some are considered so evil that we will use the coercive power of the state. Managerial negligence on quality is becoming such an issue. The moral responsibility of the firm and its employees must be considered in the corporate quality strategy. Quality and safety are the major areas in which the value system of the firm is most readily visible and easily acceptable.

The Competitive Environment

Far too often in the past, quality strategies were not targeted at specific competitors. We want to do two things: (1) meet the needs of customers; (2) exceed the quality level of competitors. The latter might not be bold enough. Some firms are building in a safety factor, which says, "We will exceed the quality level of competitors by 25%." Even being this good might not truly satisfy customers.

Although the major part of the discussion has to do with setting objectives, the managerial task of translating these into specific, short-range operational plans requires much discussion.

The Four Parts of Quality Improvement

1. Changing the culture
    Prevention is more important than detection of problems
    Never-ending improvement must be fostered
    Sustained involvement and participation by executives in quality improvement
    Being customer focused for both internal and external customers
    Improve quality in everything we do—including quality in daily, weekly, and monthly meetings

2. Providing a vehicle for change
    Strategic quality plans
    Annual quality improvement plans
    Improvement teams and councils
    Total quality assurance

3. Upgrading eduation and training
    Leadership skills
    Technology
    Team building
    Statistical methods
    Other problem-solving methods

4. Improving the reward, recognition, and ceremony systems
    Cost accounting
    Personnel performance appraisal
    Relationship to the annual quality improvement plan
    Recognition of vendors, employees, and others

The strategic quality plan is a part of structure, or part two. For it to work, the culture might have to be changed. This requires a consciousness and determination of change, rather than objectives. The other parts do fit into the planning process.

Summary

General Patton once said, "Never tell people how to do things. Tell them what to do and they will surprise you with their ingenuity." This holds after they have been given a kit bag of methods from which they can choose.

The strategic quality plan is the glue that holds customer-based plans together as we strive to overtake competitors. In governmental units, it brings unity to those conflicting goals of using funds well and providing services that satisfy most.

The best way to start strategic planning is by doing it. The plan will form an umbrella within which the annual quality improvement plan will find greater purpose. Otherwise, each unit suboptimizes its own function.

10

New Organizational Structures and New Quality Systems

PHIL ALEXANDER   Ann Arbor Associates, Ann Arbor, Michigan

MICHAEL BIRO   SARNS/3M, Ann Arbor, Michigan

EVERETT G. GARRY   L&W Engineering, Belleville, Michigan

DALE SEAMON   SARNS/3M, Ann Arbor, Michigan

TOM SLAUGHTER   International Foam and Trim, Jackson, Michigan

DUANE VALERIO   Hydra Matic Division GM, Ypsilanti, Michigan

This chapter has been written as a collaborative project by a group of six members of the Ann Arbor Section of ASQC. Envisioned as a pilot effort to demonstrate the ability of ASQC members in local sections to write publishable material by the project leader, Phil Alexander, the group has succeeded admirably in their efforts. The case studies included in the chapter represent the first published work of each member of the group (except the project leader) and stand as a testimonial to the creative talent and writing ability of the group members individually and in larger sense as representatives of ASQC membership.

We should note that although there are six authors, only four cases are included in the chapter. It was with considerable regret that we decided to drop one case when it became impossible because of corporate policy to obtain sufficient information from the firm to provide the detail necessary for comparison and analysis. Publication deadlines, unfortunately, precluded the substitution of another case.

This chapter is dedicated as the first ASQC section-level, collaborative writer's project by the Authors of Quality Literature (AQL) group to all aspiring and as yet unpublished authors among the membership of ASQC. We did it and you can do it, too!

We shall begin our examination of organizational structure with a brief historical summary and examination of the common types. These will provide us with a grounding in the more familiar and conventional aspects before launching into the newer, more interesting, and more speculative dimensions of our inquiry. Following this we shall examine four case studies that illustrate novel approaches to organizational structure and summarize their common themes. We shall then examine the outlines of a new and radically different way of understanding, a paradigm shift, and speculate on the possibility that the case studies reflect this new way of thinking as it takes root in society in general and organizations in particular.

Throughout this examination we will keep the issue of quality and the way in which the organization deals with quality as an important focal point, recognizing both its fundamental significance and the particular interests of our professional readers.

Background

Organization structure refers to the policies and procedures of the organization's administrative system as these relate to planning, organizing, directing, controlling, budgeting, resource allocations, and similar functions. The most common evidences of the organization's formal structure are the organization chart and the manual on policy and procedure. The absence of such documents does not mean that the organization has no structure, but rather that the structure is defined on a less formal basis. As a practical matter, the formal organization structure is only one aspect of the way in which the organization functions. Underlying and conditioning the organization structure are social and cultural values, the environment within which the organization carries out its function, the organization's objectives, explicit and implicit, and the strategic choices made by the organization's leaders.

These contextual, cultural, and environmental issues have, until fairly recently, been overlooked by organizational researchers and theorists who have focused largely on aspects such as span of control, number of levels (tall versus flat), concentration of power (centralized versus decentralized), information flow and the decision-making process, job definition and classification, and nature of authority (line and staff). In most organization literature there is a concern for measuring and correlating organization parameters in order to optimize organizational performance and, in turn, bring about more efficient methods of production or delivery of service. This way of thinking about organizations has come to be known as the mechanistic, rational, or bureaucratic view. As we read the literature, most of us would not be aware of this mechanistic perspective because it makes sense to us. We deal with machines in one form or another every day, from simple scissors to complex computers. Thinking of organizations the same way is, from our point of view, quite logical.

The common organizational structures are generally described from this mechanistic or bureaucratic viewpoint. These include the traditional pyramidal hierarchy, the divisionalized hierarchy, and the matrix organization. There are variations on these themes, but organizations in general, and certainly large organizations, can be categorized into these classifications.

Organic or process-focused organizational structures are of relatively recent origin and as yet are not well defined. They are taking shape in the context of the older and better articulated mechanistic organizational structures, and it is not yet clear what further evolution will bring in this area.

We shall examine the history and development of both mechanistic and organic organizational structures in the following section. In a later section of this chapter we shall examine the possibility that the organic structure is the emergence of an altogether new type of organization form rather than an adaptation of the older mechanistic form.

Development of the Mechanistic or Bureaucratic Organizational Form

The traditional pyramidal hierarchy has its origins in antiquity. In the book of Deuteronomy, we read how Moses organized the Israelites into groups of 10, each with a leader, these into groups of 100, and so on, thus creating a simple way of providing direction, communication, order, and control to a large, undifferentiated group. This same structure typified the Roman army and later the Catholic church. It is probably the most common conceptualization of organizational structure today. Like the pyramid which describes the shape of the organizational chart, it is designed for stability and to enable a single leader at the top to direct and control the efforts of a large number of individuals.

These early organizational structures were primarily for governance. They were not intended to accomplish objectives beyond maintaining their own continuity. Nor did they involve any significant percentage of the population. In short, they were not conspicuous features of the organizational landscape.

During the Middle Ages, all organizations except the church and the military were relatively small. The vast majority of the population were peasants and farmers who had no need of organization beyond the family. Such organizations as did exist, such as like the craft guilds of Europe, were typically loosely organized groups of skilled craftsmen with their apprentices. Individuals in these guilds "owned" their jobs in much the same way that independent tradesmen do today. Everyone had his or her place in the social fabric. Aside from natural disasters, unemployment was unknown. Culture, religion, and science derived from Aristotle's common sense had intertwined over the centuries to create a world view of a stable, stationary earth, the center of the universe, and a society with organizations that reflected it.

Then, in the sixteenth century, the old order gave way. In the space of a century and a half, from Copernicus' treatise on *The Revolution of the Celestial Spheres* in 1543 to the publication of Isaac Newton's *Principia* in 1687, the efforts of Copernicus, Galileo, Kepler, Huygens, Descartes, and Newton stood the world on its head. The notion that the earth turns on its axis and revolves around the sun and that knowledge derives from observation and measurement, which are so commonplace that we take them for granted, were revolutionary, heretical, and even dangerous to the men who formed them (Cohen, 1985). Descartes' *Principles of Philosophy* published in 1644, effectively divided the universe into two parts, physics (science) and metaphysics (religion). Newton then formed and gave direction to the new physics and endowed posterity with a new world view and a means of determining its intricacies, the scientific method.

Newton's new clockwork universe, which could be measured, analyzed, calculated, and accurately predicted, provided a conceptual framework for everything from astronomy, to physics, to economics, and to organizational structure. As we shall see, this is an extremely important perspective, which we shall examine in more detail later in the chapter. However, a comment by Nick Herbert, author of a popular treatment of quantum physics (1985), is instructive:

> The search for a picture of "the way the world really is" is an enterprise which transcends the narrow interests of theoretical physicists. For better or worse, humans have tended to pattern their domestic, social and political arrangements according to the dominant version of physical reality. Inevitably the cosmic view trickles down to the most mundane details of everyday life.

Herbert goes on to point out that the laws of physics that Isaac Newton and other promulgated in the seventeenth century have "inserted themselves into every aspect of ordinary life. For better or worse we live today in a largely mechanistic world." As we progress, we shall make special note of the way in which this perspective has influenced our concepts of organization structure and quality.

By the early 1800s, Newton's scientific method had given birth to the Industrial Revolution, which in turn had become the driving force behind a significant change in organizational structure. As enterprises began to take shape to exploit the new knowledge, they quickly grew beyond the limited capabilities of the small craft guilds. The new organizations took on the hierarchical nature of the church and army but with the difference that the organization became the extension of the owner-manager's abilities, a mechanism by which he could accomplish his goals from manufacturing textiles to building railroads.

As organizations became involved in more complex undertakings, no single person knew enough to provide all the answers. This gave rise to the concept of staff functions. The leader of the organization engaged knowledgeable and trusted individuals to provide advice in their particular areas of expertise so that better decisions could be made. Perhaps the best known early proponent of the staff function was Carl von Clausewitz, whose book *On War*, written in the 1820s, on the Prussian army, described the development of the principles of line and staff that are still in use today.

In this concept, the line refers to that part of the organization engaged in carrying out its primary objectives, typically manufacturing or marketing. Staff refers to individuals or groups whose special expertise is needed to enable the accomplishment of the primary objective. Thus, in an organization that manufactures widgets as its primary objective, the manufacturing organization is line, and accounting, engineering, sales, personnel, and research and development are staff. However, as the staff organizations grew, they also took on the familiar pyramidal hierarchical structure, as, for example, the quality-control function, as we shall see later.

Max Weber gave the traditional hierarchical organization its most effective delineation. The father of "bureaucracy," Weber made two singular contributions based on his study of long-lasting organizations including the Chinese civil government, the Catholic church, and the Prussian army. He introduced the notion of authority based on rational rules rather than on heredity, force, or charisma. He also defined the organization as a hierarchy of "offices" rather than individuals, each "office" with specified duties and the authority to carry out those duties. Thus, each successive level in the organization had a smaller subset of duties and a reduced level of authority (Weber, 1917). Weber's approach to organization characterization reflects the same reductionist principles associated with physics, biology, and other fields of scientific inquiry.

The American Frederick Taylor, a contemporary of Weber, gave a peculiarly American twist to organizational evolution. In the late 1800s and early 1900s Taylor developed and expounded on the principles of "scientific management." His fervor for finding the "one best way" by reducing jobs to their simplest elements, using time and motion studies, strongly influenced the mass-production industries, which found it ideally suited for integrating largely unskilled and uneducated workers into the new factories.

Taylor carried the reductionist perspective on people in organizational settings as far as it was possible to go, reducing employees to doers of simple repetitive tasks. His "scientific management" required that employees "have the mentality of an ox" and be motivated solely by pay and job security. Although his time and motion studies have endured (the basis for the practice of industrial engineering), the increasing level of education and aspirations among factory workers created a backlash of resentment against his simplified work practices, giving rise to militant unionism and the gradual disappearance of the harsher aspects of scientific management.

The turn of the century was the high point for the traditional hierarchical organizational structure. Enterprises were rapidly becoming so large that the one-man rule epitomized by Henry Ford was increasingly unworkable even with competent staff support. Furthermore, ownership through stockholders, represented by boards of directors, largely replaced owner-managers and intensified the economic or profit basis as the primary means of measuring organizational efficiency. In the 1920s the divisionalized organizational structure took shape pioneered by General Motors, DuPont, and Sears. In this concept, a relatively small corporate-level group focused on strategy, policy, and resource allocation and retained final authority and control chiefly through financial and accounting procedures. Responsibility for all other functions was vested in the managers of largely autonomous divisions, typically based on product line, geography, or market. Each division had its own complement of staff functions.

The 1950s, 1960s, and 1970s have been marked by a burgeoning of corporate-level staff functions. From relatively small staff groups focusing primarily on financial control, corporate-level activities have mushroomed into departments for manufacturing services, marketing, engineering, research and development, industrial relations, and administrative services, in addition to finance. Each of these, in turn, has developed subspecializations. Furthermore, in a sort of chicken-and-egg fashion, corporate staff functions both caused and were supported by increasing division-level staff functions (Ginsberg and Vojta, 1985). The introduction of the computer in the 1960s and 1970s has enhanced this proliferation and sharpened the type of information transfer to that which can be represented by numbers and symbols. In short, the white-collar-knowledge worker arrived on the organizational scene.

Writing on organizational design in 1960, Nobel laureate Herbert A. Simon saw no reason to believe that organizations would not continue to grow and proliferate in hierarchical fashion through the increasing complexification and subdivision of these staff departments. He based his thinking on his perception of the near universality of hierarchy in complex systems, noting the resemblance of human organizations to cosmological structures from atoms to planets to solar systems to galaxies. Regarding the staff functions, Simon observed that they could be thought of as factories for processing information regarding their particular function. Simon also observed that the assumption that any increase in the routinization of work automatically decreases work satisfaction and impairs the growth and self-realization of the worker was unbuttressed by empirical evidence and arguably false by casual observation of organizational reality. He believed that workers at all levels preferred a relatively structured situation from which to apply well-defined techniques in the accomplishment of tasks and, furthermore, that they preferred situations in which the level of novelty and uncertainty was confined to detail rather than deep structure. "Hierarchy," Simon observed, "is the adaptive form for finite intelligence to assume in the face of complexity" (Simon, 1960).

Supported by theorists like Simon, a number of corporations engaged in a further, and probably final, round of organizational structural evolution in the mechanistic tradition. In an effort to provide a new perspective for the increasingly complex organizational structures now characterized by staff functions frequently as large and complex as the line functions, several innovative efforts were made in the 1960s and 1970s to restructure the hierarchy in the form of a matrix.

The matrix organization, as the name implies, provides for two or more lines of accountability in the organization. For example, a middle manager might have a direct line of accountability both to the plant manager and to a product manager or a functional manager (engineering, marketing, finance, etc.). This organization represents a distinct break from the traditional hierarchical principle of "one person-one boss."

The brief history of matrix organizations has not been marked by success (Ginsberg and Vojta, 1985). Except in relatively small systems typified by new-product teams, matrix organizations have not found wide application. The divisional structure divided into geographical areas (typically by country) still characterizes the most highly evolved example of the mechanistic or bureaucratic organization, the international corporation.

Development of the Organic or Process Organization Form

In the 1930s and 1940s, partly as a reaction to the excesses of Taylor's scientific management, a new organizational theory appeared with the work of Elton Mayo, Fritz Roethlisberger, and W. I. Dickson. The human relations movement, as it came to be known, did not focus on the organizational structure, but rather on the organizational processes, particularly the way in which hourly workers were treated. This group attempted to show that workers integrated into small groups with a high degree of control of their own working environment would be more satisfied and hence more productive.

Beyond vague generalities such as treating workers with respect, no effort was made to change other aspects of the organizational structure. Subsequent research in the 1950s indicated that job satisfaction and productivity were not correlated, at least in the short run. From the perspective of the narrowly defined economic model of the organization, the human relations movement was a failure. However, it did provide the basis for the continued development of organizational theorists.

This concern with process and internal relationships began to insert a more humanistic perspective into organizational theory. It should be noted that this occurred within the older, and by now thoroughly entrenched, mechanistic way of thinking. Consequently, the new model was frequently described within or from the older perspective. Maslow's hierarchy of needs, the familiar pyramid of human needs from survival to self-actualization, grew out of the mechanistically based Darwinian theory of evolution, which placed survival as the fundamental value (Maslow, 1954). McGregor, building on Maslow, attempted to contrast the older mechanistic perspective on people (workers), which he called Theory X, with a new perspective, which he called Theory Y. McGregor (1960) particularly noted that Theory Y was based on assumptions derived from a different cosmology than Theory X (a fact poorly understood even today). Different cosmologies require different ways of thinking and understanding, but the vast majority of managers and organizational theorists (Simon, for example) were comfortable with the mechanistic model. Indeed, most of them were not even aware of their bias. It was simply common sense.

Through the 1960s attempts to bring a more human and organic perspective continued through the work of Argyris (1964), Bennis (1966), Herzberg (1966), Likert (1961,1967), Bennis and Schein (1965), and others. As Sashkin (1981) has noted, all of these theorists attempted to provide some sort of synthesis of the humanistic/process perspective with the older mechanistic/bureaucratic framework.

Notable in this regard were the efforts of Rensis Likert, founder and director of the Institute of Social Research at the University of Michigan. He attempted to overlay the new humanistic thinking on the older mechanistic organization structure through the concept of the manager as a link between hierarchically arranged work groups. In Likert's view, the best managers from the standpoint of long-term organizational effectiveness and efficiency were participative. They fully engaged their subordinates in the goal-setting and decision-making process on a collaborative basis. His principle of supportive relationships is a particularly good example of the humanistic perspective. "The leadership...must be such... that in all interactions and relationships within the organization, each member, in light of his [or her] background, values, desires and expectations, will view the experience as supportive and one which builds his [or her] sense of personal worth and importance" (Likert, 1961).

The "sociotechnical systems" approach associated with Emery and Trist (1973) is another excellent example of this combination of perspectives. These theorists developed the concept that the technological system used in an organizational setting must mesh properly with the social system if the organization is to operate effectively. Emery and Trist did not prescribe any particular organizational structure, although the hierarchical model was commonly used. They did, however, integrate the small groups characterized by the work of the human relations movement into their approach. A logical extension of this approach is the integration of the social and technological requirements in the planning process itself. Sociotechnical systems (STS) today are marked by an extensive planning process in which managers, engineers, and hourly employees design everything from the plant layout, to the job functions, to the organizational structure, to the work rules governing the operation.

The process focus in both planning and operation is crucial to the understanding of an STS. STS has been less effective when the organizational structure, the plant layout, job definitions, and work rules have been simply "laid on" a new or existing organization. The critical element is the direct and full involvement of the social system in planning and designing as well as operating the technical system.

A number of authors have characterized this new organic or process perspective on organizations. For purposes of illustration, the following comparison of the mechanistic system and the organic system developed by Burns and Stalker of the Tavistock Institute in London is included. Burns and Stalker (1961), working at the Tavistock Institute in London, developed the concept of an organismic system to provide an alternative way of conceptualizing organizations. In their view the mechanistic organization was appropriate to stable conditions and was characterized by:

1. A high degree of job specialization.
2. Direction and coordination of subordinates by superiors at each level of the hierarchy.
3. Precise definition of job responsibilities and authority for each position.
4. A hierarchical structure of authority, control, and communications.
5. Centralization of information, authority, and decision making at the top.
6. Communications, orders, and information flow following the vertical chain of command.
7. Insistence on loyalty to organization and obedience to superiors as a condition of employment.
8. Greater value placed on specialized (functional) rather than generalized skills.
9. Routine and repetitive tasks.

The organic system, in their view, was adapted to unstable conditions, so that the organization's goals could still be achieved when new and unfamiliar requirements came up that could not be broken down and divided among the specialists' roles. The organic organization was characterized by:

1. Definition of individual job requirements on the basis of what is required for the particular task.
2. Realistic nature and continual redefinition of individual job requirements in light of the total situation.
3. Control, authority, and communication implemented through networks.
4. Location of relevant information and authority may be anywhere in the network.
5. Open communication channels to any part of the organization.
6. Information and advice rather than instructions and decisions flow through the communication channels.
7. Commitment to organization goals and professionalism valued more than obedience and loyalty.
8. Authority and rank based on expertise rather than position in hierarchy.
9. Constantly changing and unforseen tasks.

One can infer from these characteristics that the organic organization is a constantly shifting collection of networks from a structural perspective. However, structure is significantly less relevant as an organizing principle than are process characteristics.

At this time organizations designed along organic principles are still relatively uncommon. Typically, they are found as plants, departments, or smaller portions of larger bureaucratic organizations. The case studies in this chapter have many of the elements of the organic or process model but may also be seen as exemplars of the new paradigm to be described in a later section.

This is a relatively brief and simplified history of organizational forms and structures. It is included primarily to provide a background against which to examine the organizations described in the case studies. For further reading, several good textbooks on organization development or organization behavior will provide greater detail (Gibson, 1980; Herbert, 1981; Schermerhorn, Hunt, and Osborn, 1985). Marshal Sashkin provides a very easy-to-read summary (Sashkin, 1981). D. S. Pugh (1984) has recently revised his *Organizational Theory*, which covers similar ground. Both Sashkin and Pugh provide secondary sources for most of the theorists cited. The winter/spring 1984/85 issue of *ReVision* provides a particularly comprehensive overview by Philip Murvis on "Work in the 20th Century" (a separate insert), which includes trends in organizational structure along with perspectives on management thinking, work force changes, trends in economy and politics, trends in industry, and trends in organization, governance, and labor. An excellent and recent overview on sociotechnical systems is provided by Trist (1981).

Quality Systems—History

The history of quality systems is well covered in Juran's *Quality Control Handbook*, 3rd ed, 1974 (see especially Chapters 7 and 12). Beginning with the Egyptian pyramid builders, Juran describes the evolution of the inspection function into the more sophisticated versions of quality control and reliability. Tracing the history of quality through the medieval guilds and into the twentieth century, Juran provides an overview complete with historical facts and detailed descriptions of the various configurations of organizational charts associated with the quality function. Juran's description of the elaboration of the quality and reliability function as the organization becomes larger and more complex is particularly noteworthy.

In a somewhat more recent work, Hayes and Romig (1982) offer the quality professional their explanation of organizational theory in general and the quality system in particular, through a variety of organizational charts based on the functional concept. Both Juran and Hayes and Romig use the mechanistic/bureaucratic concepts described in the previous section, notably the pyramidal hierarchical structure, one man-one boss, line and staff, levels of authority, and increased specialization at lower levels in the hierarchy. This conformity with the mechanistic perspective on organizations is understandable since inspection and quality control are fundamentally associated with mechanical processes.

The ferment that began in the general field of organizational theory in the 1930s and intensified in the 1960s and 1970s has only recently entered the province of the quality professional. Experiments with new organizational forms, which began attracting attention in the 1950s, had virtually no impact on quality professionals. It was not until the advent of quality-control circles and quality of work life (QWL) in the 1970s that the quality function began to be seen in larger terms than the classical "conformance with specifications."

Over the past 10 years, the application of quality systems in the service industry has also been taking shape. Here, too, the mechanistic perspective of quality as "conformance to specification" has met with difficulty. In both situations, the advent of quality circles and QWL and the application of quality systems in the service sector, the newer organic/process orientation has become apparent. As in the preceding general discussion, this orientation focuses on relationships rather than facts or structures. In the case of quality, the relationships are between supplier and customer or in terms of an object's relationship to its use. Thus, we describe quality in process terms as "the customer's viewpoint" or "fitness for use."

Even more recently, the concept of quality has been marked by a resurgence of interest in its historical definition, a nonquantitative description of excellence. It is in this sense that quality has been espoused by the humanistic theorists noted in the previous section. From this perspective, quality can be related to individuals, each of whom reflects a unique blend of interests, abilities, values, and goals. Thus, in the slogan "Quality people do quality work," which hangs above the aisle in a Buick plant in Flint, Michigan, the word quality has taken on this more humanistic meaning.

In terms of its historical perspective as a staff function concerned with the control of product uniformity and reliability, this new focus represents both a dilemma and a challenge. How this is being resolved will be examined in the case studies and sections on the new paradigm and implications for quality professionals which follow.

The Case Studies

Four case studies are included in this chapter covering Digital Equipment Corporation (Enfield, Connecticut plant), Chrysler Corp. (Sterling Heights, Michigan plant), People Express, and W. L. Gore & Associates, Inc. These were selected on the basis of available literature (most have been the subject of several publications), a willingness to participate, and a perception that they represent very innovative organizational efforts. Collectively, they cover both manufacturing and service industries and a range of technologies, sizes, and corporate backgrounds. One of the firms, People express, is relatively new. Two, Gore Associates and Digital Equipment, have been around for some 25 years. And one, Chrysler, is a long-time member of the corporate scene. Two organizations, People Express and Gore Associates, are examined from the perspective of the entire firm. In the others, which largely follow the traditional hierarchical pattern, a single plant reflecting the new organizational structure was chosen. All of the firms would be considered well managed, Digital Equipment and Gore Associates historically so, Chrysler on the basis of a remarkable turnaround under Lee Iacocca, and People Express on the basis of its remarkable and consistent growth. Of the four, only the Chrysler plant has union representation. Taken together, they represent a diverse group of organizations each attempting to break new ground with efforts that have both similarities and differences.

Each case was written by a different quality professional, and each reflects the author's perceptions and style as well as the facts. What this approach loses in theoretical tightness it gains in readability and ease of understanding. Quality professionals tend to see things of interest to other quality professionals and speak a common language. At the end of the case studies we will explore common themes and differences, engage in a little mind stretching by examining the origins of a new organizational paradigm, and make some observations on what all of this means to the professional reader.

DIGITAL EQUIPMENT CORPORATION—ENFIELD CONNECTICUT PLANT

Michael Biro

Digital Equipment Corporation's manufacturing facility in Enfield, Connecticut assembles printed board modules for computer storage systems. Though its 180 employees represent only a tiny fraction of the 85,000 people employed by this $5 billion electronics giant, this small manufacturing plant has received an unusual amount of nationwide attention from management personnel and publications, for it represents an innovative deviation from contemporary organizational practice. The Enfield plant's basic purpose, like that of any other manufacturing facility, is to build a quality product at the lowest possible cost and deliver it on time to achieve maximum customer satisfaction. This purpose is in keeping with the corporate philosophy, which states that "growth is not our principal goal. Our goal is to be a quality organization and do a quality job, which means we will be proud of our work and our products for years to come. As we achieve quality, growth comes as a result." The specific strategy developed by Enfield to achieve this goal is a sociotechnical design experiment, known as the "high-performance work system," which recreates the manufacturing environment from the ground up integrating such concepts as "team management," "participative management," and "job enrichment" into a truly creative organizational structure.

Much of the vision for Enfield's present structure came from Plant Manager Bruce Dillingham. "It's just the stuff I believe in," he says now. Dillingham recalls that when Digital asked him in 1980 to head the new plant being planned for Enfield, "I knew where I wanted to go, but I didn't know how to get there. So I hooked up with some people in organization design." Together they developed the values and norms that would govern the plant. The design period involved the participation of a cross-section of the plant's entire work force, as well as the usual architectural and engineering specialists. About 15 workers began the design process, and more were gradually added until the plant became fully operational in April 1983. The 77,000-square-foot physical plant, though modern in appearance, was structured in a fairly conventional manner; the simplicity and efficiency of the building alone saved $500,000 in normal setup costs for the plant.

The guiding principles of the Enfield operation are expressed not in a simple "mission statement," but in a rather lengthy, multipart document (Figure 1), which fully states the dual commitment to producing a quality product while emphasizing recognition of the work force as not just a production resource, but also as a human resource worthy of recognition and growth. Dillingham states, "We wanted to hire people with positive attitudes, minimize red tape, develop a strong commitment to community within the plant, pay above-average salaries, and expect above-average performance. We wanted never to increase costs, and to maintain a strong commitment to training and developing people." This dual emphasis on the product and the people producing it has already shown bottom-line results. The Enfield plant reaches its break-even point at 60% of capacity. Compared to other Digital facilities, overhead has been reduced by 40%, and there has been 40% reduction in the amount of time required to produce a module. Scrap is half the amount common to the industry, and the "yield"—modules that work perfectly the first time—is two to three times higher than that of other plants within Digital.

The crucial area of concern regarding the employee/product synthesis is the manufacturing operation itself. Plant Manager Dillingham oversees two support and three (manufacturing) product-line groups (Figure 2). The product-line groups consist of four teams of approximately 18 members each. The teams are totally responsible for the product they manufacture, from the receiving of raw materials, to assembly, testing, packaging, and shipping. Workers set their own hours, plan their own schedules, check their own work, and take team responsibility for each

DIGITAL
ENFIELD
CHARTER

WE HAVE THE RESPONSIBILITY OF ENSURING A CONTINUOUS FLOW OF RELIABLE MODULES AT A COMPETITIVE COST FOR ALL STORAGE SYSTEMS PRODUCTS, THROUGH:

INFLUENCING
- TECHNOLOGY
- DESIGN

RESPONSIBILITY FOR
- ALL NEW PRODUCT START UP
- TEST STRATEGY
- MANUFACTURING (SOURCING)
- QUALITY AND RELIABILITY
- COMPETITIVE SUPERIORITY

PURPOSE

DRIVE THE WORLDWIDE STORAGE SYSTEM MODULE BUSINESS TO ENABLE STORAGE SYSTEMS TO ACHIEVE AND MAINTAIN COMPETITIVE ADVANTAGE IN THE INDUSTRY.

MISSION

TO CREATE AN ENVIRONMENT THAT FOSTERS POSITIVE GROWTH FOR THE INDIVIDUAL WHICH WILL MAXIMIZE OUR ABILITY TO ACHIEVE OUR (5) MAJOR GOALS.

GOALS

WE WILL ACHIEVE EXCELLENCE IN AREAS OF
- PRODUCT COST
- QUALITY AND RELIABILITY
- TIME TO MARKET
- ASSET MANAGEMENT
- QUALITY OF WORK LIFE

Figure 1 Digital Enfield: principles of operation.

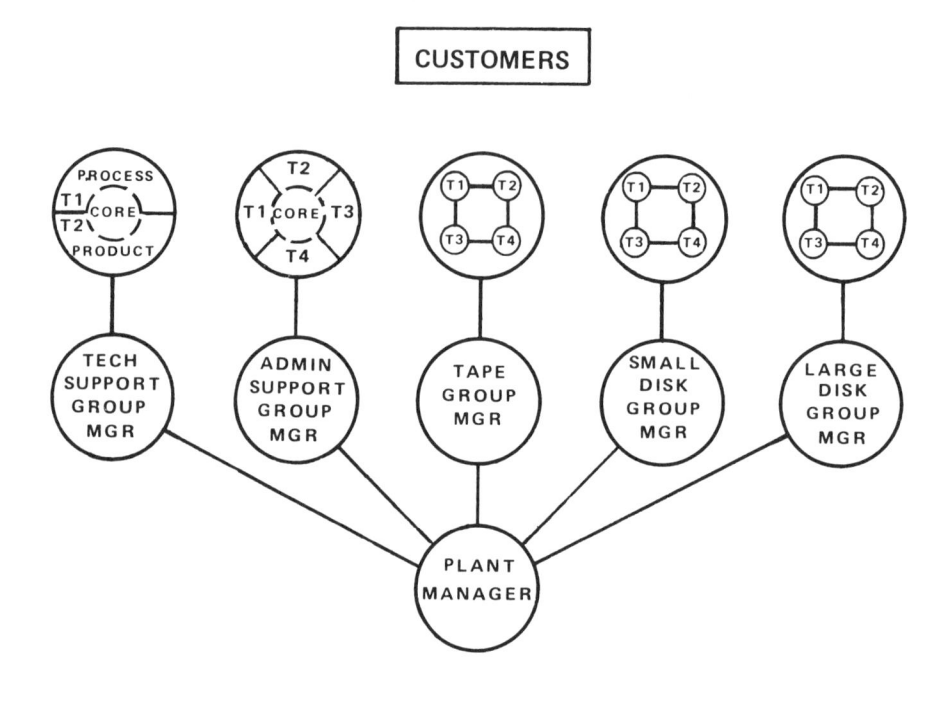

ENFIELD HIERARCHY
1985
Figure 2 Digital Enfield: hierarchy 1985.

module. Team members take on responsibility normally reserved for management, in that they select personnel, train themselves, do budgeting and costing, evaluate performance, and allocate benefits. There are no time clocks at Enfield, nor are there security guards or quality-control personnel, and each employee has a key to the building. Corporate information about how the organization functions and how an employee can influence the organization's direction is made explicit to everyone. "This is a high-trust society," says Dillingham. His goal is to have an atmosphere that is informal, relaxed, and trusting, where people are self-motivated, creative, and flexible.

In making Enfield a highly advanced manufacturing system, full advantage was taken of all of Digital's resources, thus avoiding the "not-invented-here" syndrome. A "just-in-time" production system has been implemented; there are no incoming inspection, stockrooms, or buffers in work-in-process. Teams have learned to balance the production flow of their lines, and individual workers contact vendors for daily supplies of materials. With JIT, there is a necessary emphasis on vendor quality. In its first year of operation, Enfield had 15 inventory turns, compared to the traditional one or two. The comprehensive training and responsibility taken on by the production teams make the entire operation very fluid and adaptable to change, allowing more creative possibilities for engineering.

The two support groups also operate on the team concept and provide critical information, support systems, and material, thus enabling the production teams to meet their daily schedule. The group managers themselves operate as an informal team and are responsible for allocating resources, leading the decision-making process, and managing the integration between teams. They act in a consulting role, managing the boundaries between teams, shifts, and support groups, while implementing and facilitating changes in the organizational design and evolution.

Training and development is a very serious concern at Enfield. Because each team member is expected to perform each of the 26 functions involved in making a module, 3 months of "off-line" training is required before a new team member is fully certified to make the total product. Workers also receive training in group interaction skills, such as communication, conflict management, problem solving, and interviewing. There is an emphasis on the whole person that can be seen in measures taken for employee recreation. The plant is surrounded by 50 acres of undeveloped Digital land, which contains an outdoor running path, a softball field, and a volleyball net. Aerobic exercise is taught year-round in a special area on the shop floor, and there is within the building a weight room complete with men's and women's locker rooms. The fitness program is designed to reduce stress and promote well-being among the employees. Through the training and development process, new workers become fully assimilated into the Enfield culture, learning not only the manufacturing process, but behavioral norms as well.

There are only five pay levels at Enfield. Once achieving their "floor certification," the first pay level, team members can then add other skills necessary to the team, such as budgeting, cost accounting, etc., and thus increase their pay level. The pay system offers horizontal growth and development as an incentive to the team members and is the same for all teams, though it is administered by each team in its own way. The average wage is a little higher at Enfield than it is at other Digital plants, because the competency of each worker is higher.

The emphasis of the Enfield culture is in working together in teaching one another, and in sharing the knowledge and responsibilities inherent in the entire operation. Dillingham explains that "it's the level of responsibility that you put on people that's different here. Some people don't want to have that kind of responsibility. They want to go to work, do their thing, and then go home and not worry about it. Technical engineers and other professionals have to see that their value is to teach other people—to share their knowledge—not to act as an authority figure. It takes a certain kind of engineer who would want to work in this plant."

To speak of the role of the quality professional at Enfield is, to a great extent, to discuss just one of the many important responbilities each worker assumes. The inspection, testing, documentation, and analysis functions are performed by the team members themselves, not by a separate quality function. The theme of "ownership" emerges often in the literature describing the Enfield operation. Because of the broadly based training and assembly skills utilized by the worker in assembling each module, the workers take on a feeling of ownership of the product, a pride of craftsmanship that gives each module a human face, a hallmark, so to speak, of the person who made it. Thus, quality emerges quite naturally in the inherent nature of a product built by people who, through feelings of ownership, have internalized the concern for functional fitness and customer satisfaction.

There does exist within the technical support group a number of individuals with backgrounds in the quality sciences, several of whom have ASQC affiliation and quality-engineer certifications. These people are not assigned strictly to the performance of traditional quality functions, but rather view themselves as a quality-support function, using their skills, knowledge, and experience to act as in-house consultants in facilitating and implementing quality-related activities. They assist in the design and process-related activities and also provide the interface with corporate quality personnel.

Digital's corporate quality organization is delighted with what is happening at Enfield. In a decentralized operation such as Digital, their role is not in any way attempting to "control" quality within DEC, but rather to promote the new awareness and attitude that the central goal of each individual employee should be to meet the customer needs in order to achieve customer satisfaction, rather than meeting production or deadline requirements. Enfield has provided a highly visible example of what is possible, and its role as a change agent is illustrated by the fact that the high-performance work system is now being gradually implemented in other Digital plants on a new-product basis.

It is important to realize that what has been created at Enfield is not just a new type of manufacturing system, but a very special cultural environment as well. The culture-building social skills are developed first at Enfield, followed by the technical skills. It is the high level of group dynamics, coupled with feelings of responsibility and ownership, that allows Enfield to operate as an efficient and productive manufacturing facility, not just an interesting example of social experimentation. The difficulties involved in creating a new culture are not to be overlooked. The commitment by senior management to carrying through such an endeavor is crucial to its success, as is a willingness to take risks in order to see the vision through to completion. The Enfield operation had the advantage of having been developed—quite literally—from the ground up. Other organizations with conventional management structures may find it more difficult to implement major changes in their way of doing things. The team management approach may be perceived as a threat to the role of middle management, as it involves a considerable transfer of power and responsibility. Thus, the transition within many facilities will be a gradual one, as the new forms of organization are implemented on a trial basis, prove themselves, and then slowly gain acceptance. Bruce Dillingham has often stated that it takes a certain, special kind of person to work at Enfield, one who sees his duties not as defined by a job title and description, but rather developed through strong interaction within the team framework. He describes this "management technology" as a total-system approach, one in which everyone in the organization takes on the responsibility to develop and diffuse the new technology, as knowledge and perspectives widen through horizontal growth and development. The new organizational structure at Enfield is a constantly evolving one which has already proven its effectiveness, as it stands as yet another significant development in the evolution of organizational design.

CHRYSLER'S STERLING HEIGHTS ASSEMBLY PLANT

Everett G. Garry

The mission statement for the Chrysler assembly plant at Sterling Heights, Michigan is "To be first in world automotive assembly technology and quality, using the latest concepts in employee participation/involvement, automation and design technique." The Sterling Heights plant is Chrysler's flagship in its effort to build a new spirit of participation and involvement among managers, supervisors, and hourly workers so that new technology can be implemented quickly and effectively, thus achieving greater quality and cost effectiveness for the company and a better quality of work life for the employees.

History and Organization

The history of the Sterling Heights plant has its beginning in the turbulent years following Lee Iacocca's dramatic entry to the presidency in 1978. Under his charismatic leadership, Chrysler weathered the economic storms of the early 1980s. Richard Dauch, who joined Chrysler from Volkswagen of American shortly after Lee Iacocca took the helm, quickly ascended to the position of Executive Vice President of Manufacturing and is generally recognized as the corporate driving force behind the Sterling Heights plant. The new Sterling Heights plant manager, Durward (Dur) Roller, was production manager when the plant was launched and was promoted to his present position in the spring of 1985. A staff member characterized him as "the most humanistic manager I've ever worked for" and observed that he treated board members and employees with the same respect, interest, and consideration.

The Sterling Heights plant was actually built in the 1950s by Chrysler and used for production for the Defense Department. It was purchased by Volkswagen of America in the 1970s and refurbished but never used for automobile production. It was repurchased by Chrysler for $194 million in April 1983. Between that time and the plant's reopening in September 1984, Chrysler spent an additional $456 million on training, tooling, equipment, engineering, and preproduction. Managers and employees for the Sterling Heights plant came from 20 other Chrysler facilities. In an attempt to provide a top-notch staff, middle managers were carefully screened by the plant manager and his immediate staff. These managers were further trained in an interactive management training program focusing on participative management techniques. Preference in hiring hourly workers was given to laid-off UAW members, but here too, the emphasis was placed on the new participative concept. Currently, the total number of personnel, management, supervision, and hourly staff is around 4300, of which 500 are salaried.

The plant is organized along lines pioneered by General Motors using the area manager concept. This approach basically eliminates the level of general foreman and redefines the roles of first-line supervision under the direction of area managers. This concept is currently being implemented in all Chrysler plants as a result of its success at Sterling Heights.

According to Personnel Manager Nelson Brooks, in staffing the Sterling Heights plant the intent was to provide a reasonably familiar management structure for managers and staff brought in from other plants. This structure will evolve over time to a smaller management staff group with reductions handled by attrition rather than layoff.

New Technology

Sterling Heights uses state-of-the-art production methods and technology. Over 700 suppliers are involved in their just-in-time inventory system. JIT combined with in-line sequencing provides a highly predictable and constant flow of high-quality parts from which the Chrysler Le Baron GTS and the Dodge Lancer sedans are assembled. Rather than the older method of continuous operation with sporadic breakdowns and line stoppages, Sterling Heights operates with two production shifts and one for preventive maintenance.

Over 100 robotic operations are in current use, most of which are involved with operations that were undesirable or physically exhausting from the operator's point of view. In some cases, the robots can work to tolerances that were unattainable by operators. Ninety-seven percent of the spot welds are made either by robot or by machine. Painting is similarly roboticized. There are plans to double the number of robots in 1985 with no loss of jobs for current employees. Employees replaced by robots will be retrained to perform other functions in the plant.

The entire production flow is monitored by a performance feedback system (PFS) by which operators key pertinent information into one of over 800 production data terminals at the operations stations. From these terminals, information is fed to an IBM Series One central computer, which in turn operates over 100 programmable controllers. When the operator completes a particular job, he or she keys that information into a 10-key terminal along with any specific problems or difficulties. Since the PFS provides a means of checking the work pace of operators, special contract provisions were made that no employee will be punished or reprimanded for slow cycles. Without this policy there would be considerable incentive for the operator to avoid using the terminal or key in erroneous data.

The PFS summarizes operator inputs and provides detailed information on each car at the various repair stations. In addition, every supervisor has a terminal and monitor and can check on any aspect of operations at any time. In addition, all plant facilities are monitored by a factory information system which records machines cycling slower than normal or ones which are malfunctioning or off-line.

Communications and Employee Involvement

Both the operations and policies at Chrysler Sterling Heights are highly employee oriented. On the management side the "open door" policy prevails. A variety of employee groups, including both salaried and hourly, are involved in planning new programs and activities. All work stations are no more than a 4-min walk from an air-conditioned cafeteria. (There is no executive dining room.) A toll-free "hot line" operates 24 hours a day to answer employee questions and provide information. Voluntary product quality improvement committees work on quality and other related problems and are strongly management supported. "Town hall" meetings have been held 14 times in the past 9 months. Although attendance is voluntary, production is stopped so that all employees can attend; virtually 100% do. These 30-min freewheeling sessions conducted by the plant manager cover upcoming changes and a variety of questions and concerns of employees.

Training

As a basic part of their indoctrination, all hourly employees, both transfers from other plants and new hires, receive 40 hours of training and orientation of which 12 hours are specialized.

Hourly Employee Training

All employees

8 hr	Employee orientation workshop
8 hr	Resource management
8 hr	Practical problem solving
2 hr	Plant familiarization/briefing
2 hr	Safety of work environment

Skilled trades		Nonskilled trades	
8 hr	Hazardous wastes	4 hr	Final car audit
4 hr	Statistical analysis	4 hr	Chart preparations
		4 hr	Statistical analysis

All managers participate in a 40-hr interactive management course, which focuses on participative management skills. Titled "The Winning Way," the course features a film giving a novel treatment of the Battle of Trenton in the Revolutionary War. Using a very participative approach, George Washington leads his outnumbered troups to defeat the British, whose leadership is characterized by more traditional autocratic methods.

Brooks, the personnel manager, notes that the percentage of employees attending school, for both general equivalency diplomas and college-level classes, is the highest of any Chrysler plant. He also speaks with pride about a new classroom facility being built on the property.

Union Relations

As part of the federal loan guarantee package, dramatic concessions were made by both Chrysler and the United Auto Workers (UAW) resulting in the appointment of Douglas Frazer, vice president of the UAW, to Chrysler's board of directors and a new type of contract with the UAW. Termed the Model Plant Agreement, this new contract was put into effect in Chrysler's St. Louis plant 2 in 1981 and with some modifications was the basis for the contract covering the Sterling Heights plant. This contract, negotiated by the UAW International and Chrysler Corporation, is radically different than other contracts, covering the terms of agreement in some 30 pages instead of the usual 300. In addition, there is no separate locally negotiated agreement. The contract is characterized by a staff member as "requiring considerable trust on both sides." For example, there is no contract provision for advance notification of required overtime. However, supervisors recognizing the trust on the part of the union are careful not to abuse the privilege.

Employee offenses such as absenteeism and poor performance are handled at meetings with the individual and his or her supervisor and an employee committee. The focus of these meetings is on counseling rather than punishment. Union committeemen wear beepers so that they may be called quickly to deal with any issues. Supervisors can, at their discretion, rotate personnel within their zones to different jobs. This is facilitated by a significantly reduced number of job classifications. Another new concept, single area control, provides for a union member elected by his or her peers in each zone to assist the supervisor by working with new employees and personnel from other departments to eliminate minor problems.

Nelson Brooks comments that the better union relationships have made a marked difference in the personnel manager's job. He found that 80-90% of his time was spent on labor relations problems at previous plants where he has worked. "Here, the situation is reversed and I spend about 10% of my time on these matters. It makes my job a lot more fun." He notes that grievances are less than one-quarter of what other similar plants experience and absenteeism less than half. Brooks also notes the pride of the hourly employees in being part of the Sterling Heights plant. "We sold 4000 jackets at cost with our plant name and logo to a plant with 4300 employees." Wearing the jacket "makes you one of us."

Quality System

Ron Ustruck, manager of Product Engineering and Quality Control, heads a group of 55 salaried professionals, about the same number as at plants of similar size. However, there are perhaps a third fewer hourly inspectors on the floor. Production workers are responsible for most of the routine 100% quality checking and do all of it in the body and assembly areas. Quality-control personnel conduct random quality audits on about 10 of the 450 cars assembled per shift. Ustruck notes that production supervision has taken much more responsibility for quality in their respective zones, which means that they no longer have inspectors checking defects and then "buying off" the rework. He also believes that cleanliness of the plant has improved quality. Virtually all incoming material comes in returnable containers, reducing cardboard and trash. Stock cannot be piled higher than eye level (54 in.) anywhere, allowing for "visual management" in which everything can be easily seen. Laser and optical gaging equipment is connected to computer monitors in several areas, ensuring the dimensional integrity of the vehicle in a matter of seconds. A separate building with controlled atmosphere provides a dirt- and dust-free environment for painting the car bodies. There is also a small paint test lab to continually test and maintain quality control.

Future

Sterling Heights' goals for the future are to continually improve working conditions and product quality, as indicated in their mission statement. The technology used in this facility will be applied in building new facilities and renovating other Chrysler facilities. Chrysler is also dedicated to remaining on top in technology and state-of-the-art equipment and processes. In particular, Chrysler anticipates putting over $150 million in an expansion at Sterling Heights to manufacture the new "P" cars in 1986.

Chrysler is justifiably proud of its flagship facility and has escorted some 50,000 visitors through it in the first year of operation, including representatives from all the international automobile companies. Their bid to become the world leader in automobile assembly technology rests on a firm foundation and strong commitment from the 4300 enthusiastic Sterling Heights employees.

QUALITY AND PEOPLE AT PEOPLE EXPRESS

Tom Slaughter

The logo of People Express is two human faces in profile, one in front of the other. Donald Burr, chief executive officer of People Express, explains that the first one represents the workers of the company, and the second represents the customers. When asked if, perhaps, it should be the other way around, with the customer first, Mr. Burr responds, "If you take care of the workers—give them a stake in the company, a certain amount of financial security, and opportunity for growth—then the workers will take better care of the customer than they ever would if the customer was put first."

This belief was the cause of Don Burr's dissatisfaction with the airline industry in the 1970s. Managers isolated from the customers were making decisions about how to run the airline and then passing these decisions down the hierarchical ladder to the line personnel who provide the service and deal with the customer.

Donald Burr had a better idea. He wanted to start an airline that would provide inexpensive service to his customers, reduce the amount of bureaucracy, and give the "employees" a chance to grow in their skills. His company would be based on six precepts: promote the growth and development of people; be the best provider of transportation; develop the best leadership; be a role model; have a simple structure; and maximize profits.

With some of his colleagues from Texas International Airline, Burr created People Express in April 1981 with three planes purchased from Lufthansa. From there, the company grew to approximately 4000 managers, with more than 70 aircraft, serving more than 40 cities, including London and Los Angeles.

Notice the term manager, not employee. One of the first requirements a person must meet when joining People Express is to buy 100 shares of company stock—with an interest-free loan from the company, if necessary. Additional regular stock purchases are encouraged and supported by the company. Workers now own about a third of the company. And, of course, in any company, every working owner is usually a manager.

However, having only owner/managers in the company was a part of the strategy to implement the precepts. A related strategy was cross-utilization of managers, letting them "try their wings" at skills they never had a chance to develop before. Both were to enable People Express to advance toward the goals stated in the precepts.

The goals and strategies were related. Owners would work harder, resulting in better service. Owners would also be more willing to develop skills in areas other than their own expertise, since they owned a company instead of a job. This combination of motivation, dedication, and flexibility would guarantee the development (or empowerment) of the individual and the success of the company.

Teams have also been important at People Express. Not only was the company as a whole a team, but customer service managers, flight managers, and maintenance managers were teams. In addition, teams were formed to operate the individual flights.

As the number of managers grew, however, some of the team feeling was lost as individuals lost the ability to relate to the size of the organization. To keep the company on a human scale, in 1984 the managers were divided into plane-type groups of about 400 people each. At the beginning of 1985 there were 10 such groups. The groups are almost minicompanies, in that they provide a central focus for the managers and a smaller context within which they act. In a sense, they provide a small pond. The planes assigned to the group are operated by teams drawn from the group. Functions not specific to any group are shared equally by all the groups.

Not all of the necessary functions are covered by company managers. Airplane maintenance and flight reservations are handled by subcontractors.

Regardless of position, every manager deals with customers. For some, their primary duty is providing customer service, filling in on other duties. Others have a primary duty other than customer service, but assist at various times serving drinks and snack packs on flights or checking luggage.

A concern expressed by some observers is the extent to which success depends on the president, Donald Burr. It was almost entirely his drive and fervor that got the airline its early financial backing. He is clearly the leading advocate of the new form of organization in the company, a sign of which is his regular participation in the orientation sessions for new associates.

However, efforts to increase shared decision making power are being made, which include the development of shared perceptions of reality, constraints, opportunities, and principles relevant to People Express. This is exemplified by a daily television program produced by a variety of owner-operators and viewed by all. This greatly enhances the sharing of perceptions and values.

Both London and Los Angeles terminal services were set up by managers with the authority to make decisions necessary to establish those terminals. Managers are also authorized to work on any project that is beneficial to the airline, as long as benefits are clear, measurable, and achievable in a reasonable time period. Even with higher-level authorization required, these projects give managers practice in applying the company's ideas.

Donald Burr may be People Express, but if so, he is trying to lay the groundwork for broader participation. Developing leadership does come before maximizing profits in the six precepts of the company. The perception of Burr as the autocrat who makes everything work may be as much due to the characteristics of the perceiver as of the perceived.

Quality

Before quality can be discussed and measured, it must be defined. In running an airline, conformance to specification is hardly sufficient, as anyone dealing with an unhappy flight attendant will testify. Fitness for use—more specifically, customer satisfaction—is a better criterion. If the process turns out a satisfied customer, then the process is behaving correctly. Don Burr has said, "I tell everyone, 'Make all the mistakes you want, fly the plane upside down. No problem. But just remember...we take care of the customer'" (1).

To describe and analyze the quality system at People Express, we will use a model that designates the customer as "raw material," the physical facilities as inputs affecting the "raw material," and the process as the human interactions occurring in the act of transferring (flying) the customer ("raw material") from one location to another. Using this model, we will examine the quality program in terms of control of input quality, process controls, and final inspection.

Maintenance managers handle quality control of the "inputs" (physical facilities). Maintenance of the aircraft is handled by an outside contractor, but People Express managers check the adequacy of repairs, maintenance, and cleaning, and audit the paperwork to ensure compliance with FAA regulations. This is the equivalent of incoming inspection and supplier audits in the industrial environment.

"In-process" type checks are of two types, macro and micro. Macro checks refer to statistics such as percentage of on-time arrivals and are recorded, audited, and reported by maintenance managers. Micro checks are handled by customer service managers and consist of checks to make certain customers are enjoying their flight and efforts to compensate for the nonhomogeneity of the "raw material."

The "final-inspection" stage also has two aspects. The requirement that all members of the company must serve customers in person at least part of the time leads to a better perception of their contribution to the creation of a satisfied customer. In addition, a bulletin board at the company's headquarters displays letters from customers expressing either satisfaction or dissatisfaction with the airline. Both these elements are similar to the traditional craftman's method of quality control: face-to-face interaction to determine the customers' needs and how they may fill those needs.

The second aspect of the final inspection is random market and customer surveys by an outside consultant. These surveys are to detect early signs of minor customer dissatisfaction or a lack of customer satisfaction—the type of customer feelings that may lead to a loss of business but not to a complaint.

The Role of the Quality Professional

People Express does not have anyone who has a position designated specifically as a quality professional. Various people handle certain aspects of quality control and quality auditing, but there is no position with responsibility for overall quality checks, auditing, and quality planning.

Such a role could develop in the future and be filled by an outside consultant, by training and development of people from within, or a combination of the two. However, it is useful to consider the contribution a quality professional could make.

The main contribution would be in training and tracking. Tracking takes data generated by "inspectors" and checks for trends, analyzes customer complaints for patterns, and searches for discrepancies. Training spreads the knowledge of descriptive and analytical statistics and small-group problem-solving methods in the mode of quality circles.

There would be room for a quality-control professional in an organization like People Express. It may not be called quality control or quality assurance, and one would have to take shifts serving customers, but the techniques and skills of promoting quality would definitely have a role.

Selected Readings

The airline that shook the industry, *New York Times Magazine*, Dec. 23, 1984, pp. 18-19, 24-27.
Bitter victories, *Inc.*, August 1985, pp. 25-35.
Growing pains at People Express, *Business Week*, Jan. 28, 1985. pp. 90-91.
A Passion for Excellence, Tom Peters and Nancy Austin, Random House, New York, 1985.
People Express, *100 Best Companies to Work for in America*, Robert Levering, Milton Moskowitz, and Michael Katz, New American Library, New York, 1984.
People movers, *Flying*, August 1984, pp. 36-39.
Peoples takes on the big boys, *Newsweek*, Aug. 27, 1984, pp. 52-53.
Seven who succeeded, *Time*, Jan. 7, 1985, pp. 40-41.
A squeeze at Newark could stunt People Express, *Business Week*, October 1, 1984, p. 44.

Note

1. Bitter victories, *Inc.*, August 1985, p. 28.

W. L. GORE & ASSOCIATES, INC.

Dale Seamon

W. L. Gore & Associates, Inc. was founded in 1958 to manufacture polytetrafluoroethylene (PTFE) products, better known as Teflon,* and to provide a creative means for expressing the novel organizational ideas of its founder, Dr. Wilbert L. Gore. Today, 27 years later, this company has shown a sustained growth rate surpassed by few corporations (notably People Express) and employs over 4400 people in 30 plants located in five countries. For the past 10 years sales have increased at least 35% annually.

---

*Teflon is a registered trademark of E. I. du Pont de Nemours, Inc.

Products manufactured by Gore Associates range from electronic wire insulation to Gore-Tex* expanded PTFE, a biocompatible material used for replacement arteries, vascular grafts, and other medical applications. Gore-Tex laminated to various fabrics is used in a wide range of lightweight, waterproof, "breathable" outdoor backpacking gear such as tents, parkas, sleeping-bag covers, and glove liners. And Gore-Tex was chosen by NASA for the outer protective layer of spacesuits. Other applications include protective coatings for steel and other metallic articles used in corrosive situations, industrial filtration bags, industrial seals and gaskets, and microfiltration membranes that remove bacteria and other microorganisms from air or liquids making them sterile and free from infection or disease.

The success of these products stands by itself, and the importance of the organizational system that allows the freedom and promotes the creativity necessary to achieve this success becomes apparent as we examine the founder's philosophy and goals. Bill Gore is a scientist with degrees in chemical engineering and physical chemistry, a philosopher with a doctorate in the humanities, a researcher, and an inventor. His early experience on a task force at DuPont gave him the ideas around which he and his wife Genevieve organized their company. As he puts it, "The task force was exciting, challenging, and loads of fun. Besides, we worked like Trojans. I began to wonder why entire companies couldn't be run the same way."

Noone could describe his successful management philosophy better than the founder himself. The following summary is taken from various talks Bill has given on how and why his approach works so effectively.

The Lattice Organization—A Philosophy of Enterprise

> Philosophical concepts lie at the base of decisions and actions of men. We expect that realistic concepts will lead us to attainable objectives and guide us to successful actions.

---

*Gore-Tex is a registered trademark of W. L. Gore & Associates, Inc.

A lattice organization is one that involves direct transactions, self-commitment, natural leadership, and lacks assigned or assumed authority. Concepts about the nature of man, the cooperation of groups, and requirement for governing principles are basic to his or any other form of organization.

Nature of Human Beings

We are aggressive. Our inherent aggressiveness has enabled us to vanquish threatening enemies, conquer obstacles, and overcome competitors. Our games are competitive and end with victors and vanquished.

We feel friendship and love. Our friendship, shown by affection, respect, and tolerance for our associates, is the enjoyment found in their company; love is the protective tenderness felt for our spouses and our children.

We are dreamers. We construct in imagination what might be possible and the means by which our dream can be brought to a reality. We seem to be continually dreaming. As soon as one dream is consummated, it becomes a steppingstone to another. This hierarchy of dreams (or needs) has been studied extensively by the "Third Force" psychologists led by Abraham Maslow. All of us have residual unsatisfied concerns at all levels and, therefore, are at least intermittently attentive to and active regarding each aspect of this hierarchy.

It would be foolish to contend that even an enlargement on the concepts of human beings as aggressive, loving, and dreamers can encompass so complex a subject as that of their nature. However, I believe they are basic, relevant, and quite generally applicable.

Nature of Groups

Groups are, of course, nothing but assemblages of individuals. These collectives, if voluntary, exist because the needs of the members are better satisfied by participation. If the purposes of the group involve an enterprise, considerations of efficiency of cooperation, magnitude of synergism, and utilization of individual human resources are important.

NEW ORGANIZATIONAL STRUCTURES

Cooperation and communication between two people is usually excellent. With an increase in the number of cooperators communication becomes more complex, less efficient, and limitations arise in the kinds of possible communications. When the group size becomes so large that everyone no longer "knows" everyone else, one hears "we" become "they." Beyond the level of 100-150 people it becomes necessary to impose rules, regulations and procedures that dictate how the cooperation shall be accomplished.

As the size increases from a single peron to a small group, the gain in synergism is large, particularly when a combination of capabilities (e.g., mathematician, engineer, accountant, machinist, chemist) is included. Small groups actually provide a much greater total capability than the mere sum of the number of individuals. However, as the group gets larger, loss in cooperation and communication set in so that the accomplishment per person reaches a maximum and then decreases. Some enterprises require a diversity of skills not obtainable in small groups. Others offer less opportunity for synergism and, therefore, are more heavily weighted by the cooperation factor.

One desirable feature of a good society is that each human has an opportunity to maximize his accomplishments. Enterprises designed to do this are not likely to involve large groups, usually no more than 150 persons.

Governing Principles

There are basic agreements which must be kept in order to maintain an enterprise with a viable lattice organization. I believe that four are necessary (and probably sufficient):

1. *Try* to be fair. Sincerely strive to be fair with each other, our suppliers, our customers, and all persons with whom we carry out transactions.

2. Allow, help, and encourage his or her associates to grow in knowledge, skill, scope of responsibility, and range of activities.

3. Make his or her *own* commitments—and keep them.

4. Consult with his or her associates before taking actions that might result in "holes below the waterline" and cause serious damage to the enterprise.

The Lattice Organization

The lattice organization devised by Bill Gore is not a modified organization chart, but rather a simple conceptual framework to illustrate appropriate relationships and procedures. He is quick to point out that the following chart is only for illustration and serves no formal organizational purpose.

The chart is a section of a hypothetical lattice for a plant. The entire lattice would include the names of all the associates along both axes. At Gore Associates all employees are associates. Each person in the lattice interacts directly with every other person. There are no intermediaries. Other specific attributes of the lattice organization include:

No fixed or assigned authority

Sponsors, not bosses

Natural leadership defined by followership

THE LATTICE ORGANIZATION

	A	B	C	D	E	
A						A is Al
B						B is Bob
C						C is Cora
D						D is Dave
E						E is Eva

Diagram 1 The lattice organization.

NEW ORGANIZATIONAL STRUCTURES

Person-to-person communication

Objectives set by those who "must make them happen"

Tasks and functions organized through commitments

The structure within the lattice (which is not indicated on the chart) is complex and evolves from interpersonal interactions, self-commitment to group-known responsibilities, natural leadership, and group-imposed discipline.

Special teams evolve within the lattice structure, usually led by someone particularly competent in the discipline or activity of the team. A particular individual may participate in several such teams and may even have a leadership role in one or more of them. These multiparticipant people serve an important liaison function and are often involved in the planning and coordination of projects requiring a number of different teams.

Gore believes that every successful organization has a lattice organization that underlies the facade of authoritarian hierarchy, and it is through these lattice organizations that things get done. He thinks that most of us delight in "going around" the formal procedures and doing things the straightforward and easy way. Bill also thinks that although the simplicity and order of an authoritarian management style make it particularly attractive, it results in a distinct loss of individual freedom and creative growth, values he personally prizes.

There are no corporate staff groups at Gore making decisions that impose on the freedom of individual plant operations. Each plant operates independently, making decisions at the plant level that would in more formal systems be corporate decisions. However, there is a great deal of cooperation among plants just as there is within the plant.

There is a strong psychological ownership of the firm by the associates through the commitment that the lattice organization encourages, and there is also a complementary financial ownership. All Gore Associates participate in two profit-sharing plans. One of these is a twice-a-year distribution of 15% of company profits. The second is an ASOP (Associates' stock ownership plan) in which company stock equivalent to 15% of an associate's annual income is placed in a retirement fund. The Gore family and the associates together own 90% of the stock of the privately held corporation.

It is obvious that there are major differences in the way Gore Associates is managed compared with a more traditionally managed company. These differences are not so much in actual operational functions but rather in the reliance on internal (inside the individual) controls rather than external rules and procedures, individual trust and respect, freedom to innovate, person-to-person communication, no fixed or assigned authority (natural leadership), and objectives set and organized by commitments of those who must make them happen.

The Quality System in the "Lattice" Structure

The functions that are performed at one of Gore's plants are what might be expected at any excellently managed plant. First, everyone is responsible for the quality of the product they make. This total quality system is achieved in part by complete communication and cooperation. Associate Ray Scott at one of the wire and cable division plants observes, "Everyone plays a key role—working together as a team, not as individuals. Problem solving involves all employees. They get all the disciplines together, manufacturing, quality, and engineering, and the suggestions from operators are great." Ray's title, if Gore Associates had titles, would be quality control manager.

Another important aspect of the total quality system is a thorough initial training program followed by approximately 6 weeks working closely with an experienced associate. This process is closely monitored by the new associate's start-up sponsor for the first 3 months. This ensures that the associate really knows the products, process, and overall system. Inspection associates are shown how the products they are inspecting are made in the manufacturing process, and manufacturing associates similarly understand how and why they are tested. All associates are also familiar with the products' actual application in the customer's plant. Each associate receives bulletins and flyers that describe

NEW ORGANIZATIONAL STRUCTURES

each customer and the customer's use of Gore's products. In Ray's plant there is a large banner about 50 ft long, visible to all, that says, "WHO'S THE BOSS?"—and includes the company names and logos of all of Gore's customers in the wire and cable industry.

There are also both familiar and state-of-the-art quality tools and methods in use at Gore. There is a quality manual, which is reviewed and revised periodically. There are in-process controls for "instant feedback" on the operation. Quality audits—formal quality-assurance surveys—are performed on major suppliers typically once a year. Both incoming inspection and final-process inspection are carried out, and as many as one-third of the hourly associates are involved in some type of quality-control work. All production is 100% tested before shipping, and products are expected to be 100% defect free.

In the state-of-the-art category, Gore Associates use laser gages, microscopes interfaced with digitized video monitors, computer-aided measurement systems, and a high level of statistical process control. Shanti Mekta, another associate with Ray Scott at a wire and cable plant, is an expert in statistical methodology. He provides sophisticated statistical analyses and designs experiments and process capability studies. It is easy to see why Gore is well known to it customers as a "high-quality house."

The Primary Goals

Gore believes that the productivity of the small plants using the "lattice" management philosophy is probably double that of an average manufacturing work force. With high quality, exceptional productivity, sales that double every two and a half years, and new products generated at an astonishing rate, Gore looks like a first-class money-making operation. However, Bill Gore is quick to point out that although money is important, it isn't everything. "One of the most important objectives we have is to make money." Making money, according to Bill, means "that our customers approve of what we are doing, are applauding our efforts, and that we are filling a need." But he adds, "The other key is to have fun. By that I mean to learn and make progress, and to get a feeling of satisfaction from your accomplishments. You can't make money without having fun." Those are the two primary goals at Gore—to make money and to have fun.

And how do the associates feel about them? Ray Scott agrees thoroughly. "We really believe in having fun. My enthusiasm today is the same as it was 7½ years ago [when he joined Gore]. I love to get up in the morning and go to work." And what does Bill Gore think? "I think my associates are changing the world." He just may be right.

Selected Readings

Classless capitalists, *Forbes*, May 9, 1983.
The Lattice Organization—A Philosophy of Enterprise, an internal publication of W. L. Gore & Associates, Inc., revised April 1983.
The lattice of success, *Industry Week*, July 29, 1975.
Teflon stretches out toward a bigger market, *Business Week*, May 10, 1976.
The Un-Manager, *INC.*, August 1982.
View from the top, *CHEMTECH*, April 1981.
Wilbert L. Gore, *Industry Week*, Oct. 17, 1983.

Books

Levering, Robert, Moskowitz, Milton, and Katz, Michael, *The 100 Best Companies to Work for in America*, Plume, New York, 1984.
Naisbitt, John, and Aburdene, Partricia, *Re-Inventing the Corporation*, Warner Books, 1985.
Peters, Thomas J. and Austin, Nancy, *A Passion for Excellence— The Leadership Difference*, Random House, New York, 1985.
Pinchot, Gifford III, *Intrapreneuring*, Harper and Row, 1985.

Common Themes from Case Studies

Organizational Structure

It is in this area that differences between our case studies and traditional hierarchical organizations are most apparent.

Of the four cases, two, Gore Associates and People Express, have no formal organization chart. DEC Enfield has a very simplified, inverted chart based on groups rather than individuals. Chrysler Sterling Heights has a more traditional hierarchical structure (not available at the time of publication). Furthermore, neither People Express nor Gore Associates use job titles, thus eliminating the likelihood of organizing along functional lines. Another indication of reduced structure is the union contract of Chrysler, down from 300 to 30 pages. Gore particularly avoids the one man-one boss concept of traditional hierarchies by having three sponsors for each associate. The starting sponsor, the advocate sponsor, and the pay sponsor. And none of these would hold a position of immediate authority over the individual. Except for Chrysler, there is little or no reliance on formal job descriptions, another classic element of organization structure. And even at Chrysler, the roles of the lowest three levels have been radically redefined. Job categories of the hourly level have been drastically reduced, the foreman's job has been significantly redefined, and the level of general foreman has been essentially eliminated in favor of the unit manager.

What has replaced the formal elements of structure is a vastly increased reliance on the team, task force, or work group with its clearly defined sense of mission or purpose and a personal commitment on the part of the group members. Bill Gore put it very nicely, "Commitment, not control" is the key to exceptional results.

A further structural characteristic of our cases is a strong commitment to a relatively small unit of operation. Gore Associates limits plant size to around 150 employees, and DEC Enfield employs 180. Even the large Chrysler Sterling Heights plant places primary reliance on the unit manager whose personnel complement is less than 200. And People Express has similarly organized around aircraft types to keep the relevant part of the organization small. The common denominator of these small units is human understanding and comprehension rather than the economies of scale associated with the traditional hierarchical organizations.

Leadership Style

One of the most obvious features of our four cases is the leadership style of the founders, in the case of Gore Associates and People Express, and the plant managers, in the case of DEC Enfield and Chrysler Sterling Heights.

For these individuals the radical differences of the new organizational structures are simply extensions of their own values and beliefs. These values include a fundamental belief in the importance of people, not just as primary resources for organizational goals, but in a very real sense as the primary organizational goal itself. Donald Burr's comment on the primacy of the employee over the customer is a good example.

This basic belief in people among the top executives of our case studies is an externalization of their basic belief in themselves. These leaders have enormous confidence in themselves and in their organizations. This confidence reflects a high level of self-trust and the corresponding ability to trust others. Furthermore, the high level of trust is exemplified in the specific avoidance of punishing mistakes. These leaders expect mistakes as the evidence of progress and learning and have used them as opportunities rather than occasions for punishment.

Another obvious characteristic of the key leaders in our case studies is their willingness, indeed enthusiasm, for communicating with their employees or associates. This takes place in a variety of ways—personally training new employees like Donald Burr of People Express, answering questions from the top of a cafeteria table in town hall meetings like "Dur" Roller of Chrysler Sterling Heights, trying out thoughts and ideas for public speeches by circulating them to all associates as does Bill Gore, or simply being an exemplar of management by walking around (MBWA) as is Bruce Dillingham of DEC Enfield.

These key leaders are not simply skilled managers. They are rather cultural exemplars and role models. They are, in the words of Warren Bennis, "leaders who do the right things rather than managers who do things right" (Bennis and Nanus, 1985).

Innovation

Several aspects of innovation characterize the four cases. In all of them there is the sense in which the effort itself was from its inception seen as innovative. Furthermore, all the participants involved in each of these organizations see themselves as joining a pioneering effort. To see oneself as a pioneer or innovator then becomes a selection criterion either explicitly or implicitly.

The most obvious sphere of innovation is in the character of relationships between the employees and managers or among the associates as in the case of Gore Associates. The organizational structures and leadership styles are particularly novel, as has already been pointed out.

Another aspect of innovation is reflected in the physical operations of the various organizations studied. The technology is in most cases state of the art or was when the operation was launched. This is particularly obvious in the case of Chrysler Sterling Heights. It is also important to note that the innovations in technology are designed to serve the needs of the employees or associates rather than to displace them. Again, Chrysler Sterling Heights is an example of this approach.

A final aspect of innovation is the extent to which it can be sustained. All organizations at their inception have something of this characteristic although our particular cases had a great deal of it. However, over time, the intensity associated with a pioneering and innovative effort typically begins to wane. Gore Associates is particularly instructive on this point since it has grown through infancy and adolescence into some stage of maturity. It would appear that the creation and spinoff of new products at Gore Associates provides for the continuation of this innovative spirit in terms of the organization as a whole, although how older plants in the system fare in this regard is not altogether clear. The other three cases, DEC Enfield, People Express, and Chrysler Sterling Heights, are too new to tell.

Communications

There are several characteristics of communications in our case studies that are worth noting. First, there is an enormous amount of it. It goes on everywhere, at all times, and without end. Second, the overall character is more fluid in that communication seems to link all parts of the organization on an immediate-access basis rather than through the hierarchical chain of command. This is particularly obvious at Gore Associates. Third, the communications are relatively free from organizational constraints in terms of either what can be communicated or with whom communications can take place. The classification of information as confidential or restrictions on a "need-to-know" basis are conspicuously absent. Fourth, there is a sense in which communication is broadly rather than narrowly defined. Everyone is regularly updated, sometimes formally, sometimes informally, on the situation of the organization as a whole. This can occur in novel ways as with closed-circuit video systems at People Express and Chrysler Sterling Heights. And the variety of communication elements is richer, including formal group meetings and individual meetings, informal after-hours sessions, closed-circuit TV, and newsletters. And there is less reliance on printed manuals and memos as the primary means. Finally, there is the sense in which communication is holistic. The various plants and organizations made no attempt to restrict communication to purely organizational matters. Communication is inclusive of feelings and personal, non-job-related elements.

Fun

The concept of fun as a significant organizational objective or principle will strike many as being too superficial. In the first place, it does not say what is to be accomplished. And in the second place, words like dedication and commitment seem to better reflect the serious nature of the enterprises to which we belong. That "fun" shows up as one of two guiding principles at Gore Associates and is included along with 15 other values at DEC Enfield, is, however, significant. It is also safe to say that if one were to ask the question "Is it fun to work here?" the typical employee or associate in all four of our case studies would answer with a resounding "yes." For those who find the word fun still too superficial, the word "joy" has been used by the Japanese (as in the "five joys of work"), and "passion" is coming into increasing vogue through the efforts of Peters and Austin in their current bestseller, *A Passion for Excellence* (1985). Whether it is fun, joy, or passion, a very human, positive, and energizing character is associated with the functioning of the organization. And it is this character which typifies all of our case studies.

Underlying this experience of work as fun is the attitude and behavior of the key leaders in our case studies, Donald Burr, Bill Gore, "Dur" Roller, and Bruce Dillingham. These leaders would affirm with Harry Levinson and Stuart Rosenthal (1984) that "leadership is a form of play, [and that] as play, leads to triumphs of the human spirit."

Quality Systems

All of our case studies can be characterized by high quality. Product and service standards are rigorous. These are attested to by customers and vendors alike. However, except in the case of Chrysler Sterling Heights, there does not seem to be a particularly strong emphasis on high-technology innovations to achieve this level of quality. There is instead a strong reliance on the everyday actions of all employees and managers to accomplish these results. Although the basic knowledge and skills are there as a result of training, quality seems more of an attitude than a technology.

The role of the quality professional is relatively muted. Of the four cases, in only one, Chrysler Sterling Heights, do we find a strong emphasis on the quality professional in terms of clearly defined roles, responsibilities, and departmental activities. Even here, however, there is significantly greater emphasis on the hourly personnel's responsibility for quality than one would find in comparable auto assembly plants. At the other end of the spectrum, People Express, a firm with some 4000 employees, has no one with a role specifically designated to deal exclusively with issues of quality and reliability. Specific quality functions are carried out but are parts of the jobs of about 60 maintenance managers in the case of the aircraft and the remaining 4000 customer service managers, flight managers, team managers, and general managers in the case of the passengers or customers. Clearly, quality in terms of the customers' perceptions is crucial to the success of an airline, and yet by making it no one's specific responsibility at People Express, it has been made everyone's general responsibility.

The situation is similar at Gore Associates and DEC Enfield. In these plants there is a quality presence, but it is not departmentalized and tightly defined. There are several quality professionals at DEC Enfield, but they do not appear as such on the novel organizational chart, nor do they have quality job titles even though they carry out many of the typcial functions of a quality professional. At Gore Associates, a third of the employees are directly involved with testing and other quality procedures, but only a relative handful of the 4400 employees have full-time professional responsibilities for quality. There is no corporate quality function, and there are no titles, quality or other, at Gore Associates, further reducing the association of quality with a particular job or individual. There is also a refreshing absence of job stress among those professionals in our case studies who do have specific quality-oriented job responsibilities. Teaching and coaching have replaced measuring and policing as principal activities.

A New Organization Form?

It would be relatively easy to make the case that the firms we have examined in our studies might properly be described by the organic or process organizational form described in an earlier section of the chapter. Indeed, most organizational theorists today would do so, and Chrysler Sterling Heights probably does fit this characterization.

There is an alternative perspective, however, which is worth considering. The alternative rests on the possibility that the new organizational forms exemplified by our case studies are not simply adaptations of the older mechanistic-bureaucratic organizational structure to accommodate an increasing awareness of and emphasis on the human element, but rather the emergence of a radically new different form of organization altogether. The primary difference between the new organizational form and the older one is that in the older form human beings are seen as resources for attaining organizational objectives. Even in the organic or process organizational form, people are still human resources even though they have moved to the top of the list.

In the newly emerging organization, if indeed it is that, the organization becomes the resource, perhaps even the most valuable resource, for human beings to attain their individual and collective objectives. Dr. Hans Von Beinum, Executive Director of the Ontario Quality of Working Life Center, makes this point when he observes that the current state of flux in organizations is an example of a figure-ground shift in which attention is shifting from the organization as "figure" with individuals as "ground" to the individuals as "figure" with the organization as "ground." Although this analysis loses some of the genuine novelty associated with a radically new type of organization, it serves to make the point.

We do not have the luxury of 20/20 hindsight to be able to make the assertion unequivocally that we are witnessing the emergence of such a new organizational form. However, in the following section we will examine the case for the emergence of a new paradigm and its implications for organizations. The jury, however, is still out, and the premise of a new organizational form is still speculative.

The New Paradigm

As the reader will note, this section deals with concepts that at first glance seem unrelated to the subject matter. What have perceptions of reality, clockwork universes, quantum physics, and consciousness to do with organizational structures and quality systems? A frequent reaction among those with whom we discussed the material was that we had gone off the deep end. However, in a book such as this, which is a compilation of the state of the art in human resource theory and practice, particularly as they relate to quality professionals, there seems room, indeed even the need, for a little serious mind stretching. Nor is it mind stretching simply for the exercise, valuable though this may be. There is, in our opinion, a tendency on the part of society to see change in terms of trends. On the rare occasions when a profound shift is in the process of occurring, the observable features of the change tend to be seen as a continuation of older trends. An overview of a new paradigm will set the stage for a new perspective.

It is simply not possible in the short space allotted in this chapter to give more than the briefest overview of an emerging new paradigm which has radical and profound implications for all of society as well as our particular interest in organizational structure and quality systems. The manifestations of this paradigm shift are occurring essentially on two levels. One is the level of fundamentally new knowledge. This is the level of the work of theoreticians in quantum mechanics and other esoteric realms of the natural sciences to which we may add the more controversial work in the newly established cognitive and noetic sciences, dedicated to study of the human mind, and of consciousness itself.

The second level is the level of application and popularization. It is at this level that most of us gain some knowledge of the highly technical work going on at the level of fundamentally new knowledge. Frequently, however, the popular treatments lose sight of their more basic underpinnings. Consequently, the social and cultural changes heralded in *The Third Wave, The Greening of America, The Aquarian Conspiracy, The Change Masters, Megatrends, In Pursuit of Excellence, A Passion for Excellence, Re-Inventing the Corporation*, and other popular books at times miss the mark by superficial treatment. For example, to see the computer as a primary determinant of major cultural change is true but misses the more fundamental perspective from which the creativity that brought about the computer in the first place can be explored. The creative mental processes that brought the computer about can also render it obsolete and irrelevant.

Let us begin our overview with a brief exploration at the level of fundamentally new knowledge.

Perhaps the most useful framework in the exploration of the new paradigm is found in the work of Thomas Kuhn, a theoretical physicist and professor of philosophy at Massachusetts Institute of Technology. His meticulously crafted study of the nature of changes in the realm of scientific knowledge provides a way of understanding that has powerful implications not only for scientists but for virtually all aspects of society (Kuhn, 1962, 1970). Kuhn's observations on paradigms and paradigm shifts have provided insights to theoreticians and writers ranging from the most technical to popular works like *In Search of Excellence* (Peters and Waterman, 1982).

We are indebted to Kuhn for the profound observation, buttressed by broad and insightful inquiry, that the progress of scientific knowledge is not an unbroken history of incremental additions to the facts and theories associated with that body of knowledge. It is rather to be defined in terms of periodic revolutions in perspective among communities of scientists in which the entire constellation of beliefs, values, and techniques shared by that community gives way to a new constellation. This is the paradigm shift. Kuhn further notes the importance of exemplars, those solutions to a particular problem associated with the paradigm which are employed as models or examples and can replace explicit rules as a basis for the solution of other problems from the perspective of the new paradigm.

Of critical importance to Kuhn's thesis is that when paradigm shifts do occur, the members of that community in a very real sense begin to work in a different world. When the new paradigm is accepted, the data collected in the scientific enterprise shift to support the new paradigm. Kuhn notes that these paradigm shifts are more like conversion experiences than logical and rational accretions of new knowledge for the members of the scientific community involved. Nor do all members of a scientific community experience this conversion, as Max Planck noted with his famous observation that science progresses funeral by funeral.

Kuhn points out that the view of scientific progress based on a fixed reality in which only the scientists' interpretations vary is itself an "essential part of the philosophical paradigm initiated by Descartes and developed at the same time as Newtonian dynamics." Although his primary concern is in the area of natural sciences, he further notes that "today research in parts of philosophy, psychology, linguistics and even art history, all converge to suggest that the traditional (Cartesian/Newtonian) paradigm is somehow askew."

What Kuhn is suggesting is, very simply, that when in the pursuit of scientific knowledge anomalies arise that defy interpretation by the current paradigm, it is the belief system of the scientific community which changes to create a new paradigm and a new reality. Kuhn shifts the focus from the external reality as determined by the senses to the arena of the beliefs, values, and techniques of the scientists themselves as creators of that reality.

In a previous section of this chapter the extent to which the Cartesian/Newtonian paradigm has affected all aspects of our society was noted. Following the thinking of Kuhn, it is useful to explore briefly the nature of the paradigm shift in that domain of science from which we currently draw our understanding of physical reality, notably physics itself.

In the first quarter of the twentieth century the new quantim mechanics of Bohr, Heisenberg, and other pioneers had effectively silenced the claims of physicists operating in the Cartesian/Newtonian paradigm to be able to completely describe physical reality. At the subatomic level, the world of rocks, trees, and people fades into an unmeasurable strangeness. In the intervening 60 years the strangeness has grown with the contributions of more recent physicists, Wheeler, Everett, Wigner, Bell, Stapp, Fehnmann, and others.

An excellent treatment of these strange new ways of conceptualizing our familiar world is given by Briggs and Peat (1984). With regard to Kuhn they observe:

> Kuhn's analysis of scientific history strips us of the traditional preconception that science is objective. Does that

mean that it's subjective? ("It's all in our minds?") It can't be. . . . But if science is neither objective [nor] subjective what is it?

They go on to suggest metaphorically that "we now stick our heads out into a fog-shrouded landscape—shimmering, infinitely subtle, and new" and that in this new arena the very laws of nature change with the beliefs associated with a new paradigm and are relative to the observations of the exploring scientists. This reflection, in which the observer is in some strange way the observed, they describe as the "looking-glass universe," also the title of their book.

Briggs and Peat provide an excellent overview of the work of Einstein in relativity; Bohr, Heisenberg, and Schrödinger in quantum physics; Bohn's implicate and explicate orders and the holomovement; the dissipative structures, coevolution and autopoiesis of Prigogine, Jantsch, Maturana, Varela, and Uribe; Scheldrake's morphogenetic field and theory of formative causation; and Pribram's holographic brain. These are all interrelated aspects of inquiry and exploration underlying a paradigm shift that may be every bit as all-encompassing and profound as the one launched by Copernicus, Descartes, and Newton. Briggs and Peat also provide an excellent bibliography of some 69 books and major articles, the majority of which are written for the layman.

While Briggs and Peat summarize the work of scientists through their "looking-glass" framework, Nick Herbert (1985) has written a highly readable summary of the current state of quantum physics itself. If the clockwork universe of Newton is no longer relevant, what conceptualization of reality has taken its place? The answer, according to physicist and author Nick Herbert, is that there is not one, but eight current versions of reality that meet the requirements of quantum physics, all of which are, by everyday standards, preposterous.

These range from the simple statement that there is no deep reality, i.e., everyday phenomena spring from an utterly different and unknowable kind of being (Copenhagen Convention, 1925); to Everett's "many worlds hypothesis," in which reality consists of an infinite and steadily expanding number of parallel universes in which all possible futures really happen; to the position favored by John Von Neumann and Nobel Laureate Eugene Wigner that reality is created by the act of conscious observation. According to Von Neumann's proof, if quantum theory is correct (and no physicist of any reputation today would say it is not) the world cannot be made of ordinary objects. Von Neumann postulated that physical objects would have no measurable attributes if a conscious observer were not watching them.

Fred Alan Wolf picks up this theme in his very readable *The Quantum Leap* (Wolf, 1981). He builds on Wigner's observation that "it is not possible to formulate the laws of quantum mechanics in a fully consistent way without reference to consciousness. . . . It will remain remarkable in whatever way our future concepts may develop, that the very study of the external world led to the conclusion that the content of the consciousness is an ultimate reality."

Author Nick Herbert notes that physicists propose these versions of reality as serious pictures of the world we live in. That these versions are so different, some mutually exclusive, and yet all meet the mathematical requirements of quantum physics is a commentary on both our state of knowledge and its ultimate strangeness. Herbert further observes that no one really knows how the world will seem 100 years from now. John Wheeler, a world-class physicist actively involved in determining the nature of quantum reality, describes the future of this effort in terms of magic rather than machinery.

The vast majority of us have been relatively unaware of this major change in the fundamental understanding of the way the world is. Only in the last 10 years have Fritjof Capra (1975), Gary Zukav (1979), Paul Davies (1983), Fred Wolf (1981, 1984), Heinz Pagels (1983), Briggs and Peat (1984), Alex Confort (1984), and others provided popularized versions of the quantum reality research that has taken place since 1925.

The paradigm shift in physics is, because of the nature of the tightly defined community of physicists, highly visible and relatively easy to observe. Paradigm shifts in society in general are more difficult to apprehend because of the extreme diversity of the participants, notably everyone. However, the paradigm shift in physics will have profound implications for a paradigm shift in society because it deals with both the fundamental nature of reality itself and, more important, our way of learning about reality. The new paradigm in physics indicates that the fundamental reality underlying the ordinary reality that we experience is of a different order and lies outside of and apart from our ability to perceive it by our senses or any extension of our senses through scientific apparatus. Furthermore, and more important, the rational, logical, reductionist methods of physics are of little or no value in comprehending this underlying reality, thus opening the door to new approaches centered not so much on technology but rather on the human mind and consciousness itself. It is of more than passing interest to note that a great many of those who ushered the quantum revolution into physics, notably Planck, Heisenberg, Schrödinger, Einstein, DeBroglie, Jeans, Pauli, and Eddington, were firm believers in a mystical conception of ultimate reality and equally firm in their belief that such knowledge was outside the realm of physics (Wilber, 1984).

As the new paradigm takes shape in society, it is marked by new humanistic values. As noted in a previous section, these are initially defined from the perspective of the older paradigm. However, the new paradigm is beginning to legitimize its own knowledge and exploration. The new fields of cognitive and noetic sciences, barely 10 years old, are beginning to provide a serious forum for explorations in consciousness and paranormal phenomena (Targ and Harary, 1984). The new paradigm is also having a considerable impact on psychology and psychiatry (Grof, 1985). Contrary to the older tradition in which the practice of science was neutral in terms of human values, the new paradigm builds these values into the quest for knowledge itself. This would have been impossible at the turn of the century (and even more recently) while the claim of the older Cartesian/Newtonian paradigm to fully explain all of reality from the mechanistic perspective held sway.

It has been important to paint in broad brush but unmistakable strokes the radical shift in the way physicists and natural scientists are looking at reality because the freedom to reconceptualize that this shift has provided to the community of scientists has yet to be fully understood by the rest of society. Given the all-encompassing experience of society with the older Cartesian/Newtonian paradigm in which man was simply an observer in a universe beyond his control and the possibilities of the new paradigm in which reality is a matter of man's conscious creation, it seems fair to say that the various revolutions described by the popular writers are knowingly or unknowingly built on a substantial foundation. Furthermore, if the new paradigm and infant neotic sciences have an impact anywhere near as far reaching as the older one, the prospects are absolutely breathtaking. Willis Harman, professor of engineering-economic systems at Stanford University, associate director at SRI International, and president of the Institute of Noetic Sciences, describes the implications of this new paradigm as a new Copernican revolution. He observes that "the implications of a 'consciousness-produces-reality' conceptualization are so profound and far reaching, not only for physics, but metaphysics that one can easily imagine all institutions of society being profoundly affected" (Harman and Rheingold, 1984).

John Gowan (1977) compares the importance of the coming paradigm shift in society with the shift that occurred some 9000 years ago when mankind moved from nomadic hunting to agriculture. Until that shift, people simply lived off of plants that were growing wild and animals. Gowan notes that until today mankind has similarly lived of of creativity "in the wild." The new paradigm frees us of the mechanistic constraints imposed by the older paradigm so that creativity can now be cultivated. He believes that "domesticated" creativity will bring about "a golden age. . . such as the world has never seen and . . . [that] it will occur early in the twenty-first century."

The emergence of the new paradigm is taking shape in the field of organization theory with the rise of what John Adams describes as organizational transformation. His formulation for this new arena builds on six themes: vision, new perspectives, culture and processes, leadership, performance excellence, and human empowment (Adams, 1984). Another organization researcher, Dr. Jack Gibb, whose efforts are consistent with this new organizational focus, provides the following comparison or organizational characteristics (Gibb, 1985):

Organizational Characteristics

Traditional/mechanistic (old paradigm)	Holistic/autogenic (new paradigm)
1. External motivation by reward persuasion and punishment	1. Internal motivation through identification with the organization's overarching mission
2. Competition, politics, and segmentation	2. Collaborative teams that grow out of mission; autogenic unity
3. Training, manipulation, and intervention	3. Orientation toward search, exploration, venture; new forms of creative management and structure
4. Defensiveness, use of techniques, rebelliousness	4. Dedication to the work itself artistry
5. Controls and formal hierarchy	5. Simple organic form of management and organization that flow out of the mission
6. Bottom-line efficiency	6. Internal "vision" that nurtures universal values
7. Role expectations and job descriptions	7. A deep trust in people with self-regulation occurring throughout the system

One notes that the cases described earlier in this chapter seem to have more in common with Bradford's themes of organization transformation and Gibb's characteristics of the holistic/autogenic organization than the mechanistic/rational/bureaucratic model described earlier.

The importance of "reinventing the corporation" is the central theme and title of a book by John Naisbitt and Patricia Aburdene

(1985). Naisbitt and Aburdene use examples of new companies (including Gore Associates and People Express) that have reinvented themselves as a result of the confluence of the new humanistic values and economic necessity. Among their major premises are that work should be fun—"a spiritual and mental high"—and that intuition and vision will be critical characteristics of leadership (even taught in business schools). Naisbitt and Aburdene have tried to capture the essence of Kuhn's paradigm shift in the reinvented corporation. Therefore, they have not elected to remodel it or modify it but to radically reconceptualize it.

Let us now shift our attention and look at the implications this new paradigm has for quality systems and the quality profession.

A New Perspective on Quality

From the older Cartesian/Newtonia paradigm or mechanistic perspective, quality can be understood as "conformance with specifications." From the process or organic perspective described in an earlier section, quality can be understood as "fitness for use" or "customer satisfaction." From the newly emerging paradigm or holistic perspective, "quality is a state of mind" or "quality puts meaning into work." It is not useful to debate the correctness of these various perspectives. They are not only equally valid within their various frames of reference, they are interactive. Thus, "quality as a state of mind" which "puts meaning into work" underlies the quality professional's efforts to develop new measuring techniques and statistical methodologies which enable operators to achieve closer conformance with specifications and, in turn, provide greater satisfaction to the customers. This brings us full circle and enhances satisfaction, meaning, and the quality of life for the quality professional. It is most useful to think of quality as a set of nested, interactive domains, each of which influences and is influenced by the other simultaneously.

In the present situation, the mechanistic, "conformance with specifications" perspective is, perhaps, most common among quality professionals. There is, however, little debate on the appropriateness of the newer process perspective, "fitness for use" or "customer satisfaction." The holistic perspective provides a legitimacy for both of the other perspectives while grounding them in the fundamental values held by all the participants—quality professionals, managers, workers, customers, and others—by meeting their individual needs for a sense of worth, value, and meaning in their lives.

From the perspective of the new paradigm, quality, as we think of it related to goods and services, is an expression of the quality of the lives of those who create those goods and services. Thus, quality of work life, as a particular subset of the quality of life in general, is not an interesting parallel phenomenon to product or service quality; it is the underlying fabric on which the design of product and service quality is expressed. Nor is quality of work life simply a collection of techniques and training programs, such as quality circles, important as these are. Rather it is a way of understanding individuals in their working environments such that these individuals on their own volition, individually and collectively, will create an environment commensurate with the best they know and will choose to further develop themselves in ways that will enhance their own skills, abilities, and well-being as well as society in general and the company in particular. In short, people can be trusted to create quality goods and quality services. They do not have to be coerced or exceptionally rewarded for their efforts. However, they must see themselves as being able to make creative contributions—to make real differences in the world.

To the extent that work is devoid of meaning and value for those who do it, quality will suffer. Emphasis on new technology such as robotics or sophisticated approaches to quality such as Taguchi's will not substitute. An example of this is the defense industry. In World War II, building munitions, aircraft, and the like had real meaning and value for those involved. As a result, quality was important, new technology and quality techniques blossomed, and "Rosie the Riveter" turned out high-quality work.

Today there is a different set of values. Products and services supplied by defense contractors to the federal government are not uniformly characterized by the quality and reliability available from today's vastly improved quality technology. Nor will wrangling over Mil-Specs and a proliferation of government inspectors fundamentally improve the situation. Until the work itself provides a deep sense of purpose and meaning to those involved, quality issues will be a continuing problem.

The auto industry has similarly discovered this problem. And it is no accident that improvements in technology are combined with quality circles, employee involvement, sociotech approaches, participative management, and other techniques designed to give employees at all levels a greater sense of purpose and meaning. The Chrysler Sterling Heights plant is an excellent case in point.

A trenchant commentary from this new perspective on the relevance of the founding fathers and more articulate spokesmen for quality control to the broader issue of quality can be found in this comment of Peters and Austin in their current best seller *A Passion For Excellence* (1985).

> We recommend no texts on quality as such: our subject, after all, is not quality per se but its relationship to leadership. Quality itself will always be in the eye of the beholder. Thus the most constructive book on the topic for both of us continues to be Robert Pirsig's *Zen and the Art of Motorcycle Maintenance* (Morrow, 1974).

It may be that Peters and Austin are unaware that Shewhart, Juran, Deming, Feigenbaum, Crosby, and others are very much concerned with the relationship of quality to leadership. It seems more likely, however, that they do not find much passion or contribution to an individual's personal sense of worth, value, or meaning in the works of these authors.

We do not wish to negate the contributions of these individuals, but rather to observe that although their particular quest for excellence in the field of quality gave a full measure of meaning and purpose to their own lives, this aspect was and still is largely overlooked. The focus was on the techniques and technologies rather than personal values and meaning. As we gain understanding of the inseparability of the usefulness of technique from the meaningfulness of the technique to the user, we will rekindle the excitement and enthusiasm these pioneers brought to the quality profession.

Thomas Kuhn observed that the paradigm or perspective adopted by a scientific discipline (he referred specifically to physics) can isolate that group from socially important problems when these cannot be stated in terms of the conceptual and instrumental tools the paradigm supplies. It is precisely this challenge which faces the quality profession today. Quality professionals are confronted with a need to develop this new and larger perspective on quality technology in a way in which both the socially and technically important quality problems can be seen as responding to the application of this technology. Quality technology and its associated practices must include (1) the theoretical considerations, techniques, and applications as its practitioners currently define them; (2) the more subjective aspects of quality as determined by the users of the goods and services; and (3) the quality of life, sense of meaning and value, and feeling of personal worth, competence, and influence on the part of all organizational participants, quality professionals, and others alike. Without a reconceptualization of quality technology in which the second and third perspectives are as fundamental as the first, quality professionals will increasingly find the arena in which they pursue their efforts to be defined by others.

The success of this endeavor is by no means clear. That we will have quality is beyond question. Whether it will be seen as the particular venue of quality professionals, or perhaps become a more broadly characterized aspect of the organization under the guidance of others, is an open question. The case studies in this chapter suggest the latter, perhaps because the quality profession has yet to espouse the larger aspects of quality and develop an approach, theory, and practice to accommodate these less familiar dimensions.

What makes this challenge peculiarly succinct in the arena of quality technology is that in no other technological discipline is the success of that discipline so intimately involved with everyone in the organization. Quality is not so much the result of the practice of the discipline as recorded in quality control textbooks as it is the result of the attitudes of all the organizational participants. Robert Gavin, Chairman of Motorola, has said, "people are the ultimate high technology." They are also the ultimate quality.

It is the hope of the authors of this book that it contains the information, insights, and encouragement for quality professionals to expand their vision and keep the quality profession at the cutting edge of the reawakening of society to the importance of quality in all its aspects. It is a worthy challenge.

Bibliography

Argyris, Chris, *Integrating the Individual and the Organization*, Wiley, New York, 1964.

Bennis, Warren, *Changing Organizations*, McGraw-Hill, New York, 1966.

Bennis, Warren, and Nanus, Burt, *Leaders—The Strategies for Taking Charge*, Harper & Row, 1985.

Bennis, W. C., and Schein, E. H., *Personal and Organizational Change Through Group Methods*, Wiley, New York, 1965.

Briggs, John P., and Peat, F. David, *Looking Glass Universe—The Emerging Science of Wholeness*, Simon and Schuster, New York, 1984.

Burns, Thomas, and Stalker, G. M., *The Management of Innovation*, Tavistock Institute, London, 1961.

Capra, Fritjof, *The Tao of Physics*, Bantam Books, New York, 1975.

Comfort, Alex, *Reality and Empathy—Physics, Mind and Science in the 21st Century*, State University of New York Press, 1984.

Davies, Paul, *God and the New Physics*, Simon and Schuster, New York, 1983.

Emery, F. E., and Trist, E. L., *Towards a Social Ecology*, Plenum Press, London, 1973.

Gibb, Jack R., *Self Regulation*, 1985 (publication pending).

Gibson, Cyrus E., *Managing Organizational Behavior*, Richard D. Irwin, 1980.

Ginsberg, Eli, and Vojta, George, *Beyond Human Scale: The Large Corporation at Risk*, Basic Books, New York, 1985.
Gowan, John C., Some thoughts on the development of creativity, *Journal of Creative Behavior*, Vol. 11, No. 2, 1977.
Grof, Stanislav, *Beyond the Brain—Birth, Death and Transcendence in Psychotherapy*, State University of New York Press, 1985.
Harman, Willis, and Rheingold, Howard, *Higher Creativity—Liberating Unconscious for Breakthrough Insights*, Tarcher, Los Angeles, 1984.
Hayes, Glenn E., and Romig, Harry G., *Modern Quality Control*, rev. ed., Glencoe Publishing, 1982.
Herbert, Nick, *Quantum Reality—Beyond the New Physics*, Anchor Press/Doubleday, 1985.
Herbert, Theodore T., *Dimensions of Organizational Behavior*, 2nd ed., Macmillan, New York, 1981.
Herzberg, Frederick, *Work and the Nature of Man*, World Publishing Co., Cleveland, 1966.
Juran, J. M., Ed. in Chief, Gryna, Frank M., Jr., and Bingham, M. S., Jr., Associate Ed., *Quality Control Handbook*, 3rd ed., McGraw-Hill, New York, 1974.
Kuhn, Thomas S., *The Structure of Scientific Revolutions*, 2nd ed., University of Chicago Press, Chicago, 1962, 1970.
Levinson, Harry, and Rosenthal, Stuart, *CEO: Corporate Leadership in Action*, Basic Books, New York, 1984.
Likert, Rensis, *New Patterns of Management*, McGraw-Hill, New York, 1961.
Likert, Rensis, *Managing the Human Organization*, McGraw-Hill, New York, 1967.
Maslow, Abraham, *Motivation and Personality*, Harper and Row, New York, 1954
McGregor, Douglas, *The Human Side of Enterprise*, McGraw-Hill, New York, 1960.
Murvis, Philip, Work in the 20th century, *ReVision*, Vol. 7, No. 2, Winter/Spring, 1984/85.
Naisbitt, John, and Aburdene, Patricia, *Reinventing the Corporation*, Warner Books, 1985.
Pagels, Heinz, *The Cosmic Code: Quantum Physics as the Language of Nature*, Bantam Books, New York, 1983.

Peters, Thomas, and Austin, Nancy, *A Passion for Excellence: The Leadership Difference*, Random House, New York, 1985.

Peters, Thomas I., and Waterman, Robert H., Jr., *In Search of Excellence—Lessons from America's Best Run Companies*, Harper and Row, 1982.

Pugh, D. E., Ed., *Organizational Theory—Selected Readings*, 2nd ed., Penguin Books, 1971, 1984.

Sashkin, Marshal, *An Overview of Ten Management and Organizational Theorists, The 1981 Handbook for Group Facilitators*, University Associates, San Diego, CA, 1981.

Schermerhorn, John R., Jr., Hunt, James G., and Osborn, Richard N., *Managing Organizational Behavior*, Wiley, New York, 1985.

Simon, H. A., *The New Science of Management Decision*, Harper and Row, 1960.

Targ, Russell, and Harary, Keith, *The Mind Race*, Villard Books, 1984.

Trist, Eric, *The Evolution of Socio-Technical Systems*, Ontario Quality of Working Life Centre, Toronto, Ontario, 1981.

Wilber, Ken, *Up From Eden—A Transpersonal View of Human Evolution*, Shambhala, 1983.

Wilber, Ken, Ed., *Quantum Questions—The Mystical Writings of the World's Great Physicists*, New Science Library, Boston, 1984.

Wolf, Fred Alan, *The Quantum Leap—The New Physics for Non-Scientists*, Harper and Row, 1981.

Wolf, Fred Alan, *Star Wave—Mind Consciousness and Quantum Physics*, Macmillan, New York, 1984.

Zukav, Gary, *The Dancing Wali Masters*, Bantam, New York, 1979.

Index

Acceptance sampling, 160-161
Algorithms, 152, 156
    statistical, 155
All salary work force, 10
Analysis of means (ANOM), 153,166
Argyris, Chris, 5
Artificial intelligence (AI), 152, 153-154
    human intelligence and, 155-156
Auditory systems, 57-62
    noise control, 60-61
    warning systems, 61-62

Autonomous work groups, 9

Bureaucratic organization
    work form, 206-211

Candidate specification sheet, 178
Change, preparation for, 15-48
    case study, 18-20
    communication, 43-45
    dealing with pressure, 25-28

[Change, preparation for]
  direct total participation (DTP), 22-24
  employee/management gap, 34-36
  evaluation—quality of work life survey, 32-34
  incentives, 38-39
  innovation, 39-43
  invisible organization, 31
  IQ triangle, 20-22
  organizational changes—integral management, 28-31
  planning, 28
  putting the factors together, 45-46
  quality policy, 24-25, 26
  training, 36-38
Chrysler Corporation—Sterling Heights assembly plant (case study), 226-233
  communications, 250
  innovation, 249
  leadership style, 248
  organizational structure, 247
  quality systems, 251
Communications
  in new organizational structures, 250
  participative management and, 143
  preparing for change and, 43-45
Companywide quality control (CWQC), 87-88

Computers, 156
  as heuristic tool, 167-169
  for human use, 67-72
  keyboard, 67-69
  software, 70-72
  video screens, 69-70
Construct validity, 165
Control charts, 153, 165-166

Dials, 55-57
Dickson, W. I., 211
Digital Equipment Corporation (case study), 219-226
  fun, 250
  leadership style, 248
  organizational structure, 247
  quality systems, 252
Direct Total Participation (DTP), 22-24
Displays, 55-57
Divisionalized organizational structure, 209-210

Elimination of time clocks, 9
Employee/management gap, preparation for change and, 34-36
Employee involvement, see Participative management
Employment interview, conducting, 179-181
Environment for success, 87
Exploratory data analysis (EDA), 153, 157

INDEX 271

External validity, 165

Fun in new organizational structure, 250

Gilbreth, Frank B., 140
Graphs, 158
Group motvation, leadership and management training and development and, 109-130

Herzberg, Frederick, 5, 141
Heuristics, 152, 153
   artificial intelligence and, 156
   computer and, 167-169
   statistical, 155
Human factors engineering, 49-75
   auditory systems, 57-62
      noise control, 60-61
      warning systems, 61-62
   computers for human use, 67-72
      keyboard, 67-69
      software, 70-72
      video screens, 69-70
   design of experiments, 72-74
   dials, scales, and displays, 55-57
   information presentation, 51-53
   printed materials, 53-55
   visual systems, 50-51
   work station designs, 62-67

[Human factors engineering]
   color, 66-67
   equipment location and design, 64-65
   seating, 63
   traffic patterns, 65-66
Human resources development, definition of, 9

Improved human resource application, means of achieving, 10-12
Improved quality (IQ) triangle, 20-22
Incentives, preparation for change and, 38-39
Information handling, 167
Information presentation, 51-53
Innovation
   in new organizational structures, 249
   preparation for change and, 39-43
Integral management, preparation for, change and, 28-31
Internal validity, 164

Job descriptions in quality selection system, 177-179
Job enrichment, 10
   participative management and, 147-148
Job specification in quality selection system, 177-178

Jones-Glaser Innovation Index (JGII), 41-43

Labor/management advisory board, 148-149
Leadership and management training and development, 91-137
  acquiring the skill, 95-100
  history of training and development, 97-100
  group motivational issues and performance outcomes, 109-130
  case histories, 115-130
  perceptual disparity, 112-115
  personal assessment scales, 112
  improvement through process control and breakthrough methods, 100-108
  motivational climate assessment, 105-109
  motivational climate factors, 103
  motivational system, 101-102
  perceptual process, 104-105
  self-improvement methods, 109
  nature of leadership and management, 92-95

Leadership style in new organizational structures, 248
Likert, Rensis, 6, 141, 212-213

McGregor, Douglas, 7, 141
Management commitment, participative management and, 142
Management motivation, 142
Maslow, Abraham, 7, 141, 212
Matrix organization, 211
May, Elton, 7-8, 141, 211
Mechanistics organizational form, 206-211
Morality, strategic quality planning and, 199
Motivational climate assessment, 105-109
Motivational climate factors, 103
Motivational climate scales, 109, 110
  for improvement of training and development, 115-130
Motivational system, 101-102
  perception as an integral part of, 104-105

New organizational structures, 203-268
  background, 204-205
  Chrysler Corporation (case study), 226-233

[New organizational structures]
  communications, 250
  innovation, 249
  leadership style, 248
  organizational structure, 247
  quality systems, 251
  development of the mechanistic or bureaucratic organizational form, 206-211
  development of the organic or process organizational form, 211-216
  Digital Equipment Corporation (case study), 219-226
  fun, 250
  leadership style, 248
  organizational structure, 247
  quality systems, 252
  history of quality systems, 216-218
  the new paradigm and, 253-262
  new perspective on quality, 262-266
  People Express (case study), 233-238
  communications, 250
  leadership style, 248
  organizational structure, 247
  quality systems, 251-252

[New organizational structures]
  W. L. Gore & Associates (case study), 238-246
  communications, 250
  fun, 250
  innovation, 249
  leadership style, 248
  organizational structure, 247
  quality systems, 252
New paradigm and its relationship to organizational structure and quality systems, 253-262
Noise control, 60-61
Nonalgorithmic statistics, 152

One-on-one, 145
Open door policy, 145
Opinion survey, 145
Organic organizational form, 211-216
Organizational development, 10
Ouchi, William, 7

Paradigm, new, and its relationship to organizational structures and quality systems, 253-262
Participative management, 9, 139-140
  background, 140-141

[Participative management]
  concepts, 141-142
  individual involvement processes, 145-146
  principles for implementation, 142-145
  team involvement processes, 146-149
People Express (case study), 233-238
  communications, 250
  leadership style, 248
  organizational structure, 247
  quality system, 251-252
Perception as an integral party of motivational system, 104-105
Perceptual disparity, 112-115
Performance management, 146
Personal assessment scales, 112
Pioneers in human resources development, 4-7
Preparation for change, 15-48
  case study, 18-20
  communication, 43-45
  dealing with pressure, 25-28
  direct total participation (DTP), 22-24
  employee/management gap, 34-36
  evaluation—quality of work life survey, 32-34
  incentives, 38-39
  innovation, 39-43

[Preparation for change]
  invisible organization, 31
  IQ triangle, 20-22
  organizational changes—integral management, 28-31
  planning, 28
  putting the factors together, 45-46
  quality policy, 24-25, 26
  training, 36-38
Pressure, dealing with, preparation for change and, 25-28
Printed materials, 53-55
Process organization form, 211-216
Productivity gainsharing, 10
  participative management and, 147

Quality
  the new paradigm and perspective on, 262-266
  statistics and, 154
  of work life, 9
  See also Strategic quality planning
Quality circles, 9
  participative management and, 146-147
  and performance, 77-89
  companywide quality control and quality circles, 87-88

[Quality circles]
    environment for success, 87
    major driving forces in business, 78-80
    operator-controllable or management-controllable, 81-83
    philosophy of quality performance, 83-85
    results of quality circles, 86-87
    significance of quality circles to organizations, 85-86
Quality of life work (QLW), 9
    participative management and, 147
    survey, 32-34
Quality policy, preparation for change and, 24-25, 26
Quality selection system development, 173-187
    accurate and valid job descriptions and job specifications, 177-179
    areas to probe with supervisor, 185
    conducting an effective employment interview, 179-181
    cost of guessing wrong, 175-177
    effect of telephone reference checks, 184-185

[Quality selection system development]
    making final selection decision, 185-186
    prevention not detection, 173-174
    statistical process control for human resources, 174-175
    testing and evaluation, 182-184
Quality systems
    history of, 216-218
    in new organizational structures, 251-252
Quasiexperimentation, 162-163

Recognition, participative management and, 144
Roethlisberger, Fritz, 211

Scales, 55-57
Self-assurance, participative management and, 146
Self-control, participative management and, 146
Self-improvement method, 109
Simon, Herbert A., 210-211
Sociotechnical systems (STS), 213
Statistical algorithms, 155
Statistical conclusion validity, 164
Statistical heuristics, 155

Statistical process control for human resources, 174-175
Statistical teaching, 158-160
Statistics, quality and, 154
Strategic quality planning, 189-201
   competitive environment and, 199-200
   conformance aspects of quality, 196
   design aspect of quality, 195
   four parts of quality improvement, 200-202
   morality and, 199
   planning, 189-191
   process for, 197-198
   productivity and, 196-197
   responsibility for, 198-199
Suggestion programs, 145
Synergy, 141-142

Task forces, participative management and, 146
Taylor, Frederick W., 4, 140, 209
Telephone reference checks in quality selection system, 184-185
Testing and evaluation in quality selection system, 182-184
Theory X, 212
Theory Y, 212

Time clocks, elimination of, 9
Training
   participative management and, 144
   preparation for change and, 36-38

Validity, statistics and, 164-165
Validity generalization, 182
Visual systems, 50-51

W. L. Gore & Associates, Inc. (case study), 238-246
   communications, 250
   fun, 250
   innovation, 249
   leadership style, 248
   organizational structure, 247
   quality system, 252
Warning systems, 61-62
Weber, Max, 208-209
Work life, quality of, 9
Work simplification, participative management and, 146
Work station design, 62-67
   color, 66-67
   equipment location and design, 64-65
   seating, 63
   traffic patterns, 65-66

Z-type company, 18-19